Adolescent Relations
with Mothers, Fathers,
and Friends

Adolescent Relations
with Mothers, Fathers,
and Friends

James Youniss
and
Jacqueline Smollar

The University of Chicago Press
Chicago and London

James Youniss is professor of psychology and a member of the Center for the Study of Youth Development at the Catholic University of America. His book *Parents and Peers in Social Development* is also published by the University of Chicago Press. Jacqueline Smollar is research asssociate at the Center for the Study of Youth Development at the Catholic University of America.

The University of Chicago Press, Chicago 60637
The University of Chicago Press, Ltd., London
© 1985 by The University of Chicago
All rights reserved. Published 1985
Printed in the United States of America

94   93   92   91   90   89   88   87   86   5   4   3   2

Library of Congress Cataloging in Publication Data

Youniss, James.
   Adolescent relations with mothers, fathers, and
friends.

   Companion vol. to: Parents and peers in social
development.
   Bibliography: p.
   Includes index.
   1. Youth.   2. Interpersonal relations.   3. Parent and
child.   4. Friendship.   5. Children and adults.
I. Smollar, Jacqueline.   II. Title.
HQ796.Y583   1985   305.2'35   84-28067
ISBN 0-226-96487-6

Contents

Preface

This book is a companion piece and extension of an earlier analysis of parent and friend relations, their structure and functions in children's social and personal development (James Youniss, *Parents and Peers in Social Development: A Sullivan-Piaget Perspective,* University of Chicago Press, 1980). The present book focuses on adolescents in these same relations. It presents two kinds of material: first, adolescents' own descriptions of interactions they have had in these relations, and second, theory regarding what these relations are and how they contribute to development. As before, relations are treated in the ideal typical sense as descriptions are synthesized across subjects to yield average characteristics that define structure.

Several persons helped us conduct our studies and prepare this manuscript. We wish to acknowledge them here. Fumiyo Hunter and Lois Loew supplied us with data and offered advice as we planned our studies. Alec McCosh, Nick Santilli, André Leyva, Joyce Cooper-Kahn, and Donna Klagholtz collected, coded, or analyzed data carefully and efficiently.

Our colleague Douglas Sloane gave us technical assistance and wise advice throughout this project. We are grateful for his generosity and cooperation. Catherine Cooper and Harold Grotevant, two colleagues from afar, led us to important theoretical ideas, provided criticism, and enlightened our work in other ways.

We thank the many students who volunteered to be subjects in our studies. We are grateful also to the several school principals who were interested enough in our work to allow us into their schools. They are left unnamed for the purpose of preserving anonymity.

The W. T. Grant Foundation provided four years of support for the conduct of our research. Boys Town of Omaha, Nebraska, and the Center for the

Study of Youth Development at the Catholic University of America also provided funds for our work. Paul Philibert, the director of the Center, was especially helpful and we thank him.

Ann Aubin typed the several preliminary drafts and the final manuscript. She worked with skill and good humor and went out of her way to make our task easier. We are indebted to her.

1

Interpersonal Relations of Childhood and Their Potential Courses through Adolescence

Much has been said about relations during the adolescent period. Theorists have looked at the parent-adolescent relationship in terms of change, weakening, conflict, dissipation, and revitalization. This relationship has been studied according to its internal dynamics, its socializing function, and its place in social-historical evolution. The several findings make for a rich mixture of insight, criticism, and social commentary. Adolescent friendship has received less attention. Researchers have been more interested in peer groups and peer culture. When friendship has been studied, the focus has been on differences between male and female friendships or on popularity versus isolation.

Theory is equally diverse. Three broad perspectives—psychodynamic, socialization, and cognitive—have spawned specific theories with a variety of emphases and themes. Concepts that have captured researchers' interests include emancipation, identity search, conformity, political awareness, sex roles, moral judgment, autonomy, and career choice. Two concerns cut across these concepts: one is the sociology of adolescence as a period in the life cycle; and the other is problem behavior. The latter sometimes dominates, as the institutions and persons who deal with the everyday business of adolescence must confront volatility, delinquency, egocentrism, protest, and neurotic disorders that are peculiar to the period.

In light of this array, our study may be seen as a step backward toward simplified description. Our interest is in the normal and the typical. We attempt to capture what is going on in adolescent relations as the participants in our study interact through regular contact. Our concern for structure rests on the assumption that, while interactions vary in content and momentary aim, they follow a continuing order. Persons perceive one another in a particular way, which constrains their interactions. An adolescent studied across several relationships would likely be found acting differently in each structure. For

1

example, in communicating a particular experience to a parent an adolescent might be cryptic and defensive, while in communicating the same event to a friend the adolescent is likely to be elaborative and open.

In looking for common structural characteristics we hope to contribute to an understanding of how relationships develop during adolescence and, simultaneously, how adolescents themselves develop. It is generally agreed that the parent-child relationship with which the period of adolescence begins does not remain constant as adolescence proceeds. The change can be looked at as a development in its own right. At the same time, the adolescent changes and becomes a person distant and different from the child. The change also can be considered developmental, for it is systematic and entails a reorganization of the person, who, as a consequence, perceives self, others, and reality differently. We contend that the person's development can be understood as occurring through the development of relationships, since the process of change is social and the person is an individual in relation to other persons (Furth 1983; Macmurray 1961; Youniss 1983).

A Summary of Previous Work

A previous book (Youniss 1980) derived its perspective from the writings of Piaget ([1932] 1965) and H. S. Sullivan (1953). According to their perspective, children experience life in two general relationships—one with parents, the other with peers and friends. Experience here is psychological and not objectively material, that is, the focus is on the meaning of interactions and not necessarily on the content. Each of the two relationships has a structure, which provides continuity from one interaction to the next. Thus, persons have expectations for how interactions will proceed—for example, who will take the initiative, what kinds of responses ought to be made, how the other person is likely to react next, and so on.

Two sequences depict the ideal typical form of parent-child relations. One is: request (expectation)—obedience—approval. The other is: request—disobedience—disapproval—obedience—approval. These sequences, which children described for us in their own accounts of everyday interactions with parents, imply for Piaget and Sullivan a structure called unilateral authority. This means that parents know how children should act and that they want children to learn the desired behavior. It means also that children acknowledge their parents' authority and take a position that is complementary to it (see Hinde 1979).

The broader significance is that the structure of unilateral authority is a vehicle for defining the persons in the relationship. Parents are perceived as already knowing what reality is and how it should be ordered. Children, in complement, are still learners who, by correlating their actions with parental approval or disapproval, can come to see reality as their parents do. Stated differently, children can acquire knowledge by looking to and working through their parents. One implication of this is that children see themselves as having limited agency relative to parents, who are all-knowing. According to our data, children between the ages of 6 and 12 reflect this structure by consistently describing sequential interactions that ultimately reduce to exchanges of obedience on their part for approval from their parents.

Two additional points can be made. First, children accept this structure as natural and as beneficial. When asked to comment, they say that parents use their authority to help children come to know what is right and wrong so that they can become better persons (cf., Damon 1977; Huard 1980). Second, this structure, which is found in established form early in childhood, shows signs of changing as children are about to enter adolescence. At about age 12, children repeat the same sequences as their younger counterparts but with significant modifications. Obedience is said to be "voluntary" or of "free will," and parents are described as less than all-knowing, all-powerful figures. There is realization that parents may lack knowledge in some domains and that there are occasions when parents need children's assistance because parents lack some ability or resource. Overall, however, one structure depicts the relationship for the period in question with only a slight hint that it may be changing at about the time adolescence begins.

While the relationship with parents is maintained, children are entering the sphere of peer interactions. The constituting process for friendship begins in the practice of symmetrical reciprocity between peers. The sequences consist in a duplication of acts in turn taking. When one does something, the other peer may act in the same way. Positive acts are followed by positive reciprocation; negative by negative; and neutral by neutral. Such sequences are adequate for momentary meetings but are not conducive to forming a relationship which has long-term direction. The hypothesis is that friendship is developed out of this practice, as symmetrical reciprocity is converted into the principle of fair treatment. To wit, each friend agrees to act toward the other as he or she would want to be treated. Both the practice of reciprocity and its reconstruction into a principle have been supported by findings from studies of children (cf., Bigelow 1977; Bigelow & LaGaipa 1975; Gottman 1983; Selman 1980; Smollar & Youniss 1982; Youniss & Volpe 1978).

Once this structure is set in place, a developmental series is set in motion. Since friends are equals, with neither having unilateral control of the other, they must construct procedures that allow them to manifest equality. For example, since one's opinion is no better than the other's opinion, they must find means to negotiate differences and work toward agreement. Although friends are equals, they are not identical—and individual differences require equity. Friends recognize their differences and merge strengths and weaknesses for the goal of mutual benefit. Piaget has called both aspects instances of cooperation, whereby friends co-construct reality together and in the process learn interdependence and mutual respect. Sullivan has emphasized interdependence, which deters exploitation of one friend by the other, and consensual validation, which promotes join reasoning.

A later development occurs near the end of childhood insofar as friends move toward intimacy. Intimacy is a complex concept that includes exclusive focus, openness of self-disclosure, and the sharing of problems and advice. The central notion is that friends tell one another, and get to know, just about everything that is going on in one anothers' lives. Each friend is then allowed into the other's private self-reflection and becomes part of it to the degree that reflective thinking is interpersonal as much as it is intraindividual. Hence, Piaget's and Sullivan's emphasis on co-construction and cooperation. Friends literally reason together in order to organize experience and to define themselves as persons. Again, studies of children and young adolescents agree with this depiction (cf., Berndt 1982; LaGaipa 1979; Selman 1980; Youniss 1980).

The previous study (Youniss 1980) stopped at the point where children were about to become adolescents. Their views of reality and of self were differentiated by the two relational structures—one with parents and the other with friends. These relations can be seen to offer two versions of social experience and of the self's role in two relational structures. Specifically, the procedures by which the self is a participant in social construction with parents differ from the procedures of social construction that go on in friendship. In the former relationship, the self looks to parents and constructs reality through them in a tone of conformity. In friendship, cooperative co-construction occurs as friends work with one another to reach mutually agreed upon conclusions and, thereby, come to respect one another for using these means.

Piaget is inexplicit as to the course of the two relationships during adolescence. The implication, however, is that the structure acquired in friendship is more conducive to subsequent social development. Piaget depicts the mature person as one who asserts individuality but subjugates it to the principle of reciprocity in a spirit of mutual respect. Sullivan would agree, although his writings on adolescence are deflected toward the drive for lust and, therefore, directed to heterosexual relations. Nevertheless, he describes psychiatric maturity in terms similar to those used by Piaget—the focus is on mutual needs and mutual concerns, instead of on using others to promote the self (Youniss 1980, 1983). In short, both describe the social character of the mature person who emerges from adolescence. They do this, however, without specifically saying how this state of individuality-in-relation is reached.

Reference to other theoretical positions—psychodynamics, socialization, and cognitive—is not helpful in this respect because these theories are founded on premises different from those used by Piaget and Sullivan. For example, psychodynamic theorists do focus on parent-adolescent relations whose change during the period is critical to adolescent development. They do not, in the main, use the kind of relational analysis offered by Piaget and Sullivan. For example, it is difficult to square psychodynamic theorists' emphasis on dealing with reawakened oedipal issues with Piaget's and Sullivan's focus on a shift from unilateral authority to cooperative co-construction.

A similar nontranslation across languages occurs with socialization theorists. A central issue for them is conformity to parents and counterinfluences from friends. The conformity they describe is surprisingly similar to the kind of obedience that is apropos children in a structure of unilateral authority. Further, the focus on peers and counterinfluence versus parents may have little to do with friendship and surely does not appreciate the principled form of peer interactions or the outcomes they lead to—inherent parts of Piaget's and Sullivan's view of friendship.

Cognitive theorists pose still other problems. They stress the capacities adolescents have for self-reflective reasoning that is logical in character and leads to self-reliance or autonomy. If taken literally, this framework sees relationships merely as sources of social data that the individual then organizes on his or her own. This leads to strong claims for reasoning as the means to autonomy. First, according to cognitive theorists, the means are individualistic in the sense of being the self's rational reflections on experience. Second, although reasoning leads to moral principles that clearly include social responsibility and equitable treatment, the justification for them is reasoning itself and not cooperative discourse that leads to consensus and mutual respect through the act of cooperation itself.

We pose then as an open question, what precisely happens in the course of development of these two relationships after childhood? Specifically, does the structure of unilateral authority change toward a more cooperative relation and, if so, how? Do adolescents simply distance themselves from the relationship or do they transform the relationship so that cooperation either replaces authority or is coordinated with a revision of it? As to friendship, is the structure it had in childhood retained during adolescence? Is the childhood structure of friendship, predicated on naive trust, altered when adolescents experience the hard facts of interpersonal reality? A third question is, do friends become less important as the structure of parental relations take on features that friendship once had?

As in the previous book (Youniss 1980), these questions are posed in a preliminary way as heuristic starting points. The next step is to turn to adolescents themselves for two purposes. One purpose is to have adolescents describe these relations as they know them through interactions with parents and friends. The other purpose is to use the data to discover what questions should be asked for a serious study of adolescent relationships—how these relationships develop during adolescence and why they take the courses they do.

Theoretical Approaches to Adolescence

In this section a brief review is offered of three major approaches to the study of adolescence. The purpose is to provide a point of reference for our studies of adolescent relationships. In some instances, common interests will be seen, although the terminology used is not wholly interchangable. In other cases, differences will be obvious, and there is little to say other than that the relational perspective is distinctive and cannot be readily merged with other approaches in terms of themes, emphases, or explanations.

Psychodynamic Theory

Adelson and Doehrman (1980) have reviewed recent thinking in psychodynamic theory. As is well known, the psychodynamic framework is broad in the sense that it includes a diversity of views, even views that are antagonistic to one another. What qualifies a theory to fit into this approach? One criterion would be its focus on the parent-child relationship as the constitutive basis of the adolescent. The person has been formed by this relationship, which is solidified when children resolve oedipal issues through unconscious identification with their parents. It is generally agreed that these issues come up again after puberty when adolescents once more face impelling sexual urges toward their parents (cf., Blos 1962; Douvan & Adelson 1966; A. Freud 1968). By meeting the problems of this new arousal, the relationship changes and further psychosexual development can proceed.

Theorists differ sufficiently in describing these events so that a single summary version is not possible. The general point of agreement, however, is that the revived oedipal situation may lead to regression and defensiveness (Adelson & Doehrman 1980). Further agreement is found on the point that by resolving these urges, adolescents may come to a consciousness of their beholdenness to the parental relationship. This includes seeing how it accounts for their formation and what hold parental authority has had on them. It is possible, then, for the adolescent to become emancipated from the relationship in the sense of knowing its past importance and of being free to explore other avenues of personal definition.

Offer and Offer (1975) provide descriptions of this general process as it occurs in adolescents who make the transition smoothly, with difficulty, or with serious disturbances. In the instances of success, adolescents are depicted as able to seek new definitions of themselves, while accepting the position they had in the relationship in the past. Blos (1967) offers an alternative account under the concept of individuation. He also stresses the freeing for self-exploration that occurs with realization of the relationship's formative powers. He emphasizes further reforming of the relationship by connecting back to parents in a new way. This concept bears definite similarity to the Piaget-Sullivan position on the mature person as an individual-in-relation to others.

This framework is much less articulate about friendship. Although friendship has been occasionally studied (e.g., Douvan & Adelson 1966), psychodynamic theory as a whole discounts it in its own right. Adelson and Doehrman's (1980, 107) critique seems fair: the ". . . weakness is its tendency to see friendship as merely the shadow or reflection of something else, something deeper and earlier, and thus presumably more important." That something is the parental relationship, which in a theory such as A. Freud's (1968), is the real relation that friendship substitutes for. In fleeing from the uncomfortable attraction to parents, adolescents escape to friendship where they can deal with the issues that cannot be confronted with parents.

Already the neglect of friendship and its assignment to a derivative status has begun to be connected (e.g., Wolf, Gredo & Terman 1972). It is not yet clear how that relationship will be appraised or can be synthesized with the theory as a whole. The most optimistic prospect seems to lie in object relation approaches, which, in principle, would allow relations other than those with parents to play a major role in childhood or adolescence (see Grotevant & Cooper in press). This is important because the empirical data on children's friendships are consistent and strong, as referred to above. Children begin to interact with peers at an early age (see Lewis & Rosenblum 1975) and form bonds with friends during the elementary school years. These bond consume time and interest and, in the Piaget-Sullivan perspective, provide social experiences that simply cannot be afforded within the parental relationship.

Socialization Theories

Adolescence is often called the second period of socialization; the first occurs in the protective environments of the family and elementary school. The second period begins as adolescents experience a broader sampling of society and start to prepare more specifically for the tasks of impending adulthood (Elder 1980). A key question for the socialization approaches has been how parents transmit what they know to their sons and daughters in order to prepare them for the future. The focus has been on the mechanisms of transmission, such as direct instruction, modeling, reinforcement, and communication. It is presumed that in these ways parents influence adolescents, and when parents are effective, they accomplish two things. Adolescents adopt the positions of their parents and internalize them so that, in the process, society is made intergenerationally continuous.

This view overlooks internal dynamics within the relationship. While a psychoanalytic theorist would make these dynamics central to transmission, most socialization theorists do not. How then is lack of conformity explained? One of the chief accounts is found in the hypothesis that adolescents are confronted with multiple and disparate influences which work at cross-purposes. Coleman's (1961) study is seminal in this vein because he identified a major counterinfluence to parents—the adolescent peer culture. This idea led to several studies that compared the degree of conformity to parents and to peers under the assumption that one or the other was dominant (see Hartup 1970; Berndt 1979; and Bengtson & Troll 1978).

The public protests by students in the 1960s gave the idea of counterinfluence an added directness. The notion of peer culture became clearly the image of a counterculture that flaunted the values traditionally held in society. The consequences have deepened as theorists have juxtaposed the counterculture of peers and the dissipation of the family. Divorce rates, maternal employment, and diminished intergenerational contact have become signs that families are becoming less and less able to fulfill the socializing function (cf., Advisory Committee 1976; Bronfenbrenner 1970). As this view has evolved, peers seem to take on greater influencing powers and, insofar as peers have little conscious stake in adult society, intergenerational continuity appears in jeopardy.

The only dynamic seemingly offered for peer relations is that of influence and conformity. The image is one of the adolescent not wanting to be left out or seen as different. This focus cannot be easily bridged with the Piaget-Sullivan perspective which, in fact, applies to friendship and not to peers at large. Socialization theories do not then deal with the interactions that Piaget and Sullivan address. Conformity is not the same as consensus, although they may appear similar. Conformity is motivated by wanting to be included or accepted. Consensus means reasoning together in order to find a position to which the parties can give their assent.

Cognitive Theory

A relatively new approach has been taken through cognitive theory. This approach centers on the adolescent's capacity to make sense of experience, submit it to rational self-reflection, and reach valid conclusions about reality as it is and as it ought to be. The main impetus for this approach came when classical socialization and learning theories were seen as picturing the child and the adolescent in passive roles relative to outside social forces. The correction occurred as the adolescent was acknowledged as an active agent whose experiences were only occasions for constructing reality and self. Objective experience was nondetermining. It merely provided data that the subject then organized via reasoning.

Cognitive theories quickly replaced their predecessors and came to the fore as plausible vehicles for understanding adolescents. An example of cognitive theory is Erikson's (1968) concept of identity search which has led to considerable research, as well as to a reformulation of how adolescents set sights on future roles (e.g., Waterman 1982). The adolescent was pictured at the center of multiple input in the form of feedback from other persons about the self. The adolescent's task was to organize the input to reach a version of self that was responsive to the feedback. The process shows the importance of personal reflection, the status of other persons who bring data for reflection, and self-reliance entailed in a search that begins and ends in a sense of personal consistency.

In this and other examples that could be cited, it is not clear how or whether relations have a central function. The burden of development seems to be placed wholly on the individual who must make sense of potentially confusing data. In a theory such as Kohlberg's (e.g., 1969; 1971) the relational component is embedded and difficult to isolate. There are ages in which relationships are important, for example, when young children want to be seen as good or when later, older subjects seek to maintain the existing social order. Even in the advanced stages, when adolescents would seem to be the most self-reliant, the very principles of morality that result include equity, respect for others, and social responsibility.

It is in looking closer at what is meant by autonomy that one can better appraise the cognitive framework in comparison to the Piaget-Sullivan perspective (cf., Kohlberg 1969; Loevinger 1966). As Blasi (1980) has noted, the tendency is to describe an adolescent who takes stands because they have been reached through logical reasoning. The stands are justified with direct reference to the self's appraisal. What saves the adolescent from solipsism is that reasoning has been used logically and rationally. Interestingly, Piaget who is often cited as the source for this view (Inhelder & Piaget 1958) defines autonomy differently. The validity of a principle rests on the consensus it can command from persons who jointly reason in a spirit of finding truth together. While the principle itself may refer to social responsibility, social responsibility is grounded in the cooperative procedures by which the principle is generated. That is why Piaget defines the autonomous person as the individual who "takes up its stand on norms of reciprocity and objective discussion", and finds autonomy in knowing "how to submit to [norms] in order to make itself understood" (Piaget [1932] 1965, 95–96).

A Social-Historical Outlook

For the past 20 or so years, historians have been working to reconstruct the everyday life of persons who preceded us in western societies. Three of their concerns have been the human life course, internal family relations, and relations of family members to the outside world. Adolescence has been an obvious topic of study since it captures the transition steps from the family to society, telling us how the transition occurred, and showing what was required for adulthood. Not surprisingly, this research has indicated that adolescence has undergone change over the past few centuries making this period or stage, as we know it today, a recent innovation. Studies of Europe (Gillis 1981) and North America (Kett 1977) yielded congruent findings that characteristics found in contemporary adolescence seem to have their origin in the last two or three decades of the nineteenth century.

This research covers the same topics we have reviewed from the viewpoint of psychological theories. The topics are approached differently, however, since the focus is on connections between characteristics of the adolescent period and features of the social system in which adolescents lived. Speaking generally, the result is to place psychological phenomena in context. More precisely, the goal is to discover the social-structural basis of these phenomena in the sense that they may be understood as constructions of the social structure. For example, the so called peer culture has taken various forms throughout history. In western society there has always been tolerance for peer groups, acceptance of youthful patterns of behavior, and rituals for youth (cf., Gillis 1981; Shorter 1975). There has not always been, however, compulsory schooling; industries that supplied clothes, food, and music for consumption; lack of employment that was needed for subsistence and preparatory for later employment; or money to fill adolescents' otherwise idle hours.

The available data are too extensive to permit a simple summary. However, several specific points can be made with reference to the issues raised in the foregoing theories. These are now considered, in turn, for the purpose of enriching the psychological orientation and grounding it more carefully in social-historical terms.

Parents as Socializers

Davis (1940), Riesman (1953), and other sociologists have pointed out the limited role in socialization that modern parents can have. Riesman's thesis is that in a changing society when, for example, forms of employment are shifting from industrial to technical work, parents would be doing a disservice to their children by trying to duplicate themselves in their offspring. Were conformity demanded, parents would be perpetuating society as they knew it when, in fact, the society their children face is different. Consequently, a more adaptive stance is for parents to share the socialization function with other persons, such as educators and peers, who may have a better sense of where society is headed in terms of such things as future work and mores.

Parent-adolescent Relations

Implicit in some psychological theories is the idea that parents stand in the way of the adolescent's drive for independence. There have been periods in history when this seems to have been true. For example, under the rule of primogeniture, eldest sons had to wait for their fathers to pass on the family's land before they could become economically stable, marry, and start a life of their own (e.g., Shorter 1975). However, there have been other times when adolescents left home early or parents died young, so that there was little possibility for a parental relationship after childhood (Gillis 1981; Kett 1977). Today, the pattern has become more complex since offspring are expected to become independent and leave home. At the same time, however, their adult lives will probably overlap with the extended life spans of their parents (Degler 1980).

Peer Groups

Gillis (1981) recaptures the kinds of experience adolescents have had within the communities they lived. In the main, adolescents have formed groups that were self-monitoring and were accepted guardedly by adults. At times, these groups took the form of protests against adult society (cf., Aries 1962; Kett 1977), but usually they did not threaten to overturn tradition (Gillis 1981). General fear of these groups arose in the nineteenth century when adolescents were shut out from employment and banded together (Platt 1969). These groups were perceived as having interests contrary to the interests of adult society. However, since then, the kinds of groupings that adolescents have formed have been varied in type, and many of the types are encouraged by adult society. It is no longer possible to designate all of them—for example, delinquent gangs and college fraternities—under one category (Braungart 1980).

Male and Female Adolescence

Through much of western history, males have experienced adolescence differently from females. Males were introduced into society via work outside the home at an early age. Females, who sometimes were contracted out for work, more typically stayed within the family until they married (Bernard 1981; Kett 1977). The experiences of male and female adolescents started to become more similar during the past 150 years (Cott 1977) and have become definitely more similar in recent years through compulsory high schools and enhanced job opportunities for females (Bernard 1981).

Parents

The rich body of literature on family life defies quick generalizations. However, the kind of intense relationship between parents and adolescents that some theories presume must be an innovation. As was already stated, it is only recently that demographic and economic facts and sociological conventions have allowed parents and adolescents to live together in the same residence over a long period of time. These factors, combined with the division of spousal roles that began to occur in the nineteenth century (Degler 1980; Lasch 1979), account for what we now know as the mother-child bond that begins at birth, is fostered by devoted care, and is long-lasting. These factors also account for the decreased involvement of fathers who have become oriented toward work outside the family sphere.

Friends

Aries (1962) describes a time when friendships were not so bound by class interests, family background, ethnicity, and religious beliefs. He notes that a change occurred with the establishment of capitalism and the reordering of work and wealth that followed. Sociologists who have studied friendship patterns in contemporary life have observed a definite tendency for the bond to be formed among persons with similar background characteristics (cf., Fischer 1977; Laumann 1973). Segregation of this sort is evident by the high school years (Hollingshead 1949), and bonds formed at that time are likely to be maintained well into adult life (Fischer 1977). This may account for a finding in recent studies that adolescents believe that their parents and friends hold similar values and are not necessarily sources of conflicting influence (cf., Berndt 1979; Potvin & Lee 1980).

Summary

Social-historical research both challenges and brings into broader focus several issues that are central to psychological theories. First, the questions of how, whether, and why the parental relationship changes during the adolescent period can be sharpened. One point is that parents help promote the change as they seek to encourage their children's independence. Another emphasis is that parents must cultivate independence in their children while they are living in the same household with them; parents must share interests with their children but also have interests of their own. Still another point is that parents, who have invested in the parent-child relationship from their offspring's infancy on, are likely to live long enough to maintain a continuing relationship with their adult sons and daughters.

Second, questions raised by socialization theories are informed by the following considerations. Contemporary parents probably do not perceive themselves as carrying the entire burden of socialization. Rather, they share this role with other persons including their children's peers. Further, parents realize they would be promoting a dysfunctional pattern if they insisted that their children adopt their views of society, when society as parents know it is not the society their children will have to face. Additionally, although parents might fear aspects of the peer culture, much of that culture may be self-monitored so that its principles do not conflict with those that parents hold. Conjunctively, adults not only condone but control parts of the peer world. Lastly, insofar as segregation by class, ethnic, and religious categories seems to develop in friendship patterns, the tendency is for children to form friendships with peers who have background characteristics similar to their own.

Third, cognitive theories have stressed the individual's agency and have cultivated the image of the lone adolescent struggling to sort out experience and find a place for the self. How alone is the adolescent in these tasks and to what degree does autonomy proceed? Historians emphasize that families took on their modern form, to a large extent, in order to protect their members and to insure their success against the impersonal forces of a harsh and competitive society. Seen in this light, there is an implicit closeness between parents and adolescents that supersedes the drive for separation. Given the early formation and continuing work that goes into maintaining the parent-child relationship, it seems unlikely that parents would step aside leaving the adolescent to battle the chaos of experience and to stumble alone in the search for identity. The more likely prospect is that parents remain engaged in their offspring's problems and are as concerned with their offspring's well-being as are the adolescents themselves.

Additionally, the notion of autonomy, defined as taking recourse in one's own logical appraisals of reality, can be carried too far. Adolescents living within families surely hear their parents' reasons for actions and are expected to give reasons in return. Contemporary parents typically are not authoritarian in the vein of asserting demands in a tenor of absolute parental rights (cf., Baumrind, 1975). They are more prone to create an atmosphere in which expectations and violations are dealt with through exchanges of reasons. This atmosphere is conducive to engendering a sense of social responsibility so that the consequences of one's actions are seen in terms of their effects on other members of the family and on the family as a whole.

A Framework

It would be artificial to state that past research and available theory have led to specific hypotheses about what to expect in the course of the two relationships during the adolescent period. What we have instead is a framework that is grounded in the Piaget-Sullivan perspective and outlined roughly by two general concepts: cooperative co-construction and the individual-in-relations. The former concept focuses on how unilateral authority in the parent-child relationship changes and how these changes are coordinated with cooperative procedures already established through older children's friendships.

The latter concept is applicable to parental relations as well as to friendship relations—the issue being, how do adolescents become individuals in their own right while maintaining relations that are constitutive of their individuality. For this question we find Cooper, Grotevant, and Condon's (1983) expansion of the concept of individuation a valuable heuristic. According to their view, adolescents seek to become, and to be recognized as, individuals; and in this drive, they need to become distinct from the persons they were in the parent-child relationship. However, since they have been formed through this relationship, a complete severance would undermine the self. Adolescents, therefore, also seek to remain connected to this relationship. As their movement toward individuality progresses, the old relationship becomes less suitable and the need for its revision becomes greater. The solution lies in transforming the relationship so that a balance is achieved between the two movements.

We state this concept now, in general terms, as an outline for questions that can be asked about the data. The concept seems wholly fitting to the Piaget-Sullivan perspective because its essential components include the person's formation through relationships, the realization that relationships develop, and the recognition that the outcome is an individual who is still definitionally dependent on relationships. This concept is compatible with themes found in major theories on adolescence. And, importantly, it is supported by the social-historical outlook that grounds interpersonal relationships in social surroundings.

2

The Studies and the Methodology

The studies presented in this book were designed from the perspective of a structural approach to adolescents' interpersonal relationships. As noted in the previous chapter, the basic assumptions are that adolescents' relationships with their parents and friends are worth studying because of their implications for social development, and that a structural approach to this research is valid because it can generate new insights into these relationships. The aim of this chapter is to delineate the characteristics of this approach further and to provide a description of, and a rationale for, the research design.

A Structural Approach

An analysis of relations from a structural perspective is based on the premise that interpersonal relations consist in large part of interactions that are conceptually organized by the participants into structures (Piaget [1932] 1965; Sullivan 1953; Youniss 1980). This organization of interactions as structures allows participants in relationships to order past events and to direct ongoing ones. A relational structure is knowable to an outside observer to the degree that interactions within a given relationship manifest consistency in form. In our research with preadolescents, for example, certain interactions were found to appear with regularity and to take similar form in relationships between parents and 10-year-old children. For one, parents guided their children's behavior through requests or commands, and children sought to follow these directives. In disputes or differences of opinion, parents usually insisted on or requested compliance with their point of view, and children conceded, particularly in matters of importance. In addition, children often withheld information from their parents when they felt their parents would be upset or disapproving; and if parents did find out, children offered alibis or excuses designed to put their actions in a more favorable light. Although these interactions are dissimilar with respect to their specific content, they do manifest a consistency in form that allows insights into the relationship. The consistency lies in the fact that parents appear to have exclusive rights of approval and disapproval and that children modify their behavior in response to these "rights." This form of interaction suggests that the structure of parent-preadolescent relations involves unilateral authority and the norm of complementary reciprocity.

Thus, it is through the study of interactions that relational structures can be known. It is recognized, however, that such an approach may not capture the totality of the relationships. Interactive forms, for example, may not allow inferences about the affective bond that might hold two persons together. In a similar vein, interactions may not reveal underlying motivational factors, such as guilt or fear, that may guide certain aspects of relations. Despite these shortcomings, however, interactive forms appear to be generative of general characteristics of relational structures.

Psychologists have used several methods to assess relational structures. The two most common are (1) direct observations of interactions (e.g., Bell & Bell 1983; Cooper, Grotevant, & Condon 1983; Gottman 1983; Patterson & Reid 1980) and (2) interviews, or questionnaires, in which subjects describe interactions (e.g., Bigelow & La Gaipa 1975; Chaffee, McLeod, & Wackman 1973; Kon & Losenkov, 1978; White, Speisman, & Costos, 1983). The latter method was used in our research. Both methods have advantages and disadvantages (Hinde 1979). The major advantage of the interview, or questionnaire, method is that interactions in relationships can be examined from a variety of situations and over a range of time periods, rather than being limited to one situation in a constrained time frame. Another advantage is that data obtained from questionnaires or from interviews consist of descriptions of interactions that can be scored according to regularly occurring forms. Both advantages allow for a broad framework from which to assess structures. The presumption is that descriptions ought to be congruent with actual interactions and, of course, allow insight into the meaning that the participants give to the interactions.

The disadvantages of the questionnaire or interview method are obvious. First, subjects control the data and, therefore, may generate descriptions that are distorted or otherwise affected by social desirability. However, because the data are scored on the basis of commonality of form, a large group of subjects would have to use similar distortive techniques in order to affect the results. Another disadvantage is that descriptive data represent the subjects' perceptions of what takes place in their relationships and, it may be argued, that these perceptions might differ from the interactions that actually do occur. This possible disadvantage is minimized, however, when the objective is to appraise interactions for their consistency in form, rather than for their specific content or sequences. Finally, a third disadvantage is that descriptions come from only one of the participants in a relationship, and it is not clear that the other participants hold a similar conception, although the assumption is that they do. This assumption of similarity is based on the premise that there must be a common framework from which the parties interact if their respective contributions are to be orderly and to communicate shared meaning.

Focus of Research

The selection of interactive situations for study was determined by the amount of information a situation might provide with respect to the structure of a particular relationship. The term multiplicity has been applied to relationships with parents and friends (Hinde 1978; Verbrugge 1979). This means that these relationships cover a broad range of situations and, therefore, that a wider number of situations have to be sampled if these relationships are to be fully understood. From the numerous possibilities in the available literature, a sample was chosen that met the above criteria and could be meaningfully applied to relationships with mothers, fathers, and friends. These situations are described in some detail below.

Typical and Enjoyed Interactions

Little is known about the kinds of interactions that characterize adolescents' relations with their parents and peers. Some studies, however, have shed light on adolescents' more general social activities. In their classic ecological study, Barker & Wright (1955) reported on the activities of teenagers in a midwestern community. Csikszentmihalyi and Larson (1984), using a unique methodology, enlisted adolescents to report on their own interactions at various times during the day when signaled by automatic pagers. In general, these studies found that adolescents do the kinds of things one might expect. For example, they spend more time with peers than with parents, and much of the time spent with parents is expended on routine family activities, such as eating, doing chores, and doing schoolwork.

While these techniques provide information about the distribution of time and activities in the adolescent's social life, the information does not lend itself to a structural analysis. For example, the fact that adolescents spend more time with peers than with parents does not allow inferences to be made either about the characteristics of these relations or about the level of satisfaction in each one. Time per se may be deceptive. A more telling variable may be the quality of the interactions in the available time, a point that has been stressed in the study of mother-infant relationships (e.g., Ainsworth 1969; Arend, Gove, & Sroufe 1979).

From a structural perspective, then, it was determined that a productive technique would be to focus on the kinds of interactions that characterized these relationships when the participants were together. The assumption was that, over time, interactions in particular relationships exhibit regular patterns that bear on their respective structures. For example, it has been found that the interactions that are typical in the friendships of preadolescent boys and of preadolescent girls are quite different. Boys tend to engage in interactions that center around organized activities such as sports, while girls spend their time together just talking or involved in less structured activities (Eder & Hallinan 1978; Lever 1978; Smollar-Volpe 1980). This difference in activities suggests that the structure of friendship for preadolescent boys and for preadolescent girls may also be different. Organized sports activities allow less chance for personal interchange, while unstructured activities allow more opportunity for spontaneous discussions and intimacy. A focus on typical, or characteristic, interactions, then, permits an assessment of not only the structure of relationships but also of differences in structures across gender and relationships.

Our approach also focused on the activities that adolescents most enjoyed in their relations with parents and friends. Enjoyed activities were selected for study because it was felt they might provide two kinds of information. The first of these had to do with the value of the relationship—what is it that participants get from the relationship that makes the relationship worth maintaining in a positive form. To use the example just given of the different activities that are described as typical of the friendships of preadolescent boys and of preadolescent girls: if these typical activities (i.e., sports and just talking) are also the most enjoyed activities, then it may be that the value of friendship for preadolescent boys is something like camaraderie, while for girls it may be intimacy or the opportunity for personal exchange. The second goal of examining enjoyed activities was to determine whether these activities were also typical of the relationship. It was assumed that this might provide a point of difference between relationships with parents and with friends.

Communication

Much of the literature on adolescent communication patterns deals with two areas: self-disclosure and advice seeking. Self-disclosure refers to the act of revealing personal information about the self that would not normally be disclosed in everyday conversation. The level of self-disclosure has been found to vary across relational contexts, with friends being the target of disclosure more often than parents, and with mothers being more frequent targets than fathers (Jourard & Richman 1963; Rivenbark 1971; Smollar-Volpe 1980). In addition, female adolescents and adults tend to disclose more often than do males, irrespective of targets (Rivenbark 1971; Smollar-Volpe 1980). The data for advice seeking and its complement, influence, also appear to be relatively consistent, despite some dispute (Larsen 1972). The general finding is that advice seeking and influence are distributed by domain (Brittain 1963; Burke & Weir, 1979; Emmerich 1978; Kandel & Lesser 1972). Adolescents tend to seek out friends, mothers, fathers, and others for advice depending on the specific issue—future plans, interpersonal problems, family problems, school work, etc. This suggests that adolescents seek advice based on their presumptions of how expertise is distributed in their available network and how the other persons will react to them.

Although a focus on self-disclosure and advice seeking provides information bearing on structure, it does not cover the range of communications that may exist in adolescents' relationships with their parents and friends. For example, two friends may not seek out advice from each other about their future plans, but this topic may be frequently discussed between them in order to compare objectives or simply to get to know one another better. To evaluate communication effectively in these relationships, then, part of our work involves simple descriptions of topics of conversation. A distribution of topics across relationships is expected with some topics being reserved for a particular relationship, other topics being excluded, and still others occurring in several relationships.

In addition to topics of communication, it was also determined that relational structures may be revealed through the quality of communication in a relationship. When a topic is under discussion, what are the characteristics of this discussion? Two aspects of communication were examined—the type of understanding and the kinds of general procedures used. The type of understanding was assessed with respect to whether or not participants took measures to ensure the understanding of the opinions and ideas expressed in a discussion. If both of the participants in a discussion assumed equal responsibility for ensuring understanding of their opinions and ideas, the communication was assessed as one characterized by symmetrical understanding. If only one of the participants took measures designed to ensure understanding, the communication was assessed as nonsymmetrical with respect to understanding. In a study pertaining to this issue, it was found that for adolescents, symmetrical understanding applied to friendships more often than to parent-child relations, while for young adults, symmetrical understanding also applied to relations with parents (White, Speisman, & Costos 1983).

The general procedures of communication considered in our work were related to the issue of type of understanding. Those procedures selected for study were chosen because of their potential implications for revealing structure. Of particular interest was whether or not discussion in relations were characterized by procedures indicative of openness or guardedness, of acceptance or judgment, and of cooperation or authority. It was presumed that communications involving a high level of openness, acceptance, and cooperation would have implications for relational structure that were quite different from communications characterized by guardedness, judgment, and authority.

Conflicts

In contrast to the areas of typical interactions and communications, there is an extensive literature on the degree of turmoil that adolescents experience in their relations, particularly with parents (Campbell & Cooper 1975; Cline 1980; Jacob 1974; Montemayor 1982). This has typically involved a concern with the amount of conflict experienced in relationships and with a correlation between this factor and the amount, or degree, of deviant acts committed by adolescents (Marks & Haller 1977; Potvin & Lee 1980). As such, this literature is particularly relevant to a study of adolescent deviancy ranging from suicide attempts and drug abuse to truancy from home or from school.

From the perspective of a structural approach, conflicts have a further implication. It is assumed that conflicts occur in the normal course of any relationship. Among other things, relationships involve two persons whose individual interests may at any moment detract from the needs of the relationship and bring the persons into conflict. Some of these conflicts may be significant for revealing the relationship's structure because they may represent a violation of the relationship's norms. This was demonstrated with preadolescents who frequently cited disobedience as a cause of conflict in their relationships with parents and denials of equality as a cause of conflict in their friendships. Thus, the major concern is not with the frequency of conflict in a relationship, but rather with the kinds of events which induce conflict. Also of concern, and for the same reasons as noted for conflicts, are the kinds of procedures which serve to resolve situations which cause conflict and return the relationship to its normal functioning.

Perceived Obligations

Part of our work focused on adolescents' perceptions of what they should do for their parents and friends, and why. It was assumed that these obligations would signify structure, in that they would tap the kinds of interactions required to keep a relation going in a positive manner. In this way they may reveal the structural norms of the relationship. With preadolescents, for example, it was found that obligations varied across relations with parents and friends (Ryan & Smollar 1980). For parents, the major obligation that preadolescents expressed was obedience. Preadolescents reported that they should obey their parents because if they did not, they would be punished. In contrast, they reported that they should be nice to their friends because if they did not they would lose the friendship. In both relationships, the obligation is perceived as necessary to maintain a positive relationship with the other person. The differences in the nature of this obligation, however, suggest differences in the relational structures. Relationships require that certain actions occur in order to keep the relationships running smoothly. The type of action that meets this criterion is significant for assessing structure because it provides the key event around which other activities of the relation obtain meaning.

Self in Relationships

In addition to the interactions noted above, our work also focused on adolescents' conceptions of self in the context of relationships with their friends and parents. Although self-concepts do not qualify as interactive events, it was assumed that they would provide information to complement interactive events and in that way signify structure. It was also assumed that self-concepts in relational contexts might provide insights into the emotional aspects of relationships that were not evidenced in descriptions of interactions. Feelings such as security, love, guilt, and hostility, might be motivational factors for certain interactions, and might be revealed in conceptions of self in given relationships.

It is important to note that this focus on self-concepts takes a relational perspective. It is only fairly recently that studies have shown that self-concepts vary across relational contexts (Gecas 1972; Smollar-Volpe 1981). This variation across relationships suggests further that conceptions of self have implications for understanding relationships, as well as understanding persons, since it is assumed that relationships provide the basis for the construction of a conception of self.

Summary of Approach

Our goal, then, is to describe the characteristics of relational structures. The procedure is to appraise interactions in relationships for their consistency in form. The expectation is that there will be recurrent forms of interaction and that these forms represent invariants by which relationships are structured and known.

To arrive at insights into structures, we have looked at several types of interactive events including: (1) typical and enjoyed activities, (2) topics of and quality of communication, (3) conflicts and procedures of resolution, and (4) perceived obligations. To elaborate further on structures, we have also examined conceptions of self in relational contexts. While it is believed that this approach provides insights into structures, it is acknowledged that it is but one of many and that several approaches are needed to reveal all characteristics of relationships.

The Studies and Methodology

The data presented in the following chapters were compiled from 8 research studies conducted over a 4-year period (1980–1983). In the course of these studies, 1,049 adolescents were sampled—ranging in age from 12 to 19 years and approximately equally represented by males and females. The function of this section is to provide a description of each study with respect to the aims of the study, the size and characteristics of the sample, and the methodology of data collection and analysis. In subsequent chapters, individual studies will be identified by the numerical label assigned to them in this chapter. Also, where appropriate, examples of actual questionnaires are presented in the appendices. The probability levels of significant differences resulting from statistical analyses are reported in the data chapters.

Study 1

The Sample. The sample in study 1 included 40 subjects, (20 females and 20 males), 20 each in age groups 14–15 years and 18–19 years. The subjects were from middle- to upper-middle class families living in Washington, D.C., suburban areas. All the subjects were from homes where both the mother and the father were living together with the family.

Description. The goal of study 1 was primarily exploratory with respect to adolescents' conceptions of relations. Subjects were individually interviewed in their homes, and responses were recorded on a previously prepared questionnaire form by the interviewer. The major tasks of this interview were (1) to assess adolescents' perceptions of the interactions that they felt characterized their relations with mothers, fathers and same-sex close friends; and (2) to examine adolescents' conceptions of self within each of these relational contexts. To this end, subjects were asked to provide examples of three kinds of interactions that "most commonly occur" in their relations with their mothers, fathers, and close friends. The subjects were asked to provide three descriptions of self that most characteristically typified the way they "felt or acted" when they are with their mothers, fathers, and close friends. As an example of the latter, subjects were orally presented with the statement "when I am with my mother (father, close friends), I am most likely to feel or be_____." The subjects were then asked to complete the sentence with 3 descriptions for each of the 3 relationships. Interactions and self-descriptions were organized into rationally coherent categories based on content similarity. Interrater agreement on the assignment of individual statements to categories was .91 for interactions and .94 for self-descriptions. Frequencies of category use were analyzed by chi-square tests of independence to assess differences due to sex and, or, age of subjects, and by chi-square tests for related samples to examine differences between relational contexts.

Study 2

The Sample. The sample in study 2 involved 92 adolescents, 50 females and 42 males, with each sex evenly divided into two age groups—13–14 year olds and 16–17 year olds. The subjects were from middle- to upper-middle-class suburban homes in the Washington, D.C., area. All the subjects were living with both parents and had at least one sibling.

Description. The goal of study 2 was to investigate adolescents' conceptions of the obligations they have to their mothers, fathers, and close friends of the same sex. The focus on obligations was designed to assess adolescents' views of the rules that govern these relationships. Subjects were asked to describe the kinds of things they felt they should do for their mothers, fathers, and close friends. They were then asked to select the obligation they felt was "most important" in each relationship and to explain why they felt this action should be done for the other person. The obligations and the reasons for obligations were analyzed separately for each relationship. First, responses were classified into rational categories that were suggested by the data themselves and that were based on content similarity. Interrater agreement on the assignment of responses to categories was .86 for obligations and .88 for reasons. The frequency distributions of categories across age and sex of the subjects were analyzed by chi-square tests of independence to assess for possible differences in category use as a function of these variables. The chi-square test for related samples was used to test for differences across relational contexts.

Study 3

The Sample. The subjects in study 3 were 312 high school students from a middle-sized town in upstate New York. The subjects were approximately evenly divided by sex and by the age groups 15–16 years and 17–18 years. The subjects in study 3 were from families that varied with respect to income levels (ranging from lower-class to upper-middle class), racial and ethnic backgrounds, and family structure.

Description. Study 3 served as an initial exploratory investigation of the kinds of conflicts or problems that take place in interpersonal relations and how these conflicts or problems are resolved. Again, the goal was to assess adolescents' conceptions of their relationships through their ideas about the rules that govern relationships. In study 2, these ideas about rules were probed directly by focusing on obligations. In this study, a more indirect approach was taken—with conflicts or problems assumed to arise from violations of rules. By investigating conflicts, then, the ultimate goal was to determine the rules that serve to maintain relationships in a positive form.

In study 3, these high school students were given questionnaires by their social science teachers to be filled out in class and returned to the teachers. Originally, 400 questionnaires were given out. Of those returned, 310 were usable. There were three types of questionnaires—differentiated by the specific relations being assessed. Of the 310 students, 57 females and 49 males filled out the form that asked questions about same-sex close friends and fathers; 51 females and 44 males completed the form that asked questions about same-sex friends and mothers; and 51 females and 58 males responded on the form asking questions about same-sex friends and opposite-sex friends. Thus the questions about same-sex friends were answered by all the subjects, while the questions pertaining to mothers, to fathers, and to opposite-sex friends were each answered by approximately one-third of the subjects.

For all forms, the questionnaire contained two sections. In section 1, subjects were asked to describe, for each of the two relationships targeted, two things that they did that caused conflict in the relationship and two things that the other person did that caused conflict in the relationship. They were then instructed to identify the one event of the 4 given that caused the "most serious" conflict, to give a description of how this conflict or problem was resolved, and to give a description of how this conflict or problem might have been avoided. Section 2 of the questionnaire involved a list of true-false statements designed to assess the degree of symmetry with regard to fairness, respect, and intimacy in each relationship. A sample of these statements is provided in Appendix A.

The types of conflicts and of conflict resolutions were coded and classified into categories based on content similarity by two independent coders. The categories resulting from this process were highly similar for both coders, and agreement on the assignment of responses to the categories occurred in approximately 85% of the cases. Disagreements were settled by a third coder. Responses to the true-false statements were analyzed by age × sex (two-factor) Analyses of Variance in order to assess differences as a function of these variables. Conflict categories were analyzed by chi-square tests for related samples and chi-square tests for independence.

Study 4

The Sample. The original sample for study 4 was 180 subjects. Of this sample, 120 subjects were actually used; 60 subjects were rejected because either they failed to complete the task or they came from families that did not meet the criteria for inclusion in the study. Of the 120 subjects, 60 were females and 60 males. Within each sex, subjects were equally divided into the age groups 15–16 years and 17–18 years. Subjects came from homes that varied with respect to income levels and racial and ethnic backgrounds, but all were from two-parent homes.

Description. Study 4 was designed to determine the frequency of occurrence and the seriousness of potentially problematic events in relationships with parents and friends. The events were selected from the data provided by the subjects in study 3. Twenty-one events were chosen that were relevant to relationships with parents; 22 events pertained to relationships with opposite-sex friends; and 26 to the relationships with same-sex close friends. For each relationship, about half of the events described the subject's actions (I didn't clean my room when I was asked.), and half described the other's actions (My mother . . . , or My close friend . . .). These 90 events were then compiled into a questionnaire form on which subjects were instructed to indicate how often each event occurred (never happens, happens sometimes, happens often), and whether the event caused a conflict in the relation when it did occur (did not cause a conflict, caused a conflict). Samples of the questionnaires for the mother and close-friend relationships are given in Appendix B.

The questionnaires were given to students in high school psychology and history classes by one of the researchers on the project and returned to the researcher immediately after completion. The frequencies of responses to each item were analyzed for age or sex differences, and, where possible, frequencies were compared across relational contexts.

Study 5

The Sample. Study 5 involved 95 subjects from private and public schools in the Washington–Baltimore area. All subjects were Caucasian and living with both parents. There were 40 subjects in the age group 15–16 years, and 55 in the age group 17–18 years. Males and females were approximately equally represented in each age group.

Description. Study 5 was designed to assess the procedures for resolving a conflict. One conflict was selected for each relationship, based on its frequency of occurrence in that relationship as found in study 4. The conflicts were then written up as hypothetical situations and were presented to the subjects in a one-to-one interview situation. The conflict with parents dealt with an adolescent who came home one hour after his or her curfew. The conflict with same-sex close friends involved one friend spending too much time with someone else. The hypothetical situation was read aloud to the subjects. They were then asked a series of questions: (1) Do you think this might cause a problem in the relationship? (2) What do you think might be done to resolve the problem? (3) Has something like this ever happened in your relationships with your mother (father, friend)? (4) If so, how did you and your mother (father, friend) resolve the problem?

Responses were analyzed for similarity of content and form. Resolutions were assessed with regard to whether or not they represented a compromise solution, with the end point changing the ''norms'' of the relation, or a status quo solution, with the end result being a return to the existing norms of the relation. Specific examples of each are given in the text where relevant. Types of resolutions were analyzed for possible differences due to age, sex, or type of relationship by chi-square tests of independence and related samples.

Study 6

The Sample. Study 6 sampled 180 subjects, 60 in each of age levels 12–13 years, 14–15 years, and 18–20 years. Males and females were equally represented in each age level. The subjects were from private, parochial, and public schools located in the Washington, D.C., area. They were all from Caucasian and middle-class families and lived with both parents.

Description. This study was done for a doctoral dissertation by Fumiyo Hunter (1983). Since only 2 parts of Hunter's work are discussed in this book, only these sections will be described. The methodology used was a questionnaire submitted to students by the researcher in either home room or study hall classes. One section of the questionnaire was designed to assess the range of topics of communication in adolescent relations with their mothers, fathers, and friends and the quality of this communication. To this end, subjects were presented with 7 topic areas for each relationship and instructed to indicate whether or not each topic was discussed with the target person, and if so, how often the target person (1) explained reasons for his or her ideas and (2) really tried to understand the ideas of the subject. An example of this questionnaire is given in Appendix C. The mode of analysis of these data is described in the following chapters.

The aim of another section of the questionnaire was to investigate the procedures used by the target persons when there was a disagreement between the subject and the target person. Eight procedures were described and for each one the subject was instructed to indicate how often the target person utilized each procedure when a disagreement occurred. An example of this is given in Appendix C. Responses for each procedural item were analyzed separately to assess frequencies. Responses were also factor-analyzed using principle factor analysis with iteration and Varimax rotation (Nie, et al. 1975). This analysis resulted in the emergence of 2 distinct factors. One, termed "mutual procedures," included 3 of the 8 procedures; the other, termed "unilateral procedures," incorporated 4 of the remaining procedures; and 1 procedure was found not to load on either factor. Specific details are given where relevant in the chapters presenting the data.

Study 7

The Sample. Study 7 originally involved 220 subjects. Of these, 160 were selected as meeting the criteria of completing all the tasks asked in the questionnaire and living with both of their natural or adoptive parents. All the subjects were students at a public high school in a middle-class suburban community of Cleveland, Ohio. There were 80 subjects in each of age groups 15–16 years and 17–18 years. Males and females were equally represented in each age group.

Description. Study 7 came late in the series and was designed to assess several functions: (1) to validate earlier findings, (2) to expand on information obtained in previous studies, (3) to fill in areas where information was missing, and (4) to compare relations with fathers, mothers, same-sex friends, and opposite-sex friends through a forced-choice procedure. The questionnaire generated both objective and descriptive data. It focused on styles of communication in relationships, topics of communication, concepts of self in relationships, conflicts in relationships, enjoyable activities in relationships, and how persons cause harm to relationships. A copy of the questionnaire is presented in Appendix D. Analyses of these data varied, depending on the section and the type of response, and are discussed, where relevant, in the chapters describing the data themselves.

Study 8

The Sample. One hundred and four subjects, comprising 52 father-son dyads, were interviewed for this study. All subjects were from two-parent, white, middle-class families living in the metropolitan Washington, D.C., area. The sons represented two age groups—high school and college students. The mean age for high school students was 16 years, and the mean age for college students was 19 years. Fathers with sons in high school ranged in age from 37 to 55 years, with a mean age of 45 years, while fathers with sons in college ranged in age from 42 to 61 years, with a mean age of 51 years.

Description. This study was conducted as a doctoral dissertation by Lois Loew (1982). Only 3 parts of her study are presented in this book. In one part, subjects were presented with a list of activities and asked to indicate if they shared these activities with their fathers (with their sons). In another part, subjects were asked to describe how they and their fathers (sons) resolve disagreements and how well the fathers (sons) were able to pick up on the son's (father's) feelings. In a third part, subjects were asked to describe what they talked about with their fathers (sons).These data were analyzed with respect to frequency counts and compared by chi-square tests of independence for possible differences due to age or to the position in the relationship. Further analysis is discussed in the data chapters where relevant.

Limitations of Research

These 8 studies comprise the work that is presented in subsequent chapters. They combine the methodologies of interviews and questionnaires—using each one according to the type of information needed from the study. The studies also combine scale data and descriptive data, with the former used primarily in situations where it was necessary to validate previous findings and with the latter used as an exploratory tool for assessing certain aspects of relationships. These studies allowed adolescents to generate their own descriptions of relations and to assess descriptions given by other adolescents. Although it is believed that the 8 studies provide a fairly comprehensive picture of adolescents' interpersonal functioning, there are limits to the inferences that can be made from the general findings. To begin with, most of the subjects sampled in the studies were from white, middle-class homes.

Therefore, inferences about the results need to be restricted to this group and socio-economic class. A second limitation lies in the fact that no one sample of subjects provided information on all the aspects of the relationships that were examined—although subjects in study 7 did respond to almost all of the issues. This was the result of our wish to allow the adolescents themselves to generate the design and focus for subsequent studies. In a sense, study 7 represents the culmination of this sequencing of studies, with the major issues suggested in the previous 6 studies being validated or further explored.

3

Adolescent Daughters and Their Relations with Parents

The focus of this chapter is the adolescent female's understanding of her relations with each of her parents. Included in this discussion are the kinds of interactions that take place in these two relationships, the topics and quality of communication, and the quality of certain features of the relationships. Perceptions of problems which occur in the relationships and procedures for dealing with disagreements are also discussed, as are the daughter's conceptions of self in the context of these relationships and conceptions of her obligations to her mother and father.

Typical Interactions and Enjoyed Activities

The typical interactions and enjoyed activities of parent-daughter relationships were examined in studies 1 and 7. In study 1, the females were asked to describe 3 interactions that they felt characterized their relations with their fathers and three that characterized their relationships with their mothers. In study 7, the adolescent females were asked to describe what they did with their mothers and with their fathers that they most enjoyed.

Descriptions of interactions characteristic of parent-daughter relations (study 1) took two general forms—symmetrical and asymmetrical. Symmetrical interactions indicated an equality of the participants with regard to a specific event—"We go out to eat." "We talk about problems together." "We joke around together." When the interaction reflected an inequality between the participants, it was judged asymmetrical. This general category incorporated actions directed from parents to daughters—"He tells me what to do." "She talks to me about sex."—as well as from daughters to parents—"I obey him." "I tell her all my problems."

Adolescent daughters' descriptions of their interactions with fathers were primarily asymmetrical, with 77% of the descriptions falling into this category. The most frequently reported asymmetrical interaction involved *father's attempts to exercise authority* over daughters (30%). This exercise of authority was viewed as a function of either father's protectiveness or his desire to control. Statements such as, "He is protective of me and interferes in my dating," indicate the protective aspect of authority. The desire to control was reflected in descriptions such as the following: "He always tries to order me around." "He pushes me about school." "I have to obey him." The authority position of fathers is also found in the asymmetrical interaction of *fathers giving (daughters seeking) practical advice or information* (25%). Daughters reported that father: "tells me about things, like careers," "gives good solid advice," "gives advice on how to do things," "can be trusted to help out with practical problems."

Asymmetrical father-daughter interactions, however, were not restricted to authority-related events. A small percentage concerned the *fathers' giving of support and encouragement* to daughters (14%). According to some of the daughters, father: "backs me up, gives me support and encouragement," "is always there when I need him," "defends me and sticks up for me." Other interactions classified as asymmetrical involved fathers' provisions of financial support (3%). The remainder were idiosyncratic (5%).

Although most of the father-daughter interactions were asymmetrical in form, 23% of them were classified as symmetrical. These included *conversations*, primarily on nonpersonal topics (10%); *shared activities* (10%); and *arguments* (3%). In this vein, adolescent daughters reported that they and their fathers: "have talks but not personal," "have intellectual discussions," "go out to dinner," "work around the house together," and "have disagreements about things."

As with the father-daughter relationship, most of the typical interactions of mother-daughter relationships were asymmetrical (65%). However, the predominant types of asymmetrical interactions for mothers and daughters were different from those for fathers and daughters. Mothers' *attempts to exercise authority* over daughters, whether protective or controlling, accounted for only 10% of the interactions as compared to 30% for fathers. The majority of asymmetrical interactions involved daughters *confiding in mother* (27%) and mothers *giving advice on personal matters* (20%). Daughters reported: ". . . I tell my mother almost everything." "I tell my mother my problems." "My mother tells me what to do with guys." "She gives me advice about sex." Other asymmetrical interactions concerned *mothers' giving support and encouragement* (8%) to daughters. Symmetrical interactions in this relationship included descriptions of *conversations on personal issues* (25%) and *shared activities* (10%). Thus, while both mothers and fathers typically share activities with daughters, mothers and daughters, unlike fathers and daughters, "discuss problems with each other," "have close personal talks," and "tell each other everything."

Although typical interactions in both parent-daughter relationships are primarily asymmetrical in form, the quality of the relationships appears to be different. Adolescent daughters tend to characterize relationships with fathers, for the most part, in terms of authority-related interactions. The father's authority is exercised either directly through rule-making or rule-enforcing, or indirectly through advice- and information-giving on practical matters. This view of fathers as authority figures is tempered somewhat, however, by his provision of emotional support and encouragement to his daughter. In contrast to their interactions with their fathers, daughters describe interactions with their mothers in terms of intimate exchanges. These exchanges are described as either symmetrical, with both participants sharing problems and personal information, or asymmetrical, with only daughters making self-disclosures. Advice giving by mothers also reflected intimacy since the nature of the advice concerned issues relevant to the personal domain of their daughters' lives, as well as more practical concerns. This intimacy, however, still remained predominantly asymmetrical since it was usually daughters, not mothers, who were disclosing personal information or receiving advice on personal matters.

Although characteristic parent-daughter interactions were predominantly asymmetrical, daughters' reports of their most enjoyed activities with parents, in study 7, were unanimously symmetrical. In both relationships, the common "most enjoyed activities" were *going places together, talking together,* and *performing an activity together.* In the mother-daughter relationship, 37 of the 40 *going places together* activities involved shopping. The frequencies of the interactions for both parent-daughter relationships and for the two age levels sampled in study 7 are presented in table 1.

Two results are noteworthy. First, when asked what they liked to do best with their fathers, 27% of the daughters said *nothing.* When asked what they liked to do best with their mothers, only 7% responded nothing. This difference was highly significant ($p < .01$). Also, in both relationships there was a statistically significant age difference in the types of enjoyed activities— younger girls responded with activities involving *going places together* and older girls focused on *talking together* or *performing an activity together* (in the father-daughter relation).

What do parents and daughters do together, then? From the present samples, it appears that fathers and daughters most typically engage in interactions that are authority-related. Fathers attempt to direct their daughters' behavior through control or influence, and daughters obey or disobey. Fathers advise their daughters on practical matters, and daughters seek their fathers' advice or instruction. It is this authority aspect of the relationship that may explain why 27% of the daughters were unable to provide instances of ac-

Table 1. Daughters' Descriptions of Enjoyed Activities with Parents

	Relation			
	Father-Daughter Age in years[a]		Mother-Daughter Age in years[b]	
Enjoyed Activities	15–16	17–18	15–16	17–18
1. *Going places together* (shopping, going to the racetrack, going on trips)	17	6	25	15
2. *Talking together* (talking philosophically, having an intellectual discussion, having long personal conversations)	5	13	9	19
3. *Performing an activity together* (working in the garden, riding bikes together, fishing, swimming)	5	11	3	3
4. *Nothing*	12	10	3	3
5. *Miscellaneous*	1	0	0	0

[a]$\chi^2(3) = 11.25; p < .01$
[b]$\chi^2(1) = 4.81; p < .05$
Chi-square analysis of mother-daughter data was limited to categories $1 + 2$ only because of the small numbers represented by categories $3 + 4$.

tivities they enjoyed doing with their fathers. Perhaps many adolescent females view their fathers as authority figures, and this perception precludes the occurrence of enjoyable interactions. Fathers, however, not only exercise authority, they also provide emotional support and encouragement—and fathers and daughters do go places together, share activities, and talk to one another. However, these activities are not frequently reported as typical of this relationship.

Mothers and daughters engage in interactions that differ from those of fathers and daughters with regard to intimacy. Mothers and daughters, like fathers and daughters, go shopping together, work together, play games together, and talk together. Unlike with their fathers, however, daughters talk to their mothers about personal as well as nonpersonal issues, and some mothers even reciprocate in these discussions. Thus, although mothers appear to be viewed as authorities by daughters, this authority role does not entirely inhibit the daughters', and sometimes the mothers', willingness to make self-disclosures or to discuss intimate issues.

Topics of Communication

The data reported above imply that during adolescence, communication between fathers and daughters is, for the most part, limited to practical or objective social issues. Communication between mothers and daughters appears to incorporate personal matters, as well as practical concerns. This section focuses more specifically on the topics that daughters talk about with their parents. It includes responses from studies 6 and 7. In study 7, adolescent girls were presented with a list of 22 topic areas and 4 persons representing significant others—father, mother, close female friend, close male friend. The girls were asked to indicate the person they were most likely and least likely to talk to about each of the 22 topics. In study 6, there were 7 general topic areas—schoolwork, friendship, future school and job plans, dating, family, religion, and social issues. In study 6, adolescent girls were asked to indicate whether or not they discussed each topic area with their fathers and mothers.

In study 7, of the 4 significant others, the father was most frequently selected as the person the daughters would be most likely to talk to on only one topic area—*political beliefs* (41%). In contrast, the father was most often selected as the person the daughters would be least likely to talk to on 20 of the 22 items, the exceptions being *career goals* and *political beliefs*. More than 60% of the girls said they would be least likely to talk to their fathers about their *views on sex* or *marriage*, their *feelings about close male friends,* and their *problems with their fathers.* Over 50% chose the father as the person they would be least likely to talk to about their: *feelings about friends, feelings about mothers and fathers, doubts about their abilities, problems at school, problems with female and male friends,* and *fears about life.*

In comparison, adolescent girls most frequently selected the mother as the most preferred communicant when the topics were *how well I'm doing in school* (59%), *my problems with father* (53%), *my feelings about father* (50%), *my problems with brothers or sisters* (49%), *my views on religion* (45%), and *my career goals* (44%). Mothers were selected with equal frequency as close female friends in discussions of *feelings about brothers and sisters* and *hopes and plans for the future.* The mother ranked third or fourth as the least preferred communicants on all but 5 topic areas. For these 5 topics, they ranked second behind father. However, the percentages of daughters selecting the mother for these topics were considerably smaller than those selecting the father.

Fathers were the preferred communicants for daughters, then, only when the topic was political beliefs. Adolescent daughters, however, sought communication with their mothers when the topics concerned problems and feelings about family members, as well as school issues, career goals, and hopes and plans for the future. This suggests that daughters preferred to talk to their fathers when the issues concerned objective social matters. When issues involved the personal domain of the lives of adolescent females, mothers were often the preferred communicants.

Despite these findings with regard to preferences, the results from study 6 indicate that many parents and daughters do discuss both social matters and personal issues. Eight-three percent of the daughters, for example, reported that they discussed with their fathers the way they handled their *schoolwork* or what they should do to make better grades. Other topic areas frequently discussed with fathers were "future school and job plans" (82%), "the way you behave toward your *family* or problems you may have with your family" (83%), "the way you behave toward your *friends* or problems you may have with friends" (61%), and *social issues* (58%). This last topic area was discussed significantly ($p < .01$) more frequently by the oldest girls (18–20 years) in study 6 than by the two groups of younger girls (12–13 years and 14–15 years). Topic areas less frequently discussed with fathers were *religious beliefs* (48%) and "what you should or should not do on *dates*" (33%).

Similar results were found for discussions with mothers in this study. Frequencies of discussions with mothers were slightly higher than for those with fathers for the general topic areas of *school* (90%), *future plans* (92%), *family* (87%), and *social issues* (61%) and were considerably higher for the topic areas of *friendships* (85%), ($p < .01$); *religious issues* (71%), ($p < .01$); and *dating* (50%), ($p < .01$). As with the father-daughter relationship, discussions of social issues with mothers varied significantly with the age level of the daughters ($p < .05$). While 80% of the 18–20-year-old girls indicated that they discussed social issues with their mothers, only 53% of the 14–15 year olds and 50% of the 12–13 year olds reported discussions of this topic.

In summary, it appears that more mothers and daughters than fathers and daughters talk to one another about each of these specific topics, and mother-daughter conversations, in general, appear to cover a wider range of issues than do father-daughter communications. Again, father-daughter communications seem to focus primarily on objective social issues and the practical aspects of the daughters' lives (politics, school, future plans, and societal issues). In contrast, mother-daughter discussions cover the personal as well as the practical domains of the daughters' lives—although the daughters' dating behavior and views about male friends appear to be less frequently discussed. Mothers are also the preferred communicants, over both fathers and friends, when topics involve family issues, school, and future goals. The reason for this discrepancy in communication between fathers and daughters and mothers and daughters is not clear at this point. One possible explanation may be that father-daughter communication is more limited than mother-daughter communication because the quality of communication differs in the two relationships. This issue is discussed in the following section.

The Quality of Parent-Daughter Communication

This section includes responses from studies 6 and 7. In study 6, adolescent females who indicated that they did discuss particular topic areas with their parents were asked to report how frequently (often or not very often) their parents explained reasons for their ideas on a particular topic and how frequently their parents really tried to understand their daughters' ideas on this topic. Responses to these items were analyzed separately, but individual subjects' responses to both items were compared to assess for general types of communication. Communication in a particular topic area was judged to involve *symmetrical understanding* if parents were reported to often explain their reasons and to often try to understand their daughters' ideas. An assessment of *nonunderstanding* was made if daughters indicated that parents did not often explain reasons or try to understand their ideas. If parents were described as often performing one function but not often performing the other, a judgment was made of *asymmetrical understanding*.

In study 6, the majority of girls who indicated that discussions with their fathers did take place on each topic area reported that their fathers often explained reasons for their ideas in discussions of *future plans* (76%), *schoolwork* (70%), behavior in the *family* (65%), and *social issues* (65%). (Percentages are based on the number of girls reporting that discussions on a particular topic did take place with parents. The *N* for each of these is provided in Table 2). Less than 50% of the girls, however, reported that their fathers often explained reasons in discussions of *religious beliefs* (47%), *dating behavior* (43%), or *friendships* (47%). Similarly, more than 50% of the daughters indicated that their fathers often "really tried to understand their ideas" when discussions involved *future plans* (69%) and *social issues* (61%), but less than 50% reported this to be true in discussions of *schoolwork* (47%), *family (41%), friendship* (38%), *dating* (30%), or *religious issues* (39%). Overall, fathers were seen as more often explaining their reasons for ideas than as trying to understand the ideas of their daughters.

Similar patterns emerged in the mother-daughter relationships. Here, however, over 50% of the girls noted that their mothers often explained reasons for their ideas in the discussions of all 7 topic areas—ranging from 77% in discussions of family issues to 56% in discussions of social issues. Like fathers, mothers were viewed as less frequently "really trying to understand daughters' ideas" than as explaining their own reasons and ideas.

The results of the assessment of the form of communication are shown in Table 2. In general, communication based on symmetrical understanding was slightly more frequent in the mother-daughter relationship than in the father-daughter relationship. In the father-daughter relationship, symmetrical understanding appeared to characterize discussions of *future plans* (57%) and *social issues* (54%), while conversations regarding *schoolwork* and *family* were more frequently typified by asymmetrical understanding. Finally, father-daughter discussions of *friendship, dating,* and *religion* were most frequently characterized by nonunderstanding. For the mother-daughter relationship, the

Table 2. Type of Understanding Characteristic of Parent-Daughter Discussions of
Seven Topic Areas

Topic Areas	Type of Understanding		
	Symmetrical	Asymmetrical	Nonunderstanding
Schoolwork			
Father (N=74)	35%	48%	17%
Mother (N=81)	37	36	27
Friendship			
Father (N=55)	25	35	40
Mother (N=77)	42a	35	23
Future			
Father (N=75)	57	30	13
Mother (N=83)	46	33	21
Dating			
Father (N=30)	20	33	47
Mother (N=52)	28	40	32
Family			
Father (N=75)	35	37	28
Mother (N=78)	45	41	14
Religion			
Father (N=43)	28	30	42
Mother (N=64)	39	28	33
Social Issues			
Father (N=52)	54	21	25
Mother (N=55)	42	25	33

[a] $\chi^2(1) = 7.68$, $p < .01$ for differences between mother and father regarding symmetrical understanding.

most frequent type of communication for all topic areas, except dating, was symmetrical understanding. However, not more than 46% of the daughters indicated this type of communication for any topic area.

Study 7 addressed more general procedures characterizing parent-daughter communications. These were divided into categories reflecting openness and intimacy, acceptance, and the use of either cooperation or authority in settling disagreements. The subjects in study 7 were presented with items pertaining to each of the procedural categories and asked, for each item, to select the person with whom they were most likely to communicate in that manner. The persons they were to choose from were mother, father, close female friend, and close male friend. The percentages of daughters selecting the mother and the father for each item are shown in table 3. Overall, the father was selected more frequently than were any of the other three persons when the items reflected a closed or guarded form of communication, a nonacceptance of the daughter's point of view or the value of her advice, and the use of authority procedures in resolving disputes. In contrast, the father was selected less fre-

Table 3. Percentage of Daughters Selecting Fathers and Mothers on 16 Items Representing Procedures of Communication

	Selecting Father	Selecting Mother
Openness & intimacy		
1. This person and I always talk openly to each other	1%	10%
2. This person and I are not embarrassed to talk about our doubts and fears to each other	0	9
3. I am usually very careful what I say to this person	31	21
4. I usually hide my true feelings from this person	36	21
5. This person has never admitted any doubts or fears to me[a]	57	9
6. This person does not express his/her true feelings to me[a]	49	10
7. I would never admit my doubts and fears to this person[a]	44	14
8. This person does not talk openly to me[a]	56	11
Acceptance of other's point of view		
9. I am not interested in any advice this person has to offer[b]*	25	11
10. This person does not consider my advice worth seeking[b]	54	12
11. This person always accepts my point of view even if it is different from his/hers	6	11
12. When we don't agree, this person always listens carefully to my side of the issue[a]	5	22
Use of authority in resolving disagreements		
13. When we don't agree, this person usually insists I change	37	34
14. When we don't agree, this person says I should change my opinion because he/she knows more	36	32
Use of cooperation in resolving disagreements		
15. When we don't agree, this person usually talks out differences with me	6	15
16. When we don't agree, this person usually gives me good reasons why I should change my point of view	16	27

*Only 50 of the 80 subjects answered this question.
[a]$p < .01$
[b]$p < .05$

quently than any of the other persons on items representing mutual openness or intimacy, acceptance of the daughter's point of view, and use of cooperative procedures in the settlement of disagreements.

While the mother was selected only slightly more frequently than the father on items reflecting mutual intimacy, mothers were chosen far less frequently than fathers on items pertaining to guardedness in communication. Mothers were also viewed as more likely than fathers to accept their daughters' points of view, and less likely than fathers to reject the value of their daughters'

opinions or advice. Mothers and fathers were selected with about equal frequency on items representing the use of authority in settling disputes, but the
mother was chosen more often than the father when the items pertained to the
use of cooperative techniques.

The results of studies 6 and 7 indicate that from the daughters' perspectives, communications with mothers were more likely to be characterized by
symmetrical understanding, openness, acceptance, and cooperation than were
communications with fathers. When specific topic areas were examined,
however, discussions of *future plans* and *social issues* with fathers were reported by over 50% of the girls as characterized by symmetrical understanding, if not by openness and acceptance. These findings correspond to the
results reported previously concerning the topics of parent-daughter communication. Father-daughter communications appear to center around topics that
reflect practical concerns or objective issues and, correspondingly, are the
kinds of topics that many fathers and daughters discuss at a level of symmetrical understanding. In contrast, mother-daughter communications include
topics that cover both the practical and the personal domains of their daughters' existence. They are also more likely to involve symmetrical understanding across topic areas, less guardedness, and more acceptance and
cooperation regardless of topic area.

Despite these differences between the father-daughter and the mother-
daughter relationships, communication in neither relationship can be said to
be characterized by a high level of symmetrical understanding, mutual openness, acceptance, or cooperation. Thus, differences in the quality of communications with parents, in general, cannot fully explain the discrepancy
between fathers and mothers with respect to the range and frequency of communications with daughters. To examine this issue further, the next section
will deal with specific qualities of the relationship itself.

The Quality of Parent-Daughter Relationships

This section presents daughters' perspectives on specific aspects of their relationships with their parents. These aspects are: Do parents meet the daughters'
material and emotional needs? Do parents and daughters share similar expectations and have respect for one another? And, is self-disclosure a major part
of the relationship? The data presented in this section are from studies 3 and 7.
Study 7 focused on whether or not parents meet their daughters' material and
emotional needs and what daughters do in return if these needs are met. The
daughters were asked to respond *true* or *false* to the statements: "My moth-
er(father) usually makes sure that I get the things I need. For example, she(he)
gives me money to buy things, like food and clothes"—material need. "My
mother(father) is usually sensitive to my feelings. For example, she(he) listens when I have a problem"—emotional need. They were then asked to

describe what they do in return for the parent if they answered *true* for these statements.

Study 3 addressed the relational features of *fairness, respect,* and *self-disclosure.* These features were assessed with regard to positive symmetry, negative symmetry, and asymmetry. Adolescent females were given a list of 6 true-false statements, 3 statements presenting their behavior (e.g., I usually expect more from my father(mother) in our relation than I am willing to give back), and 3 statements depicting their parents' behavior (e.g., My father(mother) usually expects more from me in our relation than he(she) is willing to give back). In this study, about 50% of the daughters answered these questions in reference to their fathers and the other half in reference to their mothers. When an individual subject answered a pair of statements in a positive way, a judgment was made of *positive symmetry* (neither person expects more than they are willing to give back). When a pair of statements was answered in a negative way, the assessment was for *negative symmetry* (both persons expect more than they are willing to give back). Finally, if one statement was answered in a positive way and the other one in a negative way, the feature was assessed as *asymmetrical* in the relation (one expects more but the other does not).

The results for study 3, shown in table 4, indicate that parent-child relationships do not differ considerably with respect to the symmetry of these features of the relationship. Relationships with parents appear to be positively symmetrical with regard to *respect,* (both persons consider the other to be as important as the self in the relationship). They are characterized, however, by asymmetry in *fairness* and by negative symmetry with regard to *willingness to self-disclose*—since neither person feels free to tell the other everything. With regard to fairness, daughters frequently describe themselves as expecting more from their fathers (21 out of 30) and mothers (17 out of 24) than they were willing to give back. While negative symmetry of self-disclosure was the most frequent category in both relations, some type of self-disclosure was reported as occurring significantly more often in the mother-daughter relationship (60%) than in the father-daughter relationship (31%).

Table 4. The Symmetry of Parent-Daughter Relations with Regard to Respect, Fairness, and Willingness to Make Self-Disclosures

Type of Symmetry	Fairness		Respect		Self-Disclosure[a]	
	Father	Mother	Father	Mother	Father	Mother
Positive symmetry	17	17	28	30	8	13
Negative symmetry	5	9	12	8	36	20
Asymmetry	30	24	12	12	8	17

[a]$\chi^2(2) = 8.96; p < .05$

In study 7, the majority of the 80 daughters (70%) described the father as meeting their material needs, but only 35% said the father met their emotional needs. When asked what they do in return for their fathers if they do meet their material needs ($N = 56$), 32% of the daughters provided responses reflecting symmetrical reciprocity (e.g., "Help him out with his work." "Help him around the house."), while 57% offered responses indicating asymmetrical reciprocity (e.g., "Obey him." "Do well in school." "Thank him." "Tell him I love him."). Eleven percent did not answer this part of the question. Similarly, when asked to report what they do for their fathers in return for meeting their emotional needs ($N = 28$), 61% of the daughters gave asymmetrical responses ("Thank him." "Obey him." "Tell him my problems." "Listen to his advice."), while only 14% gave examples involving symmetrical reciprocity ("Listen to him when he has a problem." "Do the same for him.") On this part of the question, 25% of the daughters did not answer.

In contrast to fathers, the mother was reported by the majority of daughters as meeting both material (84%) and emotional (72%) needs. The difference between mothers and fathers with respect to meeting emotional needs was significant ($p < .01$). In addition, instances of symmetrical reciprocity were far higher in the mother-daughter relationship than in the father-daughter relationship. Of the 67 girls reporting that the mother met their material needs, 72% said they reciprocated in a symmetrical manner ("Help her out around the house."), while only 25% reported asymmetrical reciprocity ("Thank her." "Obey her."). This pattern was the reverse of that found in the father-daughter relationship. Instances of symmetrical reciprocity were less frequent in the mother-daughter relationship when the issue concerned meeting emotional needs ($N = 58$) but still occurred more often than in the father-daughter relationship. Forty percent of the daughters indicated they reciprocated to their mothers in a symmetrical manner in response to meeting their emotional needs as compared to only 14% reporting this form of reciprocity in the father-daughter relationship. However, even in mother-daughter relationships, reciprocation to emotional needs was primarily asymmetrical (55%) with most of the daughters indicating that they "tell her my problems," or "listen to her advice." With respect to reciprocation to their mothers for meeting material needs, 3% of the daughters did not answer this part of the question. Five percent did not answer this question in response to meeting emotional needs.

Adolescent daughters, then, generally viewed their relationships with both parents as similar with regard to *respect, fairness,* and *meeting material needs.* Discrepancies between the relationships with the two parents arose, however, when issues pertained to self-disclosure, meeting emotional needs, and the type of reciprocity that occurred when both material and emotional needs were met. The first difference is that self-disclosure, whether symmetrical or asymmetrical, occurred more frequently in mother-daughter than in father-daughter relationships. This is consistent with the findings reported in the previous sections. Correspondingly, mothers were perceived as more likely than fathers to be "sensitive" to their daughters' feelings or to meet their emotional needs. When given the statement, "My father is sensitive to my feelings. . . ," 65% of the daughters sampled in study 7 marked this statement *false*. Although these findings were obtained from different studies, they are consistent in that self-disclosure is unlikely to take place in a relationship where one member is perceived as insensitive to, or not interested in, the feelings of another.

A different view of parent-daughter relationships is indicated in the discrepancy between the types of reciprocity characteristic of each relationship. The results suggest that daughters are more likely to reciprocate in a symmetrical manner to their mothers than to their fathers. In fact, reciprocation to their fathers was generally asymmetrical in that it was not related to the act that was being reciprocated. That is, if fathers meet material or emotional needs, daughters do not reciprocate in kind, but rather "obey him" or "thank him." In contrast, daughters were more likely to reciprocate in kind if mothers met their needs. This suggests that daughters perceive mothers as having needs and perceive themselves as able to respond to these needs, at least in part. Fathers, however, are either not perceived as having these needs, or daughters do not perceive themselves as able to respond to these needs in their fathers.

The general findings with regard to the quality of the relationships indicate a failure to deal with emotions in father-daughter relationships that is not commonly found in mother-daughter relationships. This emotional distance is consistent with the findings for fathers and daughters with respect to the types of interactions and the topics and quality of communication. It also suggests that problems may occur in the father-daughter relationship more often than in the mother-daughter relationship and that these problems may differ in form in the two relationships. This issue is discussed in the following section.

Problems in Parent-Daughter Relationships

Problems in parent-daughter relationships were examined in studies 4 and 7. In study 4, adolescent females were presented with 21 possible problem situations and asked to indicate whether or not each situation occurred in their relationships with their fathers and mothers, and if so, whether or not it caused conflict. Study 7 provided 18 conflict situations. Daughters were to indicate whether or not the situation occurred in their own relations with their parents, and whether it occurred more frequently with their father or with their mother. An example of a situation presented is: "My parent gets upset if I don't do my chores when I am asked." In addition, these same daughters were asked to describe (1) what they do that hurts their relationship with their father(mother) and (2) what their father(mother) does that hurts the relationship.

In study 4, contrary to expectations, only 3 out of the 21 problem situations were reported to occur with fathers by over 50% of the daughters. These were: "I don't do what my father tells me to do" (57%). "I got lower grades than my father expected" (52%). And, "There are some things about my father's personality that I don't like" (62%). The problem situation, "I went some-place my father told me not to go," was said to have occurred by 50% of the older girls (17–18 years) in study 4, but by only 12% of the younger girls (15–16 years) ($p < .05$). For almost all problem situations, if the problem was reported to have occurred, it was also reported to have caused a conflict in the relationship. The major exception that did not necessarily cause a conflict in the relationship was the problem situation of disliking aspects of the father's personality.

In contrast to the problem situations with their fathers, the majority of daughters reported an occurrence of 12 of the 21 problem situations when the parent was identified as the mother. The most frequently reported situations were: "I don't do what my mother tells me to do" (90%). "When my mother scolds me, I talk back to her" (82%). "My mother won't let me go someplace I want to go" (77%). And, "I got lower grades than my mother expected" (70%). Other commonly occurring problem situations in the mother-daughter relationship were: "When I'm in a bad mood, I yell at my mother" (67%). "I didn't clean my room like my mother asked" (63%). "I didn't tell my mother something important" (60%). "I went someplace my mother told me not to go" (58%). And, "My mother is unfair" (50%).

The discrepancy between the occurrence of problem situations in parent-daughter relationships was supported by the findings of study 7. In this study, 15 of the 18 conflict situations were reported as occurring in relations with parents by more than 50% of the daughters. Of these 15, only 4 were said to occur more often with fathers than with mothers, with none of the differences being significant. One conflict situation occurred with equal frequency, and the remainder were reported to have occurred more often with mothers than with fathers. Situations causing problems with fathers more often than with mothers were: "My parent gets upset if I get into trouble at school" (35% father, 29% mother, 36% neither). "I get upset when my parent yells at me" (53% father, 39% mother). "I get upset when my parent doesn't try to understand my point of view" (46% father, 35% mother). And, "I get upset when my parent criticizes me" (46% father, 35% mother). Conflict situations occurring with mothers considerably more often than with fathers were: "My parent gets upset when I don't help out when I'm asked" (51% mother, 32% father). "My parent gets upset when I don't tell her (him) what's going on in my life outside the home" (45% mother, 7% father [$p < .01$]). "My parent gets upset when I yell at her (him)" (52% mother, 35% father). "My parent gets upset when I don't do my chores after I've been told to" (59% mother, 25% father [$p < .01$]). "My parent gets upset when I don't let her (him) know I'm going to be late coming home" (65% mother, 18% father [$p < .01$]). "I get upset when my parent won't let me go out somewhere when I want to" (51% mother, 29% father [$p < .05$]). And, "I get upset when my parent makes me do something I don't want to do" (56% mother, 27.5% father [$p < .01$]).

From the two studies discussed above, it appears clear that despite the findings that father-daughter relationships involve limited communications and are perceived primarily in terms of authority-related interactions and communication and by a lack of meeting emotional needs, daughters and fathers do not become involved in a large number of problem situations. Those situations that do seem to occur with any frequency in the relationship involve the father's failure to treat the daughter with respect (yelling at her, criticizing her, or not trying to understand her) or the daughter's performance in her schoolwork. In contrast, problem situations occur frequently in the mother-daughter relationship and cover a wide range of issues. Particularly frequent are problems arising out of rules that govern the daughter's behavior and from expectations of assistance around the house. Daughters also reported that they fail to treat their mothers with respect (yelling at her, talking back to her) and perceived their mothers as being unfair in their expectations.

The reason for this discrepancy between mothers and daughters and between fathers and daughters with respect to conflicts or problems is not clear. It is possible that the emotional and psychological distance between daughters and fathers may prevent conflicts from occurring as well as deter positive types of interactions. It is also possible that the kinds of problem situations depicted in these studies did not tap those that may occur in father-daughter relationships. The data from study 7 concerning what it is that parents and daughters do to hurt their relationship may shed some light on this issue.

Daughters reported that they hurt their relationship with their father primarily by *ignoring him* (42%). More specifically, they said: "I don't talk to him." "I ignore him." "I never talk to him." "I stay away from him, try not to talk to him." And, "I avoid him, pretend like he's not there." They also indicated that they *act insubordinate* (25%) and to a lesser extent are *abrasive* (11%) to their father. In this vein daughters noted that they "talk back to him," "don't do what he says," "argue with him," "yell at him," "say mean things to him," and "act rude to him." A few daughters reported they hurt the relationship with their father by *not living up to his expectations* (6%), and 14% said they did *nothing* to hurt the relationship or did not answer the question. Two percent of the responses were idiosyncratic (i.e., "I'm not willing to go out in public with him.")

Correspondingly, fathers were described as hurting the relationship with their daughters mainly by *ignoring them* (32%). Daughters indicated: "He doesn't talk to me." "He never listens to me." "He doesn't ever talk." "He ignores me." And, "He never openly talks to me." Fathers were also frequently seen as hurting the relationship by being too *critical* (19%) of or *verbally abrasive* (16%) to their daughters. In this vein, fathers were said to "belittle me," "put me down all the time," "criticize me," "yell at me always," and "insult me." Other daughters indicated that fathers hurt their relationship by being *too authoritarian* (11%), or having a *character flaw* (15%) in their personalities (e.g., drinking, going out with other women, being too religious). Seven percent of the responses were idiosyncratic (e.g., "He is there!" "He does everything wrong." And, "He opens his mouth.").

In contrast to fathers, mothers are rarely reported to *ignore* their daughters (6%), ($p < .05$), and daughters do not frequently describe themselves as *ignoring* their mothers (9%), ($p < .01$). Instead, daughters report that they hurt their relationship with their mother mainly by being *insubordinate* (39%) or *verbally abrasive* (24%). For example daughters said that they "talk back to her," "yell at her," "don't do what she says," "say I hate her when I'm mad," and "fight with her." Other daughters indicated that they hurt their relationship with their mother by *not meeting expectations* (11%) and by *not telling her everything* (9%). Thus with respect to mothers, daughters hurt the relationship by "doing something I know she disapproves of," "not telling her everything," "not living up to her values," and "going out too much." Eight percent of the daughters either said they did *nothing* to hurt the relationship or did not answer the question.

Mothers were most frequently described as hurting the relationship by being *too authoritarian* (30%). This category included statements, such as "tells me I can't have the car," "makes me break up friendships," "doesn't let me go out," and "tells me who to hang around with." Mothers were also reported to hurt the relationship by being too *critical* (16%) or *verbally abrasive* (15%). Some daughters indicated that their mothers hurt the relationship by being *unwilling to talk about personal or serious things* (6%). Fourteen percent noted that their mothers had *flaws in their personalities* which caused problems in the relationship (e.g., "she's a dingbat," "has a demanding personality," "unreasonable person," or "drinks."). Thirteen percent either said *nothing* or did not answer the question.

These findings suggest that the major problem in the father-daughter relationship is simply that fathers and daughters do not talk to each other and often do not openly acknowledge each other's participation in the family. This lack of contact may explain in part why the problem situations presented in studies 4 and 7 were found to occur infrequently in father-daughter relationships. Other problems in the father-daughter relationship concerned the fathers' failure to treat their daughters with respect (verbal abrasiveness and criticism) and the daughters' reciprocation of this lack of respect (insubordination and verbal abrasiveness). Although fathers are clearly viewed as authority figures in the relationship, the fathers' "misuse" of authority was not frequently perceived as hurting the relationship.

In contrast to fathers, the mother's exercise of authority over her daughter was perceived as a major cause of problems in the relationship, as was the mother's failure to treat her daughter with respect (criticism and verbal abrasiveness). In complement, daughters hurt the relationship with their mothers by failing to show respect (insubordination and verbal abrasiveness). This is consistent with the findings of studies 4 and 7 with regard to the types of conflicts that take place in mother-daughter relationships—that is, conflicts over rules and conflicts arising out of insubordination and lack of respect. In summary, conflicts occur more frequently in the mother-daughter relationship, but the amount of contact between mothers and daughters is also greater than that between fathers and daughters—thus allowing for more problems to arise.

The major violation in the father-daughter relationship, then, is the apparently mutual failure of the participants to acknowledge each other. Thus the emotional distance that is characteristic of this relationship, and that was reported in the previous section, is further elaborated by a physical distance created by fathers and daughters simply not talking to each other or generally ignoring each other. While this violation may not reveal much information about the structure of this relationship with respect to the rules which govern it, it does have implications for an understanding of the structure of the relationship with regard to the connectedness or detachment characteristic of the relationship. The violation suggests that fathers and daughters are to a large extent detached from each other and that this detachment is harmful to their relationship.

The second most frequent violation in the father-daughter relationship, and one that was most characteristic of the mother-daughter relationship, concerns the issue of respect. Mothers fail to show respect for daughters and thus violate the relationship by being too controlling, critical or abrasive. Daughters violate this rule of the relationship by being insubordinate or rude. Part of this violation reflects a structure of unilateral authority in that daughters fail to show respect by disobeying their mothers, and mothers fail to show respect by not treating their daughters as equals (i.e., attempting to control their behavior). The other part of the violation reflects a more symmetrical aspect of the relationship in that neither party is allowed to criticize, or to be verbally abrasive to, the other without hurting the relationship. Thus, the kinds of situations that cause conflicts in parent-daughter relationships indicate that father-daughter and mother-daughter relationships have both unilateral and symmetrical components. The father-daughter relationship involves the additional factor of a general detachment of the participants from each other. It remains to be seen, in the next section, if procedures to work out problem situations reveal similar elements of the relationship.

Procedures for Dealing with Problems in Parent-Daughter Relationships

This section includes data from studies 5 and 6. In study 6, daughters were presented with the following statement for each parent: "When your mother(father) wants you to do something, and you want to do something else, how often does your mother(father). . .?" This statement was followed by a list of 8 procedures: 4 describing ways of dealing with the issue by indicating a respect for the other person's point of view, and 4 suggesting an authority position vis-à-vis the other person. Procedures indicating respect were "Keep talking about it hoping I would start wanting to do it," "Try to convince me I would enjoy doing what he(she) wants me to do," "Say he'll(she'll) do favors for me at other times if I go along with him(her) how," and "Ask me if I would be willing to do it." Those procedures suggesting an authority relation were "Say I'm supposed to do what I'm told," "Simply tell me to do it," "Say he(she) expects me to do what I'm told," and "Keep telling me to do it until I do it." For each procedure, daughters were asked to report how often (*not often* or *often*) each parent utilized the procedure in the situation that was described. In relationships with both fathers and mothers, the procedures were found to load on two major factors (c.f., Chapter 2, Study 6). One factor, mutual procedures, included all procedures that indicated respect for the other, except "asks me if I would be willing to do it." The other factor, unilateral procedures, included all four statements that indicated an authority position.

In the father-daughter relationship, mutual procedures were not frequently described as utilized by fathers. Less than 35% of the daughters said that when there was a disagreement between them, their fathers often "keep talking about it hoping I would start wanting to do it" (32%), "say I would enjoy doing what he wants me to do" (34%), and "offer to do favors for me in return" (22%). Surprisingly, unilateral procedures were also not frequently reported as utilized by fathers. Only 51% of the daughters said that their fathers often "say he expects me to do what I'm told," and less than 50% noted that their fathers often "say I'm *supposed* to do what I'm told" (42%), "simply tell me to do it" (43%), and "keep telling me to do it until I do it" (40%).

Similar to findings for fathers, mothers were reported to not often use mutual procedures when there was a disagreement with their daughters. The procedure "keep talking about it hoping I would want to start doing it," however, was more frequently reported as used by mothers (47%) than by fathers (32%). In contrast to findings about the fathers, over 50% of the daughters said that their mothers often used unilateral procedures—that is, "say she expects me to do what I'm told" (54%), "keep telling me to do it" (57%), and "simply tells me to do it" (57%).

In general, then, mutual procedures for dealing with disagreements are not utilized frequently by either mothers or fathers. Mothers, however, appear to utilize unilateral procedures slightly more often than do fathers. It may be the case, however, that the type of situation presented does not occur often between fathers and daughters or that if it does occur, fathers simply do not deal with it.

To assess procedures of resolution further, female adolescents in study 5 were presented with two hypothetical situations describing a situation that caused a conflict between a daughter and her parent. The mother was the target parent in one situation, and the father in the other. The situation was described as follows:

> Mary is a girl your age. Mary and her mother (father) usually get along well. One night, however, Mary came home very late from a party. She had done this a few times before and her mother (father) was very upset. She (He) felt that this caused a serious problem in her (his) relationship with her (his) daughter.

For each parent-daughter relationship, the task for the subjects was to indicate whether or not they felt this situation would cause a problem in the relationship; what they believed would have to take place to make things better in the relationship; whether or not a similar situation had ever occurred in their own relationship with the target parent; and, if it had, what was done to resolve the problem.

When the father was the parent presented in the hypothetical situation, 86% of the daughters reported that the event would probably cause a problem in the relationship. Descriptions of how this problem might be resolved fell into two general categories—*compromise resolutions* and *status quo resolutions. Compromise resolutions,* accounting for 30% of the descriptions, included procedures leading to the father's extension of the curfew hour. This was usually agreed to after a discussion of the daughter's reasons for being late or after her straightforward request for a later curfew. In contrast, *status quo resolutions,* accounting for 70% of the responses, incorporated procedures designed to make things better in the relationship without changing the curfew hour. The most frequently reported procedure in this category (N = 35) involved *fathers explaining why they are upset* (40%). An example of this is: "Her father should tell her why he wants her in on time—not just to be mean—it's for her own safety and she should understand this." Other procedures leading to *status quo resolutions* were: *father stands by rule,* either through punishment or threat, and daughter accepts this position (23%); *daughter apologizes or provides reasonable explanations* (23%); and *daughter proves herself trustworthy on future occasions* (14%). Regardless of the specific procedures, however, inherent in all the *status quo* resolutions is the daughter's acceptance of the validity both of the rule and of her father's enforcement of it.

Despite the finding that all the daughters were able to provide clear solutions to the hypothetical problem with fathers, only 36% reported that this type of situation had ever occurred in their own relationship with fathers. In addition, resolutions to these actual situations rarely involved *compromise* (17%), with the end result more frequently being a maintenance of the *status quo* (83%).

Results for the mother-daughter hypothetical situation were similar to those found for the father-daughter relationship. Again, most of the daughters reported that the situation was likely to cause a problem in the relationship (84%) and solutions provided for the problem were more frequently *status quo resolutions* (62%) than *compromise resolutions* (38%). Also similar to the father-daughter situation, the most common procedure leading to a *status quo* solution involved mothers' explanations of their fears and worries (50%).

In contrast to the father-daughter relationship, however, 68% of the daughters reported that a similar event had in fact occurred in their own relationships with their mothers. Twelve percent of these girls ($N = 34$) indicated that the problem was resolved through *compromise solution,* 68% provided *status quo solutions,* and 20% noted that the problem was not resolved. It is interesting to note that none of the actual *status quo solutions* involved mothers explaining their reasons to their daughters. Instead, procedures leading to a *status quo solution* were *punishment and acceptance of punishment, obedience to the curfew on future occasions,* or *provision of an acceptable explanation* for lateness.

In summary, for both fathers and mothers, resolutions of this type of problem situation most commonly involved procedures that improved the relationship while at the same time maintained the status quo with respect to rules and expectations. This suggests that daughters view their parents as persons who construct rules for the daughters' benefit and who are basically concerned for their daughters' welfare. Daughters, in complement, are viewed by the female subjects in the study as required to understand this concern and to accept these concerns as valid. The major difference between the mother-daughter and the father-daughter relationship is that the event described in the hypothetical situation was said to occur with their mothers in "real-life" by almost twice as many daughters as those who reported it occurring with their fathers ($p < .01$). In fact, of the girls who indicated that this situation had not occurred with their fathers, 53% reported that it had occurred with their mothers. This suggests that daughters do break the rules on occasion but that breaking a rule is more likely to bring them into conflict with their mothers than with their fathers. One explanation for this may be that mothers are the family "rule makers" and, therefore, are the ones who take action when a rule is broken. This finding is consistent with the results on conflicts that were reported in the previous section. It is also consistent with the finding that fathers are not frequently reported as using either mutual or unilateral procedures to resolve disputes over what their daughters want to do. It may be that this type of situation—father wants daughter to do something, but daughter does not want to do it—simply does not frequently occur in father-daughter relations.

Self-Conception and Obligations in Parent-Daughter Relations

The previous sections have dealt primarily with daughters' conceptions of their mothers and fathers with regard to specific aspects of parent-daughter relationships. This section focuses on how daughters conceptualize themselves in these relationships and what they feel are their obligations to their parents. The data presented are from studies 2 and 7. Prior to study 7, 40 adolescent females in study 1 were asked to provide three descriptions of the way they usually act or feel when they are with their fathers, mothers, and friends. Thirty of these descriptions were then presented to the subjects in study 7 who were asked to indicate the person—father, mother, close female friend, close male friend—with whom they were most likely to feel or act this way.

When they were with their fathers, the majority of daughters described themselves as *distant* (64%), *uncomfortable* (65%), *withdrawn* (64%), and *insensitive* (44%). They also selected father more often than the others when the descriptions were *argumentative* (46%), *dishonest* (33%), *careful what I say* (42%), *phony* (38%), *critized* (45%), and *insecure* (40%). One percent or less of the daughters said that they were likely to be *open* or *playful* or to feel *accepted* when they were with their fathers. Self-descriptions in the mother-daughter relationship were not so clear cut. However, mothers were selected more often than were the others when the self-descriptions were *helpful* (53%), *loved* (36%), *judgmental* (34%), *selfish* (32%), and *cooperative* (32%).

In general, daughters appear to feel primarily distant, uncomfortable and withdrawn when they are with their fathers. This is consistent with the findings on the lack of contact and communication and the emotional distance that appears to exist between fathers and daughters. Descriptions of self in the mother-daughter relationship reflect the more complex nature of this relationship. Here, daughters are helpful and cooperative and feel loved, but they are also judgmental of their mothers and act selfish when they are with her.

In study 2, daughters were asked to describe what they felt they should do for their fathers and mothers and why they felt this was important. For their fathers, 56% of the daughters said they should *obey him* or *meet his expectations,* 34% reported that they should *talk to him* or *spend time with him,* and 10% said they should *help him out.* The reasons given for why it was important to fulfill these obligations fell into 4 general categories. Thirty-four percent of the daughters felt they should do a specific thing for their fathers because it *makes him feel good*—"He needs it, he has a hard time of it." "Makes him feel that you love him." "It makes him feel good." "He has feelings too." Twenty-six percent of the daughters fulfilled obligations to their fathers because they felt it was a *repayment of their debt* to him. This debt was described in terms of the amount of money that fathers provided in support of their daughters—for example, "He put a lot of money into raising me," "He's making all the money to support me," and "He has provided a lot for me." In addition to these reasons, 24% of the daughters said that meeting obligations *keeps the relationship smooth*. Ten percent of the daughters said that they should meet their obligations to their father, because he *acts in the best interest* of the daughter—for example, "He knows best," "He is smarter than you and can keep you out of trouble." Twelve percent of the reasons given could not be classified into any one category.

In contrast to the obligations daughters reported they have to fathers, only 32% of the daughters said that they should *obey mother* or *meet her expectations*. Instead, the most frequent obligation that was felt toward the mother was to *help her out* (42%). Similar to feelings toward their fathers, some daughters also felt obliged to *talk to* or *spend time with* their mothers (28%). The major reason daughters gave for fulfilling obligations to mother was to *make her feel good* (46%)—"Mother needs it (help)." "Shows I love her and adults need a lot of love." "So my mother won't feel bad, unloved." Another reason that daughters gave for fulfilling obligations to their mothers was that it *keeps the relation smooth* (30%). This category included responses such as "so she won't get mad at me," and "to make a good relationship." Fewer daughters described obligations to their mothers as *repayments of debts* (16%). When they did, however, the debt did not refer to financial provisions—as it did in their relationships with their fathers—but rather to their mothers' personal involvement: "She has given me so much time and energy, it's the least I can do (to help her out)," "She does so much for me," and "She raised me and everything." Even fewer daughters (8%) felt that obligations should be met because mothers *act in the best interest* of their daughters—for example, "so I can grow-up right," and "because mother knows what's best for me."

Overall, the results of our studies about obligations and why it is important to fulfill them underscore the unilateral aspect of the father-daughter relationship and are consistent with the indications that the mother-daughter relationship has both unilateral and symmetrical components. In general, daughters felt obliged to *obey* their fathers or to *meet his expectations for their behavior*. The reasons for fulfilling these obligations were to repay their father's financial support and to keep the father-daughter relationship smooth. The concept seems to be that to show respect for their fathers and to maintain positive relations with them, it is necessary to do so on their terms. For some of the daughters, however, their fathers were persons with whom they should talk and spend time, as well as obey because it makes their fathers feel good. This suggests that even in this unilateral relationship, daughters recognize fathers' needs as persons as well as their positions as authority figures. However, this awareness of their fathers' needs does not extend to perceptions of their fathers as persons who need help, or can get help, from their daughters.

In contrast to the obligations daughters felt toward their fathers, the major obligation daughters felt toward their mothers was to help them out. This obligation was performed because it made their mothers feel good or it kept the relationship running smoothly. Daughters viewed their mothers as persons whose expectations should be met to make them feel good or to repay them—not for their financial support, but for their personal support. These findings suggest that adolescent females are more aware of their mothers as persons with feelings and needs of their own than they are of similar feelings and needs of their fathers. This implication is consistent with previously reported findings pertaining to differences in the mother-daughter and father-daughter relationships with respect to communication and the quality of the relationships.

Adolescent Daughters' Perception of Parents

Basically, the data from our studies provide a fairly clear-cut and consistent picture of how daughters perceive their realtionships with their fathers. Fathers are perceived as authority figures who provide advice on practical matters and guidelines for their daughters' behavior. Some fathers also encourage and support their daughters, but this support is from a distance and lacks emotional content. Contact between fathers and daughters occurs infrequently, and when it does occur, it usually lacks intimacy, understanding, and acceptance. Daughters describe themselves as uncomfortable and withdrawn in this relationship but at the same time, actual conflicts occur infrequently. Thus, their relationship with their fathers may more aptly be described as a "nonrelation" than as a negative one.

The data for the mother-daughter relationship present a more complex picture. This relationship appears to involve a combination of authority and equality, intimacy and conflict. Mothers, like fathers, are viewed as authority figures but not as distant ones. Daughters feel free to confide in their mothers, as well as to fight with them and to disobey them. Mothers meet their daughters' emotional as well as material needs, and daughters often reciprocate in kind. Mothers and daughters also appear to talk about a variety of topics, although the quality of their communication may not always be ideal. In addition, daughters appear to perceive their mothers as persons who need their help as much as they perceive them as persons who can help them. This perception of "need" with respect to their mothers may explain why the authority aspect of this relationship is tempered by intimacy and moments of equality.

4

Adolescent Sons and Their Relations with Parents

The aim of this chapter is to summarize the data on parent-son relationships. The results cover the same aspects of the parent-child relationship that was reported in the chapter on daughters and parents: typical and enjoyed interactions, topics of conversation, communication style, quality of the relationship, conflicts, self-descriptions, and obligations. As was seen previously, daughters' perceptions of relations with their fathers differ markedly from their perceptions of relationships with their mothers. The general question for the present chapter is whether sons also differentiate between the two parents and, if so, whether or not the differences are similar to those found in parent-daughter relations.

Typical Interactions and Enjoyed Activities

The data presented in this section are from studies 1, 7, and 8. In study 1, adolescent males were asked to provide 3 interactions that typically occurred in their relations with their fathers and 3 interactions that were typical of their relations with their mothers. For fathers, 48% of the responses were classified as *instrumental interactions*. In this category, sons reported that their fathers "help with homework," "teach me things," "give me advice about my future," and "give knowledge to me." Twenty-five percent of the interactions specified *conversation,* which typically focused on common interests or practical matters; and 17% involved shared *recreational or work activities,* such as playing sports, fishing, hunting, camping, working together on projects, and working in the yard. Finally, 7% of the interactions described fathers as *exercising authority* over sons—3% were idiosyncratic. Overall, 42% of the interactions indicated a symmetry between the participants (conversa-

52

tions or recreational and work activities), while 58% implied an inequality or asymmetry between father and son.

In contrast to interactions with fathers, the most common interactions with mothers involved *conversation* (42%). In this category, sons were seen as either confiding in their mothers or providing their mothers with information about their activities. Eight of the 25 responses included in this category described mutual sharing of problems and advice. In addition, 25% of the mother-son interactions depicted *instrumental interactions*. In this vein, mothers, like fathers, "help me with homework," "give me advice, like on how to meet people," and "help me when I need it." Mothers were also described as *nurturing* (15%) and as *exercising authority* (8%). The former involved "cooking for" and "taking care of when sick"; the latter included "ordering" the sons to do things or "pushing him" about school grades. Only 2 responses described mothers and sons sharing an activity together other than talking, and 7% of the responses were idiosyncratic.

In summary, sons perceive fathers primarily as persons who give them advice or knowledge and as persons with whom they can converse on objective issues or practical matters. Mothers are also seen as "advisors" but far more frequently as persons in whom the son can confide. Unlike with their fathers, with their mothers sons feel free to "talk to her about anything," "talk to her openly," and "tell her my problems." Sons, however, appear to share activities with their fathers more often than with their mothers. Thus while fathers and sons play sports together, work together, and go camping and fishing, the major activity for mothers and sons seems to be talking.

Interactions between fathers and sons were further examined in study 8. This study did not sample mothers and sons. In study 8, adolescent sons and their fathers were given a list of 10 activities to be judged for frequency of occurrence. Over 70% of the sons reported that their fathers and they regularly *ate together, worked together on chores,* and *watched television together.* In addition, 50% reported that their fathers frequently *watched sons play athletics* either in the past or currently. Other frequently occurring activities were *play sports together* (50%), *go to sports events together* (42%), and *just talk* (48%). Thirty-three percent of the sons said they *shared hobbies* with their fathers, and 27% said they *participated in their fathers' work.* On the remaining item, *family activities,* there was a difference according to age group: 80% of the younger age group (mean age 16 years) said that they participated with their fathers in family activities, while only 58% of the older sons (mean age of 19 years) said that they did so.

These results were matched by judgments made by fathers of the same activities. There was little disparity in the percentages between sons' and fathers' judgments. The matching held even to the point of there being a difference on *family activities* between fathers of the younger boys and fathers of the older boys. Apparently, sons and fathers had similar perceptions of what they did or did not do together. Generally, apart from daily family activities, such as eating, watching T.V., and doing chores, most of the activities of fathers and sons appear to center around sports or recreational events. Fewer sons "just talk" to their fathers or share in their hobbies or their work.

Study 7 assessed parent-son interactions by focusing on the following question: What do you do with your mother (father) that you most enjoy? The most frequently cited enjoyed activity with their fathers was *joint recreation* (25%), which included activities such as fishing, camping, hunting, or playing sports. Sons also reported that they enjoyed *working with* their fathers (19%)—usually on projects around the house—*talking to* their fathers (16%), and *going places* with their fathers (14%). Twelve percent of the subjects said that they most enjoyed *unstructured* or *casual* activities, such as "watching T.V.," "driving around together," "telling dirty jokes" and "watching girls." Fourteen percent of the sons gave the response *nothing* to this question or did not answer it.

Sons did not report *joint recreation* as an enjoyed activity with their mothers. Instead, the most frequently reported enjoyed activity with mothers was *talking* (36%). Other enjoyed activities were *going places together* (30%)—primarily shopping—and *unstructured activities* (15%), such as "joking around," "watching T.V." or "just being together." Seven percent of the sons indicated they enjoyed *working* with their mothers (cooking, cleaning). Nine percent said *nothing* or did not provide an answer. Two responses could not be categorized.

From the sons' perspectives, then, both mothers and fathers are persons from whom they can seek guidance, assistance, and information. The major difference between the activities enjoyed with fathers and those enjoyed with mothers is that fathers and sons share recreational and some work activities, while mothers and sons talk. Conversations between mothers and sons also appear to cover both the personal and practical domains of the sons' lives, while conversations with fathers appear to be limited to practical matters or to objective social issues.

Topics of Conversation

A variation in the topics of conversation between fathers and sons and mothers and sons was found in the results of studies 6, 7, and 8. In study 8, adolescent sons were asked to describe what they were likely to talk about with their fathers. This study did not include data pertaining to mothers. The major topic was the son's *school performance*, stated by 66% of the subjects. Over 25% of the sons mentioned *sports* (46%), *politics* (35%), *events of the day* (29%), and *special interests* (27%). Less than 20% also noted *father's work* (19%), *advice* (17%), *household chores* (16%), *money* (14%), and son's *social activities* (8%).

These results are notable for the rare occurrence of discussion of personal matters and for the emphasis on school performance and sports. This finding is supported by the results of study 7. In study 7, sons, similar to the daughters discussed in chapter 3, were presented with a list of 22 topics that they might discuss with other persons. All of the topics referred to the adolescent's personal interest—for example, *my fears about life, my feelings about my girlfriend,* or *my career goals.* For each topic, the adolescents were to designate the person with whom they were most likely to discuss the topic and the person with whom they were *least* likely to discuss the topic. These choices were to be made from among four potential discussion partners: father, mother, close male friend, close female friend.

The father was selected more often than the other target person as the person that sons would be most likely to talk to when the topics were *my career goals* (41%), *my hopes and plans for the future* (33%), and *doubts about my abilities* (29%). For a fourth topic, *problems with my mother* (34%), the father was tied with the male friend as the preferred person to talk to. In all cases, however, less than 50%, and usually less than 40%, of the sons selected the father as the preferred discussion partner—thus indicating that even on these topics, there is little consensus among sons about their preference for fathers as discussion partners. Over 40% of the sons did select the father as the person they would be least likely to talk to when the topics were *my problems with my father* (51%), *my feelings about my father* (48%), *my problems at school* (44%), and *my attitudes toward marriage* (41%). Fathers were also the most frequent least preferred partners in discussion of *my problems with my girlfriend* (35%), *my feelings about my close male friend* (33%), *how well I'm doing in school* (34%), *my feelings about my girlfriend* (31%), *my moral standards* (30%), *my views on religion* (29%), and *my fears about life* (28%).

There were 8 items for which sons selected the mother more often than the other three persons as the most likely discussion partner. These items clustered in an interesting way. First of all, 4 items pertained to the family. These topics were *my problems with father* (56%), *my feelings about father* (55%), *my problems with brothers or sisters* (53%), and *my feelings about brothers and sisters* (41%). A second cluster included two items: *how well I'm doing at school* (49%) and *problems I'm having at school* (39%). The two remaining items dealt with *my views on religion* (45%) and *my attitudes toward marriage* (31%). The 4 topics for which the mother was the least preferred discussion partner over the other target persons were *my problems with my mother* (40%), *my feelings about my mother* (34%), *my views on sex* (39%), and *my views on society* (24%). For the remaining 18 items, the mother ranked 3rd or 4th as the least preferred discussion partner.

Topics of conversation between parents and sons were assessed a third way in study 6. Here sons were presented with 7 general topic areas each focusing on the son's behavior or perspective. These areas were (1) the way you handle your *schoolwork* or what you should do to make better grades, (2) the way you behave toward your *friends* or problems you may have with your friends, (3) your *future* school and job plans, (4) what you should or should not do on *dates,* (5) the way you behave toward your *family* or problems you may have with your family, (6) *religious beliefs* such as what you think about God and other religious teachings, and (7) *social issues* such as racial and sexual discrimination, draft for military service, or a social welfare program. The question was whether or not these topics were discussed between parents and sons. Over 80% of the sons indicated that they did discuss *family* (90%), *future plans* (88%), and *school* (87%) with their fathers; and over 60% reported discussions of *friends* (74%), *social issues* (71%), and *religion* (61%) with their fathers. Only 40% indicated that they discussed *dating* behavior with their fathers. In a similar vein, over 80% of the sons discussed *family* (91%), *school* (90%), *future* (89%), and *friends* (81%) with their mothers. Topics less often discussed with mothers were *religious beliefs* (77%), *social issues* (69%), and *dating* (47%). Overall, for 6 of the 7 topics, more sons talked with their mothers than with their fathers—however, this difference was negligible.

Data from these three studies are quite consistent. Adolescent males agree that their futures are a topic of discussion between them and their fathers. They and their fathers also discuss family issues, especially the problems that sons may be having with their mothers. Sons also discuss their school performance with their fathers, but fathers were clearly not the preferred discussion partners for this topic. Perhaps discussions of this topic are initiated by fathers, not by sons. The data are also consistent as to the topics fathers and sons rarely discuss. These topics are problems that sons have with their fathers, sons' social life outside the home, and feelings the sons have about other persons and themselves. The exception here was that fathers were the most frequently preferred discussion partners for the item regarding self-doubts about abilities. It is noteworthy, however, that only 34% of the sons chose the father for this topic. However, only 85% of the sons answered this item, which suggests that possibly 15% of them are not likely to discuss this topic with any of the target persons.

The data regarding mother-son conversations are also quite consistent. Discussions with mothers appear to cover a wider range of topics than those with fathers and include the personal as well as the practical domains of the sons' lives. Two topics, however, are rarely discussed between mothers and sons. These are *views about sex* and *dating.* Thus, with mothers, sons discuss family issues and problems, religious beliefs, issues concerning school, and to some extent, friendships with other males.

In summary, conversations not only are more typical in mother-son relationships than in father-son relationships, but also cover a wider range of topics. This is similar to the differences between the two parental relationships found for daughters. For the daughters, however, conversations with their fathers were even more limited and constrained than were those between fathers and sons.

The Quality of Communication

In this section, data from studies 6 and 7 are presented in a discussion of the style or quality of communication that characterizes parent-son conversations. In study 7, male adolescents were given a list of 17 items representing three general procedures of communication and were asked to select for each item the person with whom they were most likely to communicate in that manner.

Table 5. Percentages of Sons Selecting Father and Mother on Items Representing Procedures of Communication

Procedures	Selecting Father	Selecting Mother
Openness and intimacy		
1. This person and I always talk openly to each other	4%	17%
2. This person and I are not embarrassed to talk about our doubts and fears to each other	7	11
3. I am usually very careful what I say to this person	33*	16
4. I usually hide my true feelings from this person[a]	33*	14
5. This person has never admitted any doubts or fears to me[b]	34*	5
6. This person does not express his/her true feelings to me[a]	39*	11
7. I would never admit my doubts and fears to this person	30*	12
8. This person does not talk openly to me	31*	10
Acceptance of other's point of view		
9. I am not interested in any advice this person has to offer	14	11
10. This person does not consider my advice worth seeking	30*	14
11. This person always accepts my point of view even if it is different from his/hers	6	15
12. When we don't agree, this person usually listens carefully to my side of the issue	8	23
Use of authority in resolving disagreements		
13. When we don't agree, this person usually insists I change my point of view	29*	28
14. When we don't agree, this person usually says I should change my opinion because he/she knows more	44*	26
Use of cooperation in resolving disagreements		
15. When we don't agree, this person usually talks out differences with me	19	31†
16. When we don't agree, this person usually gives me good reasons why I should change my point of view	18	31†

*Father is most frequently selected person
†Mother is most frequently selected person
[a]$p < .05$
[b]$p < .01$

Again, the target persons were mother, father, close male friend, and close female friend. The items for each procedure and the percentages of sons selecting fathers and mothers for each item are shown in table 5.

The father was selected more frequently than were the other target persons when the items reflected a guardedness in communication and far less frequently than were the others when the items indicated openness or intimacy. Similarly, the father was chosen more frequently than were the others on all items that reflected the use of authority in disagreements and least frequently on items that focused on the use of negotiation. In addition, the father was rarely chosen for items that reflected acceptance of the son's point of view (items 11 and 12) but was the most frequent choice for the item pertaining to disregard for the son's advice or opinions (item 10).

Sons most frequently chose the mother as the person who *talks out differences with me* and who *gives me good reasons why I should change my opinion*. The mother was selected less often than were the others on all but two items that reflected a guardedness in communication. When compared to fathers and sons, mothers and sons were more likely to talk openly to each other and to tell each other their true feelings. In general, mothers were also more likely than fathers to respect their sons' opinions when there were disagreements. In contrast, sons and mothers were far less likely to *hide feelings* from each other than were sons and fathers, and mothers were less likely than fathers *not to consider their sons' advice worth seeking*. Mothers were also viewed as less likely than fathers to deal with disagreements by ignoring the validity of the sons' perspective.

The sum of these data suggests that while fathers and sons do talk to each other, their communication rarely involves openness; and fathers appear rarely to show respect for their sons' points of view. Instead, communication is guarded, and disagreements are dealt with through the fathers' exercise of authority. Discussions with mothers, in contrast, are not only more frequent than those with fathers, but also are characterized by a higher level of openness and a willingness on the part of mothers to consider their sons' points of view or opinions as valid. The obvious inference is that mothers are perceived as less judgmental than fathers are, more likely to listen with open minds, more amenable to talking out differences, and more willing to share their own feelings and thoughts with their sons. Fathers, on the other hand, are perceived as judgmental and closed.

The quality of parent-son communication was also assessed in study 6. In this study, the sons who reported that they discussed any of the 7 topic areas were asked to indicate how often (*not often* or *often*) mothers and fathers explained their reasons for their ideas and really tried to understand their sons' reasons and ideas. The 7 topic areas concerned *schoolwork, future plans, family, friends, dating, religion,* and *social issues*. As with the data for parents and daughters, responses to the two questions were analyzed separately but were also combined to assess the type of understanding. Understanding was judged to be *symmetrical* if parents often explained their reasons and often really tried to understand their sons' ideas. If parents did not often explain reasons or often try to understand their sons' ideas, a judgment was made for *nonunderstanding*. Understanding was said to be *asymmetrical* if parents often did one but not the other.

At least 50% of the sons said that their fathers often explained their reasons in discussions of *future plans* (71%), *schoolwork* (68%), *family* (59%), *social issues* (53%), and *religion* (51%); but less than 50% said that their fathers often explained their reasons in discussions of *friendship* (43%) or *dating* (42%). Fathers were reported to often try to understand their sons' ideas only when the topic was *future plans* (59%). Trying to understand the sons' ideas was reported particularly infrequently in discussions of *friendship* (37%), *dating* (33%), and *family* (42%). Mothers were reported , by at least 50% of the sons, to often explain their reasons and to try to understand their sons' ideas in discussions of all topics except *dating* (43% explain, 48% understand). The order of frequency for explanations was *family* (72%), *future* (68%), *school* (65%), *religion* (65%), *friendships* (55%), and *social issues* (50%). The frequencies for understanding were *future* (59%), *school* (58%), *religion* (54%), *friends* (52%), *family* (50%), and *social issues* (50%). For all the topic areas except dating, mothers were reported to explain more often than to understand.

The results for the assessment of type of understanding in father-son and in mother-son communications are shown in table 6. Symmetrical understanding occurred most frequently in father-son discussions of *future plans, school, family,* and *social issues,* and in mother-son discussions of *school, friendships, future plans,* and *religion.* Nonunderstanding appeared to characterize father-son discussions of *friendships, dating,* and *religion,* and mother-son conversations about *dating.* Asymmetrical understanding was found to be most typical of mother-son discussions of *family.* In the other cases, the distribution did not clearly favor one form of understanding over the others. One interesting finding, also shown in table 6, was that symmetrical communication decreased significantly with the increasing age of the sons in father-son discussions of schoolwork and family while asymmetrical and nonunderstanding communications increased with the increasing age of the sons.

These finding are consistent with those of study 7. While fathers are perceived as frequently explaining their own ideas, they are less likely to try to understand their sons' ideas. Thus the perception of fathers as judgmental and closed is supported by the view of them as unwilling to often try to understand their sons' perspectives. Similarly, the perception of mothers as more open-minded and accepting is complemented by a view of them as often trying to understand their sons, as well as explaining their own views. For both parental relationships, however, less than 60% of the sons reported that their par-

Table 6. Type of Understanding Characteristic of Parent-Son Discussions of Seven Topic Areas

| | Type of Understanding | | |
Topic Areas	Symmetrical	Asymmetrical	Nonunderstanding
Schoolwork			
Father[a] (N=79)	38%	35%	27%
Mother (N=81)	44	35	21
Friendship			
Father[b] (N=67)	24	33	43
Mother (N=73)	40	27	33
Future			
Father (N=79)	52	26	22
Mother (N=80)	46	34	20
Dating			
Father (N=36)	22	31	47
Mother (N=42)	26	26	48
Family			
Father (N=81)	37	27	36[c]
Mother (N=82)	37	49	14
Religion			
Father (N=55)	35	25	40
Mother (N=69)	48	23	29
Social Issues			
Father (N=64)	44	14	42
Mother (N=62)	37	26	37

[a]$\chi^2(2) = 10.05; p < .05$ (for age)
[b]$\chi^2(1) = 6.26; p < .05$ (for age)
[c]$\chi^2(1) = 6.26; p < .05$ (for mother-father difference)

ents really tried to understand their ideas regardless of the topic area; and symmetrical understanding occurred fairly infrequently. Thus the open-mindedness of, and acceptance by, mothers in communications with their sons may be assessed as greater than that for fathers—but not necessarily as characteristic or typical of mother-son communications.

The Qualities of Parent-Son Relations

The previous section presented sons' perspectives about the quality or style of communications with their parents. This section deals with data relevant to certain qualities of the relationships themselves: What kinds of reciprocity characterize the relationships? Do parents meet their sons' material and emotional needs? To assess this last question, sons were presented with two true-false statements about each parent: "My mother (father) usually makes sure that I get the things I need. For example, she (he) gives me money to buy things like food and clothes" (material needs). "My mother (father) is usually sensitive to my problems, for example, she (he) listens when I have a problem'' (emotional needs). The sons were also asked to describe what they do in return for their parents if they answered *true* to the statement.

For the most part, both fathers (74%) and mothers (80%) were reported to meet the material needs of their sons. However, when the question dealt with emotional needs, only 49% of the sons reported that their fathers were *sensitive to feelings* or *listened when I have a problem* as compared to 70% who indicated this quality in relationships with their mothers. This difference was significant at the $p < .05$ level. The sons' responses to what they do for their parents in return, if parents do meet these needs, were assessed for symmetry of reciprocity. For material needs, statements such as ''do the same for him,'' ''help her around the house,'' ''run errands for him,'' and ''do anything I can to help out'' were judged to involve *symmetrical reciprocity*. The parent gave the son money and in return the son did the same for the parent or helped the parent out in a ''goods for service'' type arrangement. Responses such as ''obey him,'' ''get good grades in school,'' ''thank her,'' ''tell him I appreciate it,'' and ''spend the money carefully'' were classified as *asymmetrical reciprocity*. In a similar fashion, when emotional needs were met, responses indicating that sons performed the same function for the parent, such as ''do the same for her'' or ''listen to her when she has a problem'' were judged *symmetrical*. Statements such as ''thank him,'' ''listen to her advice,'' and, most commonly, ''tell her my problems'' were considered to be examples of *asymmetrical reciprocity*.

In the father-son relation, 51% of the sons who reported that their fathers met their material needs ($N = 59$) gave descriptions that reflected symmetrical reciprocity; 34% of the descriptions involved asymmetrical reciprocity; and 15% of the sons did not answer this part of the question. Of the sons who indicated that their fathers met their emotional needs ($N = 39$), only 20% indicated that they reciprocated in a symmetrical way, 62% noted asymmetrical forms of reciprocity, and 18% did not answer. In contrast to the father-son relationship, examples involving symmetrical reciprocity were more frequent in the mother-son relationship. Of the sons reporting that their mothers met material needs ($N = 64$), 74% reciprocated in a symmetrical manner, 20% in an asymmetrical manner, and 6% did not answer. Concerning mothers' meeting their emotional needs ($N = 56$), 50% of the sons gave examples of symmetrical reciprocity, 38% gave examples of asymmetrical reciprocity, and 12% did not answer.

These finding are consistent with other data reported for these parent-child relationships. Fathers were perceived as dealing with the emotional aspects of their sons' lives less often than were mothers—mothers were seen as very much involved in this domain. In addition, when material needs were met, symmetrical forms of reciprocity occurred more frequently in the mother-son relationship (74%) than in the father-son relationship (51%). This discrepancy

Table 7. Type of Reciprocity in Parent-Son Relations Pertaining to Respect, Fairness, and Self-Disclosure

Type of Reciprocity	Fairness		Respect		Self-Disclosure	
	Father	Mother	Father	Mother	Father	Mother
Positive Symmetrical Reciprocity	16	16	25	23	6	13
Negative Symmetrical Reciprocity	4	3	7	7	25	17
Asymmetrical Reciprocity	21	22	9	11	10	12

was maintained when the issue referred to reciprocating emotional needs. Here 24% of the sons reported reciprocating to their fathers in a symmetrical way, while 50% of the sons reciprocated to their mothers in this manner ($p < .05$). This suggests that sons not only perceive their fathers as less likely than their mothers to meet their needs, but also perceive themselves as less able to meet these same needs for their fathers than for their mothers.

The quality of relationships was also assessed in study 3. Three aspects of relationship were addressed: *fairness, respect,* and *willingness to self-disclose.* Subjects in this study were presented with 6 true-false statements: 3 presenting the son's perspective (e.g., ''I expect more from my mother in our relationship, than I am willing to give back'') and 3 presenting the parent's perspective (e.g., ''My mother expects more from me in our relationship than she is willing to give back''). Half of the sons in this study responded to statements pertaining to their mothers only, and half pertaining to their fathers only. If both statements of a pair were answered positively, the response was assessed as positive symmetrical reciprocity—neither one expects more than he(she) is willing to give back. If both statements were answered negatively, the judgment was for negative symmetrical reciprocity—both expect more than they are willing to give back. And, if one was positive and the other negative, the judgment was of asymmetrical reciprocity—one expects more but the other does not.

The results of this analysis are shown in table 7. For both parents, positive symmetrical reciprocity characterizes the aspect of *respect;* asymmetrical reciprocity is more typical for the aspect of *fairness;* and negative symmetrical reciprocity characterizes the aspect of *willingness to self-disclosure.*

In summary, when parents are perceived as meeting the needs of their sons, sons are more likely to reciprocate in symmetrical ways with their mothers than with their fathers. However, when the issue concerns more abstract aspects of the relationship, sons perceive the relationship with both parents in quite similar ways. Parents and sons treat each other as equals with regard to respect and self-disclosure but are less likely to be perceived as being equal with respect to fairness.

Problems in Parent-Son Relations

The data in this section come from studies 4 and 7. In study 7, sons were asked to name one thing that your mother (father) does that hurts your relationship and to name one thing that you do that hurts your relationship with your mother (father). Sons most frequently described themselves as hurting the relationship with the father by *failing to treat him with respect* (42%)— either by acting *insubordinately* (31%) or *abrasively* (11%). *Insubordination* was exemplified by statements such as "disobey him as much as possible," "talk back to him," "don't do what he says," and "argue with him." *Abrasiveness* usually involved yelling or swearing at the father. The next most frequent category included the response *nothing,* or instances where sons did not answer the question, (30%). Sons also reported that they hurt the relationship with the father by *not talking to him* (12.5%) or by *not meeting his expectations* (12.5%). This latter category included statements that reflected poor performance in school or behavior that the sons knew the father disapproved of. Three percent of the responses were idiosyncratic (e.g., "I beat him at golf").

How do sons perceive their fathers as harming their relationships? The most frequent answer, given by 31% of the sons, depicted the father as *failing to treat the son with respect* by means of "yelling," "criticizing," or "insulting." Twenty-three percent of the sons either said that the father did *nothing* to harm their relationship or did not answer the question; 16% attributed problems to the father *not listening,* or *not paying attention* to sons; and 16% specified *character flaws* in the father as the cause of problems. These *character flaws* were "drinking," most often "bad temper," "laziness," or general "orneriness." Finally, 11% of the sons said that the father was *too authoritarian*—that is, "too strict" or "unfair." Three percent of the responses to this question could not be classified.

As with their fathers, sons most frequently reported that they hurt their relationships with the mother by *failing to treat her with respect* (43%). This category again included acts of *insubordination* (23%), as well as *abrasiveness* (20%). Twenty-six percent of the sons said *nothing* or gave no answer to this question; 23% said that they did *not meet her expectations;* and 7% said that they did *not talk to her enough* or *ignored her.* One response could not be classified. Mothers were seen as hurting relations with their sons primarily by *failing to treat them with respect* (28%)—"yelling," "putting me down" or "criticizing." The next most common response was that the mother caused problems in their relationship by acting *too authoritarian* (24%). The mother "nags too much," "interferes in my business," and "is too protective and restrictive." Twenty-three percent of the sons either said that the mother did *nothing* to harm the relationship or did not answer the question; 6% said that the mother *ignored* them; and 13% attributed harm in the relationship to *character flaws* in the mother. For this latter category, specific responses were: "She gets angry too quickly," "She talks too much," and "She's not serious." Six percent of the responses could not be categorized.

The results are similar for both of the parent-son relationships. Sons perceive their parents and themselves as harming the relationships primarily by treating each other disrespectfully. The only noteworthy difference was that sons were more likely to describe the mother as harming the relationship through acts of authority (24%) than they were to describe fathers as hurting the relationship in this way (11%).

The kinds of situations that cause problems in parent-son relationships were assessed in a different way in study 4. Here, sons were presented with 21 possible problem-causing situations—11 initiated by the sons and 10 initiated by the parents. They were asked to indicate for each situation whether or not it occurred in their own relationships with their parents (*never happens* versus *does happen*) and, if so, whether or not it caused a conflict in the relationship (*caused a conflict* versus *did not cause a conflict*). The situations were sorted on the basis of frequency of occurrence. Situations were judged to be frequent if over 50% of the sons said they occurred and infrequent if less than 15% of the sons said the situation occurred in their own relationships.

Of the 21 situations, only 3 were found to occur frequently with fathers. These were: *there are some things about my father's personality that I don't like* (60%); *I don't do what my father tells me to do* (52%); and, *I got lower grades than my father expected* (53%). All of these situations were judged to cause conflicts when they did occur. Infrequently occurring situations were *I yell at my father when I'm in a bad mood* (13%); *I stopped talking to my father for a week* (13%); *My father searches my room* (10%); *My father won't listen when I have a problem* (12%); and *My father lied to me about something important* (13%).

In general then, the three major conflict areas with the father appear to involve the son's insubordination and failure to meet the father's expectations and the father's character flaws. These events were also reported frequently in the open-ended descriptions given in study 7. Unlike study 7, however, situations involving the father's disrespectfulness to the son were not reported as occurring in study 4 by over 50% of the sons. The situation *my father criticizes me a lot,* however, was reported as occurring by 45% of the sons.

In contrast to the occurrance of these situations with fathers, 12 of the 22 situations were found to occur frequently with mothers. The son-initiated situations were *I don't do what my mother tells me to do* (92%); *I got lower grades than my mother expected* (70%); *I went someplace my mother told me not to go* (68%); *I didn't clean my room when my mother asked* (69%); *I came in two hours late* (62%); *when my mother scolds me, I talk back to her* (62%);

I lied to my mother about something important (60%); and *I didn't tell my mother about my feelings when I was depressed* (60%). The mother-initiated events were *my mother won't let me go someplace I want to go* (73%); *there are some things about my mother's personality that I don't like* (53%); and *my mother expects me to do too much work around the house* (52%). With respect to the mother-son relationship, none of the situations could be judged as infrequently occurring. In all cases, over 15% of the sons reported that the situation had occurred at least once in their relationships with their mothers.

In the mother-son relationship, then, problem-causing situations not only occur more frequently than in the father-son relationship but also cover a wider range of issues. In both relationships, acts involving the son's insubordination occurred frequently, but in the mother-son relationship, this involved acts of rule-breaking and verbal disrespect, as well as not doing what the son had been told to do. In addition, the mother's "misuse" of her authority was also frequently reported to occur, again consistent with the findings of study 7.

Problems in parent-son relationships were compared more directly in study 7. In that study, sons were presented with 18 situations already described as causing problems in their relationships with parents (e.g., I get upset when my parent . . . or my parent gets upset when . . .) and were asked to indicate whether or not each situation had ever occurred in their relationships with their parents, and, if it had, whether or not it occurred more often with one parent than with the other. Of the 18 situations, 14 were said to have occurred with parents by more than 50% of the sons. The exceptions were *my parent gets upset when I don't tell him(her) my problems* (35%); *I get upset when my parent doesn't listen* (45%); *I get upset when my parent doesn't tell me the truth* (36%); and *my parent gets upset when I don't tell her(him) what's going on in my life* (42%).

Of the 14 frequently occurring situations, 4 were reported to occur more often with mothers than with fathers, 6 happened with fathers more often than with mothers, and 4 occurred with equal frequency with both parents. The 4 situations occurring more frequently with mothers than with fathers all involved son-initiated problems. These were *my parent gets upset when I stay out too late* (44% mother, 29% father); *my parent gets upset when I get into trouble in school* (48% mother, 36% father); *my parent gets upset when I purposely ignore him(her)* (40% mother, 27% father); and, *my parent gets upset when I don't let him(her) know when I'm going to be late* (54% mother, 26% father [$p < .01$]).

In contrast, of the 6 situations occurring more frequently with fathers than with mothers, only 2 were son-initiated while 4 were father-initiated problems. The son-initiated situations were identical to the ones reported in study 4 as occurring frequently. They were *my parent gets upset when I don't help when I'm asked to* (57% father, 32% mother [$p < .05$]); and *my parent gets upset when I don't do well in school* (51% father, 41% mother). For this last situation, there was a significant age difference ($p < .05$) with the younger boys more likely to say "mother" and the older sons more likely to say "father". The parent-initiated situations reported as occurring more frequently with fathers than with mothers were *I get upset when my parent criticizes me* (51% father, 20% mother) ($p < .01$); *I get upset when my parent yells at me* (46% father, 20% mother); *I get upset when my parent doesn't understand my point of view* (45% father, 34% mother); and *I get upset when my parent says one thing but does another* (39% father, 29% mother). Again, for these last two situations, there were significant age differences ($p < .05$) with the younger sons (15–16 year olds) more often reporting "mother" and the older ones more frequently reporting "father".

In summary, problems in father-son relationships appear to arise out of the fathers' failure to treat their sons with respect and from the sons' failure to treat their fathers with respect, as well as from the sons' failure to meet expectations by doing as they are told. Problems in mother-son relationships also arise out of situations such as the ones reported above, although mothers' failure to respect their sons was seen as occurring less frequently than fathers'. In mother-son relationships, however, there were also a number of problems that arose out of the sons' failure to obey a variety of household rules and, in complement, out of the mothers' exercise of authority in establishing these rules. Mother-son relationships, then, not only involve greater and more open communication than do father-son relationships, but are also open to more problems concerning authority and obedience in the day-to-day activities of the family. This suggests, despite the findings about symmetry of reciprocity and greater intimacy of communication, that the mother-son relationship is still very much an authority-based relationship.

Procedures for Resolving Difficulties in Parent-Son Relations

The data in this section come from studies 6 and 7. In study 6, sons were presented with a situation described in the following manner: *When your mother (father) wants you to do something and you do not want to do it, how often does your mother (father) . . . ?* This was followed by 8 procedures. These procedures were factor-analyzed and 7 of them were found to load on two distinct factors (c.f., chapter 2, study 6). One factor, termed mutual procedures, included the procedures "keep talking about it hoping I would want to do it," "say he(she) will do favors for me at some other time if I do this for her(him) now," and "say I would enjoy doing what she(he) wants me to do." These procedures demonstrate situations where the parent considers the son's unwillingness to do what he or she wants as a valid stance and attempts to change the son's mind while maintaining respect for his opinion. Less than 50% of the sons reported that their fathers or their mothers used these procedures frequently.

The other factor, unilateral procedures, included statements which did not show consideration or acceptance of the son's opinion on this issue. They were "say I'm supposed to do what he(she) tells me to do," "simply tells me to do it," "say he(she) expects me to do it," and "keeps telling me to do it until I do it." The first 3 of these procedures were reported by at least 50% of the sons to occur often in their relationships with the father (53%, 54%, and 68%, respectively). The last 2 procedures were noted by over 50% of the sons to occur often in their relationships with the mother (62% and 54% respectively).

Overall, then, when sons are reluctant to do what a parent wants them to do, both mothers and fathers are seen as responding without consideration of the validity of the son's stance. Sons say either that their parents *expect sons* to do what they are told, or that their parents simply *tell them to do it* until the son finally complies. Again, both parents are clearly perceived as authority figures in this type of situation.

Resolutions of difficulties in parent-son relationships were assessed in a different way in study 5. Here, sons were presented with the following hypothetical situation:

> John, a boy your age and his mother (father) usually get along well and have a close relationship. One night, however, John came home very late from a party. He had done this a few times before and his mother (father) was very upset. She(He) felt that this caused a serious problem in her(his) relationship with her(his) son.

The sons were then asked to describe if they felt this situation would cause problems in the relationship between John and his mother or father; how the participants might resolve the problem; whether or not this type of situation had ever occurred in their own relationships with mothers and fathers; and, if it had, how they and their mothers or fathers resolved the problem.

With respect to the "father" situation, 85% of the sons indicated that it would probably cause a problem in the relationship. Resolutions to the hypothetical situation were classified either as *status quo solutions* (73%), where the end result involved no change in the curfew rule, or as *compromise solutions* (27%), where the end result was an extension of the curfew. *Compromise solutions* were usually attained after fathers and sons discussed the problem or after sons simply asked for a later, more reasonable, curfew. *Status quo solutions* ($N = 33$) were reached either by the son *apologizing* or *proving himself trustworthy* in the future (45%), or by the father simply *restating his expectation* that the rule be obeyed (55%). When asked if this situation had ever actually occurred in their own relationships with their fathers, only 49% of the sons said *yes*. In addition, of the actual resolutions ($N = 22$), only 4% involved *compromise,* with the remainder being *status quo solutions.* In these procedures of actual resolution, solutions were reached most frequently only after fathers had punished their sons (50%).

Responses to the mother-son situation were somewhat similar to those for the father-son situation. Seventy-six percent of the sons felt that the situation would cause a problem in the relationship. Seventy-eight percent of the resolutions involved *status quo* solutions, while only 22% incorporated *compromise solutions*. However, 73% of the sons reported that a similar situation had actually occurred in their relationship with their mothers as compared with only 49% of sons reporting an actual occurrence of the event with fathers (*p* < .05). Again, the problem was more likely to be resolved in a *status quo* manner (85%) than by a *compromise solution* (15%). Punishment, however, was infrequently cited in the mother-son relationship as a procedure of resolution (12%). Instead, the problem was most frequently resolved by the son proving himself trustworthy on future occasions (57%).

These results suggest that, with respect to procedures for resolving disagreements or conflicts, sons do not differentiate markedly between their mothers and their fathers. Both parents are more likely to utilize unilateral procedures than mutual procedures in attempting to attain their sons' compliance with their wishes. Also, in both relationships, procedures leading to a *status quo solution* are more likely to occur in the face of the sons' rule violations than are procedures involving a compromise solution. The major difference between the parents seems to be that when sons violate rules, these violations are more likely to bring them into conflict with their mothers than with their fathers. In addition, these conflicts with mothers are most likely to be resolved through a somewhat long-term process whereby sons have to prove themselves to their mothers. In contrast, conflicts with fathers are settled more quickly, with fathers punishing the sons and the sons accepting the punishment as "fair" or "deserved."

Self-descriptions in Parent-Son Relations

The data in this section are from study 7. In this study, sons, like daughters, were given a list of 30 adjectives describing actions or feeling states and a list of 4 relational persons—father, mother, close male friend, close female friend. The task was to select the person with whom the subject was most likely to feel or act in a specific manner—for example, I am *most likely* to feel or be . . . when I am with my (father, mother, close male friend, close female friend). The goal was to assess self-description as a function of relationships.

Sons selected the father considerably more frequently than they did any of the other persons on 9 of the adjectives. With respect to father, sons most frequently reported that they were *judgmental* (40%), *withdrawn* (39%), *insensitive* (34%), *careful what they said* (44%), *serious* (45%), *uncomfortable* (41%), *criticized* (38%), *unwanted* (25%), and *distant* (39%). Sons, when with their fathers, rarely described themselves as *playful* (3%), *relaxed* (4%), *loved* (8%), *open* (7%), *sensitive* (8%), or *myself* (8%). When compared with other important persons in their lives, then, sons appear to feel most distant, uncomfortable, and fearful when they are with their fathers. Perhaps most telling was that only 8% of the sons said that they were likely to be themselves when with their fathers.

In contrast, the mother was selected considerably more frequently than any of the other persons on only 2 adjectives—*helpful* (50%) and *loved* (38%). Mothers were tied with close male friends as first choice when the adjectives were *honest* and *trusting*.

These data are consistent with the findings regarding typical interactions and the quality of communications in these relationships. Fathers were perceived as judgmental and closed, and sons reacted to this perception by being judgmental and closed themselves. Fathers were seen as not commonly meeting the emotional needs of their sons, and in response, sons withdraw and are equally insensitive to their fathers. Father-son relationships then involve a guardedness and a lack of acceptance that is not found in mother-son relationships. In the latter, sons are helpful and feel loved. They are honest with their mothers and in return perceive her as honest with them. Thus, the authority aspect of this relationship coexists with the aspects of openness and trust.

Sons' Obligations to Parents

The data in this section are from study 2. In this study, sons were asked to describe (1) obligations they felt they had toward their parents, and (2) why they felt these obligations were important. The primary obligations that sons indicated they had toward the father were *obedience* or *meeting expectations* (49%) and *giving assistance* (28%). Other sons indicated that they should *talk to* or *spend time* with the father (21%). Most of the sons felt that these obligations were *repayments* for all that the father had done, or was doing, for them (43%): "Do what he says . . . it's your responsibility to father for what he has done for you." "Help him around the house . . . because he has helped you in the past." "Don't talk back to him . . . cause he supports you." Some sons indicated that the function of their obligations was to *improve the relationship* between father and son (26%). Examples of this type of answer are "Talk to him . . . to make relationship better," "be honest . . . to be closer to him," and "talk to him understand him . . . makes for a smoother relation." Other sons reported that the reason for carrying out obligations was either to *make things better for yourself* (12%) or to make things *better for father* (19%). For example, "do things with him . . . because it makes him happy" was a benefit for the father, while "don't talk back . . . so he will love you" was a benefit to the self.

Forty-three percent of the sons said that they were obliged to *obey* the mother or to *meet her expectations,* 36% indicated that they should *help* the mother, and 21% said that they should *communicate* with her or be understanding of her. *Reciprocity* was the most frequent reason (43%) for the sons' feeling of obligations. It referred to the return to mothers of acts equivalent to what they had done for their sons. Examples of *reciprocity* were "she's done a lot for you, you owe her"; "she has done so much for you, she deserves it"; "returning favors—it's your obligation"; "she taught you everything you know, you should pay her back"; "so that his mother will help him too"; and "because she supports him and does a lot for him." Seventeen percent of the sons cast reasons in terms of their *mothers' need* for their sons' help. Specific statements included " 'cause it's a rough time of life for the parent," "she needs to feel appreciated," "she ain't getting any younger," and "so she can get her work done." Lastly, 24% put their reasons in terms of *closeness* or improving the relationship: "because you love her," "to maintain a close relationship," "to enjoy your relationship," "to keep the relationship between you and your mother good," and "to make things go smoother in the relationship."

Summary

The data provide a fairly consistent picture of sons' perceptions of relationships with their parents. Fathers are seen as persons with whom sons share recreational or work activities and with whom they can discuss objective issues or practical problems. The relationship is primarily asymmetrical, or unilateral, in form. Fathers meet the material needs of their sons and in return merit obedience and respect from the sons. Problems in father-son relationships appear to revolve around grades in school, the failure of sons to do what they're told, and the failures of both fathers and sons to treat each other with respect. The relationship may be best described as distant but respectful. Sons do not feel comfortable or open with their fathers; however, they do share activities together, and they do appear to respect their fathers as advisors on practical matters.

Relationships with mothers also involve authority, but these relationships are often not distant. Many mothers and sons appear to have a close relationship based on openness and the sharing of confidences. At the same time, mothers are clearly rule makers who require obedience and respect. Problems in mother-son relationships revolve primarily around this rule-making role. Mothers place restrictions on their sons' conduct, and mothers handle violations of the rules. Despite this disciplinary position, sons agree that their mothers are concerned about them. Sons tell their mothers about their activities and about problems they may be having. Thus the majority of sons see their mothers as monitoring them from perspectives of concern and love—although occasionally this concern may be seen as too intrusive.

Thus, both parental relationships may be described as authority relationships. Sons do not perceive themselves as equals to their parents nor do they suggest that their parents view them as equals. Both parents are viewed as advice givers rather than as advice seekers; both parents are described as objects of respect and as persons to whom the son is obligated to show this respect; and both parents use their positions of authority when they have disagreements with their sons and when they are making rules or setting guidelines for their sons' behavior. While the "authority" label is sufficient to describe father-son relationships, it is only descriptive of part of the mother-son relationship. This relationship has another side to it. Mothers not only give advice and make and enforce rules, but they also listen to problems, share confidences—and at times, show respect for their sons' points of view. In this sense, mothers can be "friends" as well as parents.

These differences between the two parents are similar to the differences found for parent-daughter relationships. For the latter, however, the distinctions between the father-daughter and the mother-daughter relationships are more extreme.

5

Adolescents and Their Relations with Parents: Conclusions

The aim of this chapter is to present a cohesive summary of the foregoing data and to discuss their bearing on the issues outlined in chapter 1. In keeping with our perspective, focus is placed primarily on the characteristics of parent-adolescent relationships. The assumption is that a clear understanding of relationships, as structures, can contribute to theories that address either the dynamics or the results of these relationships. The attempt here is to look at what occurs in the relationships and estimate how they are structured. From this vantage point, we can begin to address other psychological functions that may follow.

It should now be apparent that for any question we posed, there were a variety of answers that could be construed as reflecting individual variations in the relationship. It is equally apparent, however, that when responses were assessed by form, the data showed clear consistency. This was true for the majority of answers given in any study, and it was true for the recurrence of forms that occurred across studies. On these grounds, it is possible to discuss two modal parent-adolescent relationships—one of sons and daughters with their fathers, the other with their mothers. This is not to deny individual differences, but to deal for the present with structures that include the majority of the subjects we sampled.

Unilateral Authority

The assumption was that during the adolescent period, parents and their sons and daughters move away from a structure of unilateral authority and begin to interact more cooperatively. Adolescents seek and parents grant greater independence than was true during childhood. There is no question that, for the adolescents in our samples, parents retain the position of authority. These adolescents view their parents as having the right to monitor, direct, and control their behavior; to set rules and demand that they be followed; and to present expectations for performance in matters such as school work or chores around the house. In addition, adolescents say that they seek advice from their parents, especially about their plans for careers and other plans for their futures.

Two aspects of parental authority seem to differ from its status during childhood and may, therefore, imply a developmental change during adolescence. First, parental authority is restricted to, or specialized by, areas of adolescents' lives rather than being applied universally to the whole of adolescents' lives. The key data on this point came from results on communication. There are some topics that adolescents discuss with both parents, other topics that they discuss with only one parent, and still other topics that they discuss with neither parent. It is plausible to say that parents have little authority when they are unaware of what their sons or daughters are doing, or thinking about, in an area of their lives. Whether lack of knowledge is due to adolescents controlling information or to parents granting privacy, the result is the same. Adolescents gain independence from parental authority when they are allowed to act outside their parents' ken and without their parents' intervention (e.g., Wright & Keple 1981).

Second, while parents can assert their authority unilaterally, adolescents perceive that they can also partake of cooperative decision making with their parents. Examples of obvious unilateral authority were found in the ways that parents settled some disagreements with their sons and daughters. On the other hand, in some matters parents are clearly ready to discuss differences and seek compromises. The distinction seems to depend to some degree on the matter at hand. On topics such as school performance, parents appear to have strong expectations for their sons and daughters to meet. There is not much negotiation on such topics, but more of a presentation of goals and reasons on the parents' parts. On the other hand, in matters of personal problems, if parents are involved at all, they act less as unilateral authorities and more as advisors willing to listen, seeking to understand.

On both of these points, there is an additional factor of differences between mothers and fathers. If authority is represented by communication, then the authority of fathers is quite restrictive relative to that of mothers. The involvement of fathers in their sons' and daughters' lives is usually perceived as restricted to the domains of academic performance and future plans, although it may also include an interest in the adolescents' views on social and political issues. In contrast, the involvement of mothers extends beyond these issues and includes issues pertaining to household rules, emotional states, and the interpersonal domains of the adolescents' lives. Although the issue of household rules is generally handled by mothers through the imposition of rules for conduct with the expectation of compliance, the other issues are those for which no objective standards apply.

Mothers and fathers are differentiated, then, with respect to their domains of involvement. This differentiation leads to a further discrepancy between them regarding their exercise of unilateral authority. While both parents act unilaterally when issues involve objective performance, (academic performance, adherence to rules) the mothers' extension to domains for which no objective standards apply, allows them greater opportunities to engage in more cooperative forms of interacting. Indeed, according to our results, fathers are generally viewed as acting unilaterally and being judgmental, while mothers are perceived as being accepting, understanding, and acting cooperatively as well as unilaterally (cf., Siegelman, Block, Block, & Von der Lippe, 1970).

The two major changes discussed above suggest that the structure of unilateral authority that is characteristic of parent-child relationships is revised somewhat in adolescence. In some matters, the structure is maintained with parents keeping their role as validators and authorities for their adolescents (Bell & Bell 1983; Cooper, Grotevant, & Condon 1983; Krosnick & Judd 1982). In other matters, unilateral authority gives way to a more cooperative stance. And, for still other matters, parents simply exclude themselves or are excluded by adolescents from any involvement. In addition, there is a difference between fathers and mothers in the extent to which they are authorities. Fathers' authority seems limited to the domains that center on objective performance by adolescents—those indicating that the adolescent is becoming a productive member of adult society. Mothers share that aspect of authority, but also extend their role to that side of adolescents' lives that includes their personal and emotional well-being. Either fathers leave these things to mothers, or adolescents consciously exclude fathers—or both happen. The data do not provide a definite answer. In any case, mothers express themselves, and adolescents seek their mothers' council in these matters on a somewhat regular basis. This finding is important because it highlights an elemental distinction between fathers and mothers. A good deal of adolescents' lives and interests are centered on how well they are doing socially and on how comfortable they feel emotionally. These issues are as important, or more important, than how much progress they are making toward some future image of adulthood. Mothers engage themselves in these interests. As a rule, fathers do not—except in particular instances when adolescents are experiencing difficulties, such as problems with their mothers that they cannot seem to handle (cf., Burke & Weir 1979).

From Figure to Person

The changes that occur in adolescence with respect to the unilateral-authority structure of parent-adolescent relationships correspond to changes that also occur concerning perceptions of parents as persons. There is a striking absence from children's and preadolescents' descriptions of interactions with their parents of a view of parents as being persons with personalities entailing likeable and unlikeable traits, variable moods, and a scale of competencies (Youniss, 1980). Children are prone to perceive their parents as *figures* who have knowledge and power to get things done, especially those things children need or want. This perception may be seen as the logical consequence of the structure of unilateral authority. This structure is conducive to imposing a veil of mystification between parent and child so that neither really comes to appreciate the other as he or she truly is. One would expect that as the relation shifts toward cooperation, this gap in understanding is bridged so that each comes to be seen more validly as a particular personality.

Present data bear on this prospective developmental achievement in two ways. First, the obvious behavioral basis for mutual understanding of personalities is reciprocal self-disclosure. The minimum prerequisite is simple conversation in which two persons express their thoughts and feelings nondefensively. The findings indicate in several ways that this kind of discussion occurs more frequently between mothers and adolescents than between fathers and adolescents. Simple conversation is a high-frequency item for mother-adolescent interactions. Conversations with mothers are not characterized by guardedness and distrust as are conversations with fathers. Reciprocal understanding is more common with mothers than with fathers. And, as noted above, the topics that mothers and adolescents discuss are inherently conducive to mutual disclosure and the sharing of experiences (cf., White, Speisman, & Costos 1983).

The results that bear on the shift from seeing parents as figures to seeing them as personalities begin with adolescents' statements of their obligations to parents. The majority of the adolescents perceived their primary obligation to their fathers in terms of conforming to their fathers' wishes and meeting their fathers' expectations. In contrast, the same adolescents stated that they felt obliged to reciprocate to their mothers for all that mothers had done for them. This result is duplicated in adolescents' descriptions of whether or not parents met their material and emotional needs and how they should respond in return if their needs had been met. The latter descriptions are particularly precise in showing that adolescents feel that they understand their mothers and are able to serve their mothers' needs (Burke & Weir, 1979).

These results suggest that fathers are still viewed as figures while mothers are perceived more concretely in terms of their actions, ideas, feelings, and needs. It would be excessive to conclude that mothers are fully understood as persons apart from their position as mothers. This is unlikely because relations with mothers show a mixture of both unilateral and mutual components. What is clear, however, is that mothers are not simply perceived as figures and that mothers' personalities are appreciated to a greater extent than are fathers' personalities. The exception is the notation of character flaws in both parents, when such flaws may be sources of conflict.

A second point concerns the more precise steps that comprise the shift from viewing parents as figures to viewing them as persons. It is assumed that the process is gradual with adolescents abandoning the naivete of childhood and beginning to see reality as more complex and problematic. One of the steps toward appreciation of personalities seems to be articulation of *role* (Furth 1980). Adolescents indicate that much of what their mothers do, how they act, and why they act is a function of mothers fulfilling their role as mothers. In this regard, they describe their mothers as disciplinarians and as conversational partners, as caring for their needs and as helping them solve personal problems. A grasp of these diverse functions helps adolescents to see their mothers as persons rather than just as figures. This grasp of role, then, helps adolescents to give order to their mothers' actions but falls short of a full appreciation of them as particular personalities.

Undoubtedly, adolescents also begin to see their fathers from the perspective of their roles. If this is correct, it holds an important implication for parental roles as they are divided by gender. As the data show in many ways, fathers are elusive persons in that they administer authority selectively and often indirectly. Further, fathers reveal little of themselves through free-form, self-disclosing conversations and, simultaneously, they manifest little involvement in the several personal areas that are of central concern to adolescents. The resulting perception of the paternal role, then, is likely to be restricted to a narrow domain that views fathers as providers, advisors about how society works, problem solvers, and arbiters of serious disputes. Not only is this a stilted perspective of the role of fathers, but it obviously falls short of an understanding of fathers as individual personalities.

Individuation

The revision of the structure of unilateral authority, which is characteristic of parent-child relationships, to a structure that incorporates both unilateral authority and cooperation allows (2) for the increasing independence of adolescents from parental authority and (2) for the construction of a self separate from parental influence. At the same time, the change that occurs during adolescence from a perception of parents-as-figures to parents-as-persons—with needs and feelings of their own—implies a connectedness between parents and adolescents that is based not on authority, but rather on respect for one another as persons. This dual process is expressed in the concept of *individuation* (Cooper, Grotevant, & Condon 1983; White, Spersman, & Costos 1983). It is a process whereby adolescents move away from dependence on parents while attempting to remain connected to them.

The present data help to provide evidence that makes the dual character of individuation more behaviorally concrete. The findings include several indications of separation. Perhaps the clearest signs of this are limited contact with parents and possession of private lives apart from the family. Time spent away from parents is surely a common feature of contemporary adolescent life. Adolescents spend six or more hours in school, frequently hold part-time jobs after school, and have active social schedules that often consume evenings and weekends. Time away from parents is time not monitored or directly controlled by parents. It is also time when ideas are formed and decisions are made without parental involvement. Of course, parents need not be physically present to influence what adolescents think or do. Nevertheless, as the data show, much of what goes on in this private sphere is monitored only loosely by parents, for example, through anticipatory instructions or after-the-fact admonishments. Further, many activities in this private sphere take place without parents' knowledge and are not discussed with parents.

The likely prospect is that parents grant this freedom with the provision that adolescents can have private lives as long as they meet other demands, such as academic success, and do not harm themselves or other persons. The point is that separation, the process of which proceeds by way of parental consent, allows adolescents to explore their own ideas and values in situations from which parents are absent. This point is reinforced by the fact that adolescents become reporters of their own extrafamilial activities. They have, then, the power to control the information that they give to their parents about themselves. While parents have other means of learning about their sons' and daughters' activities, some portion of these activities remains private and under the adolescents' own control (cf., Fox 1981; Sullivan & Sullivan 1980).

As the studies on friendship will show, time spent outside the family is indeed time expended in self-exploration. Friends discuss ideas about reality, about values, and about moral standards. They also discuss their feelings and share their experiences. These activities must be considered essential to self-definition. This is glimpsed in the present data through the reports on the frequency with which adolescents discuss friendship, dating, and personal feelings with parents. The frequency is low, especially with fathers. Hence, it is clear that separation occurs through the license that parents grant adolescents to have private lives and through the activities that adolescents undertake when they are apart from their families.

While separation is occurring, a large proportion of adolescents still maintain definite connections with their parents. First, they feel respect for, and are respected by, their parents. Second, they clearly desire to please their parents, to meet the expectations that parents have for them, and to seek their parents' approval. Third, although parents grant them freedom through privacy, many adolescents keep parents informed about their lives and even consider parents as advisors on personal matters. Fourth, the majority of adolescents appreciate both parents' roles—insofar as they view them as an expression of concern for their own well-being. In summary, adolescents have a sense of being members of a family, of having obligations to the family, and of feeling an attachment to their parents (Greenberg, Siegel, & Leitch 1983; Hirschi 1969; Offer, Ostrov, & Howard 1981).

One of the difficulties in psychological theories is a tendency to hone down the parent-adolescent relationship to the extent that it is stripped from context. A valuable correction comes from looking at the relationship from a broader perspective—in which it becomes one of several relationships that the individuals in it are experiencing, and in which the family is seen with regard to the society surrounding it. From this perspective, parents and adolescents can be seen as in alliance together against society. This alliance is designed as an adaptive action to help adolescents meet demands of society that cannot be dismissed. The entrance of adolescents into adult society is made easier when their parents provide support and lay down guidelines. For example, the planning of one's son's or daughter's future may involve not only explaining the contingencies among academic achievements, credentials, and jobs, but also discussing strategies and means. While there is no paucity of evidence that adolescents have disagreements that help to separate them from their parents, these differences tend to pale in light of the alliance that parents and offspring have on the matter of the latter's successful movement into society (Douvan & Adeleson 1966; Lin, Ensel, & Vaughn 1981; Reiss, Oliveri, & Curd 1983). Such a compact in the face of a problematic future in society is not new but is recognized by historians as a fact of family life since the late nineteenth century (cf. Gillis 1981; Katz 1981; Kett 1977).

There is a second way to look at the individuation process in terms of the difference in roles that adolescents see for their fathers, as opposed to their mothers. It is not an oversimplification to say that relations with fathers may help to contribute to separation. Fathers tend to make demands without modifying them in light of the adolescents' views. Fathers tend to administer authority indirectly and from a distance. And, fathers do not typically keep accounts of adolescents' activities—leaving adolescents to develop their interests without parental engagement. Insofar as fathers hold to standards, adolescents have clear targets against which to evaluate themselves. At the same time, fathers' noninvolvement in the adolescents' daily experiences allows adolescents to test tentative definitions of self through means other than the paternal relationship.

On the other hand, the typical actions of mothers would seem to work for cohesion or connectedness. Both sons and daughters express a a deep debt to their mothers and state the reasons for their feelings of obligation in terms of "all she's done for me," "she needs time for herself," "to show you care and she needs help," "to keep good relations with her." One is tempted to add that adolescents' relations with their mothers are in fact more clearly relations based on concrete interactional terms than are their relations with their fathers. The latter come close to being nonrelations in the sense that they are based on impersonal standards that often miss the here-and-now interests of their sons and daughters.

The concept of individuation is relatively new to theories of adolescence but serves an obvious function by tempering the traditional emphasis on autonomy and the tendency not to see the relationship in its own development. These corrections are needed but do not make up for the fact that the concept requires more precise specification than it now has. Present data contribute to that need if only because adolescents themselves sense the duality of their relationships with their parents. They made this point particularly in their responses to the following question: How do you think your relationship with your father (mother) has changed over the past five years?

A 15-year-old female said the following about her father: "I respect him more; know that he has work to do and needs to rest. I know he's there to help. Still he sees me as his little girl. He respects me more—more demanding. He expects more of me."

Another 15-year-old female said: "We can now talk and express feelings freely without feeling we are going to hurt each other. I don't treat him as this father figure—treat him like a person. He doesn't have as much power over me. He realized there was a communication gap and tried to overcome it. It made us closer."

A third 15-year-old female said: "Now I'm really not a little girl and he's beginning to realize it. Now, if he's in a bad mood, I understand. I know he's a person too. I'm not as afraid and can understand him. . . ."

An 18-year-old female said: "I still see him as my father. He gives me more freedom but still demands a certain amount of respect from me."

Another 18-year-old female said: "I used to be 'daddy's girl'. We talk now but avoid issues where there's going to be conflict. I thought he could do no wrong but then I started to get my own ideas. We used to have the same views but now they are different. He tries to be more possessive as I get older. He doesn't want me to grow up."

A 15-year-old male said of his father: "There's more friction now; more conflict. I've started to question why he wants me to do certain things. He puts more responsibilities on me now, but not more freedom."

An 18-year-old male said: "He accepts me as mature; gives me more freedom, but still expects a lot of me. I know how to handle him better—how to talk and understand him without getting into fights."

Another 18-year-old male said: "I understand now what my father is like. I want to please him more. He demands more of me now. And he gives me more freedom and privileges."

A 15-year-old male said the following about his mother: "She's grown more flexible with me. She trusts me more. I don't idealize her anymore. She's not a god-like figure, just a person."

A 16-year-old male said: "She expects more now. She's more critical. She also accepts that I'm getting older and gives me more freedom and responsibility. I can talk to her about more grown-up things."

An 18-year-old male said: "She accepts me as a mature person. She gives me more freedom. She expects more from me now. I accept her more as a friend. We talk about deeper things."

A 15-year-old female said of her mother: "She respects me more and lets me be on my own more. Treats me like a person, consults my opinion. I am a voice that is heard. Five years ago she was just a mother, now she's a person."

Another 15-year-old female said: "Now she treats me like an adult. Gives me more freedom. If I have really big problems I can come and talk to her. She brings her problems to me now also. I can talk to her about a lot of things. She understands."

An 18-year-old female said: "I'm more independent of her. Also, I am more free with my opinions even when I disagree. I realize she's not only my mother but an individual herself and I take her more on that level now. We still turn to each other when we have problems. We're still close."

Another 18-year-old female said: "She expects more from me. She's realized that I grew up. I'm not a little kid. I'm a person, my own person. She still tries to help me and now I know I can help her."

These excerpts help elaborate the mixture of separateness and connection that constitutes parent-adolescent relations. Parents' granting of freedom is not incompatible with maintaining elements of connectedness. Indeed, adolescents see freedom and connectedness as working together, insofar as parents are respected both as persons and in their role as parents. The result is that parents interact more cooperatively while they retain their authority status. The grounds for continuity may lie in the distribution of authority across areas so that cooperative discussion in one area is seen as fitting with unilateral assertion in a different area. The underlying theme to all of this is the adolescents' general belief that their parents act from a position of wanting to help their sons and daughters and, thus, operate at times from their roles as parents and at other times as persons.

Conformity and Influence

The issue of conformity and influence has been of concern to socialization theorists who tend to think of parents as transmitters of culture to the younger generation. These theorists have emphasized parents' teaching function and the styles of instruction that are the most efficacious in leading to internalization of norms. A side issue has been whether or not modern parents have reneged on this function and have given it over to others, in particular, to their sons' and daughters' peers (Bronfenbrenner 1970). A more recent concern has been voiced regarding the evidence that contemporary family structure has deteriorated to the point that parents and peers do not even constitute opposing forces. As Shorter (1975) has expressed the matter, contemporary parents no longer care to exert control, and their sons and daughters no longer care whether or not their parents approve or disapprove of their actions.

Stated thus, socialization theory seems an exaggeration only too ready to be knocked down by forthcoming evidence. At least for the adolescents in our samples, disinterest by parents is not typical. Indeed, the recurring theme is that adolescents seek their parents' advice and approval and that parents give advice and approval because they are very much concerned about their children's socialization. One of the grounds for pessimism by socialization theorists is that they believe that contemporary parents, especially mothers, have sacrificed their authority and roles for the purpose of preserving the relationship. According to socialization theorists, mothers seek to be friends with their sons and daughters and thus may compromise their authority.

This claim is also not supported by our data—at least not as socialization theorists analyze the relationship. Mothers undoubtedly assert their authority; in fact, they are the major disciplinarians, continually monitoring adolescents' conduct. At the same time, mothers are somewhat like friends in that they try to maintain contact with adolescents' personal lives and work toward cooperation with them. Authority and cooperation are not mutually exclusive functions, especially when they are distributed across domains of interest and emanate from a common source of interest in adolescents' well-being. This conclusion comes directly from adolescents' responses to the question of why they feel a sense of obligation to their parents. The most common response from sons and daughters about their mothers focused on reciprocity. Obligations consisted mainly of two types: (1) meet her expectations and (2) be understanding of her. Reasons for fulfilling obligations were also of two types. One dealt with what mothers have done for their children—"because she's done so much for you," "because she supports you," "she raised you," "it's the least you can do for her," "you owe it to her," and "you should pay her back." The other reason referred to mothers as having needs and feelings as persons—"to make her feel good," "to make her happy," " 'cause she needs your help."

If these statements reflect the normal dynamics of reciprocity in interpersonal relations, (e.g., Youniss 1980), they may represent the consequences of a pattern that is conducive to mutual respect. Mothers are somewhat ubiquitous in the services they perform for their adolescent offspring. They are empathetic to adolescents' personal problems. At the same time, mothers are the disciplinarians of adolescents' misdeeds. If both types of action are perceived to spring from the same motive of concern, then, mothers' authority is as believable as their friend-like sharing of personal experiences. It is not unreasonable to suggest that actions which establish mothers' credibility can enhance their authority. That adolescents feel they can reciprocate to their mothers probably indicates a sense of growth in their own competencies. That adolescents feel they should reciprocate probably signifies a growing sense of person-to-person understanding.

Socialization theorists' dismal prospect for the transmission of cultural values by contemporary parents to their children is not supported by our data. Fathers and mothers are perceived as having standards and expectations that they want their sons and daughters to meet. Sons and daughters, in turn, articulate a clear sense of wanting to live up to their parents' expectations. It was rare to find adolescents who said they did not want approval or who thought their parents' standards were irrelevant. A few adolescents said that their parents were hypocritical because they themselves did not live up to the standards they espoused. But the majority of adolescents stated that parental standards were designed for their own good. This perception can be understood when it is recognized that parents do not try to exert control over the full range of adolescent experiences. Parents express authority selectively, presumably in areas that they think are the most important.

Family Dynamics

Family systems theory is a relatively new approach within social science. It originated in clinical settings with the insight that an individual's behavioral patterns were sustained by interactions with other individuals with whom the individual had regular contact (Watzlawick, Beavin, & Jackson 1967; Minuchin 1974). This insight led to the clinical treatment of whole families and recently to theories of ways that individual family members function in systematic concordance (e.g., Reiss, Oliveri, & Curd 1983). These theories are conceptually rich in providing new perspectives on how to assess individual behavior, its establishment, maintenance, and correction. These concepts are novel and in need of empirical precision. At this time, they are more heuristic than definitive. One of their uses at present is to suggest ways in which the mixture of facts about adolescence may be organized (Cooper, Grotevant, & Condon 1983).

Our studies of parent-adolescent relationships are undoubtedly too broad to capture the detailed dynamics that family-system theorists have documented in actual family interactions. However, one general result of our studies is quite consistent with these theories: Fathers and mothers may have separate but conjunctive functions within the family system. The functions of the two parents are not duplicative, but in their separation, keep the family system intact. In the present case, this conception deters emphasizing the adolescents' separate relationships with their fathers and mothers without considering their synchrony from the system's perspective. We have already reviewed several of the differences that distinguish paternal from maternal relationships. We will now discuss how the two relationships might be reflections of total family functioning.

In our samples, adolescents depicted their families in a traditional manner. One is immediately reminded of Talcott Parsons' (Parsons & Bales 1955) and David Riesman's (1953) characterizations of families roughly three decades ago. In his effort to bring Freudian theory into the then current sociology, Parsons looked at American families of the post–World War II era in the following terms. Contemporary society was structured according to principles of modernity. One of its features was that persons were not valued for who they were, by way of status or family background, but for what they could do and had achieved. Another feature was that social institutions and individuals were divisible into segregated or specific functions. These, among other features, were brought to bear on the family by Parsons in a division of labor between fathers and mothers. Fathers were assigned *instrumental* functions that were designed to socialize children into modern society, so that they could adapt as adult members upon their entrance to society. Mothers were assigned *expressive* functions that were generally defined as caring for the psychological well-being of children and other family members.

Parsons's analysis of modernity has met with controversy and criticism within the sociological-historical discipline (cf., Johnson 1975; Tilly 1981) as well as with observers of contemporary families, in particular for its identification of adult womanhood with motherhood (e.g., Bernard 1981). Despite these criticisms, it is evident that adolescents' depictions of their mothers and fathers come close to recapitulating Parsons's assessment. The fathers in our studies fit Parsons's instrumental characterization with their central interest being adolescents' performances that bear on their functioning as productive adults. The mothers in our studies were shown to take care of expressive functions—specifically, emotional well-being, social acceptance, and other psychological needs. The difference between mothers in "traditional" families and the mothers in our studies is that the latter ones also have an instrumental orientation and that often their participation in this function is greater than that of the fathers.

According to Riesman (1953), contemporary parents face a problem that was not always the lot of parents. There were times in the past when society seemed stable and parents could project that their children would spend their futures in occupations, and with values, that were similar to those of the parents. At those times, socialization by parents was directed toward teaching skills that the parents had and toward instilling values that the parents held. In contemporary times, which began approximately in the latter decades of the nineteenth century, change in society rather than stability became the rule. The likelihood then, was that children would have occupations that differed from those of their parents and would have to adopt values that their parents did not accept. Concrete examples abound. For instance, today's adolescents are likely to move into service occupations that stem from technology while their fathers have held jobs in an economy geared toward industrial production (Bell 1973). Another obvious example concerns women. A large proportion of female adolescents today can look forward to careers that were not available to their mothers.

Riesman noted that societal structure, and how it is perceived, bears on the techniques parents employ for child-rearing and socialization. For example, during 1880–1920, increasing numbers of parents began to prepare adolescents for future jobs by sending them to school, rather than putting them directly into the work force (cf., Katz 1981; Kett 1977). According to Riesman, modern parents realize that the skills and values they have, and that were sufficient for them, may not be the skills and values their children will need to adapt to the future. As a consequence, parents do not try to duplicate themselves in their children. Instead, parents act more like managers who provide their children with experiences that will prepare them for the future. In this regard, parents enlist the aid of others, such as their children's teachers and peers, who might know better what the future holds.

This analysis bears on the present data in several ways. First of all, it helps to emphasize again the common alliance among parents and adolescents who, despite individual differences and details of interaction, are as a family unit working toward the adolescents' adaptive entrance to society. Second, it helps to explain the seeming distance that parents, especially fathers, have from the adolescents' daily affairs. Parents are not unaware that socialization is, in fact, occurring outside their own view. The likelihood is that they want this to occur and keep track of it by checking overt markers such as grades or signs of personal crisis. Third, fathers and mothers may be co-managers who divide their functions—with mothers carrying the greater load by attending to everyday details. Fathers' main duties are outside the home, and they are brought into personal matters only when special advice is needed.

Unfortunately, our studies of parent-adolescent interactions were not sufficiently refined to allow assessment of some of the innovative concepts about family systems. They were, however, adequate in yielding data indicative of the central concept that paternal and maternal relations, while different, are coordinated. In this regard, the separate relationships have a common purpose and are directed toward the same end. What we have done here is to add sociological context to the notion of the family as a system. This addition was suggested by the adolescents' descriptions that came surprisingly close to being restatements of post–World War II sociological theory. It might be noted here that the connection is not so obtuse, given the time of assessment and the ages of these adolescents. Their parents were born in the 1930s and early 1940s, as a rule. The parents of our adolescents, then, were products of families extant at the time that Parsons, Riesman, and others were writing their characterizations.

Personal Relationships

At several times in this chapter, one might have noted the hint of a paradox between adolescents' attachment and detachment from parents. It may have been apparent in the conjunction of separation and attachment, or in the foregoing view of parent-adolescent alliance against society and of parental distance in managerial functions. The argument has been that parent-adolescent relationships are, in fact, complex in makeup and cannot be described as having a single theme without serious risk of distortion. Our view is that the parent-adolescent relationship is not an entity in itself but is a product of social construction. This would follow from historical data that show how family structure and parental roles have changed in accordance with deep shifts in overall societal structure (e.g., Cott 1977; Degler 1980; Shorter 1975; Stone 1981).

Some historians and sociologists who have tried to build historical results into a psychological theory have noted that individuality is a central mark of modern society. The notion is that individual identity has replaced the older definition of self as a member of a lineage or of a family. The implications for psychological theory are rather clear. Implicit in many of these theories is the concept that maturity requires taking a stand as an individual who can think rationally and act self-sufficiently. This concept may underlie emphases that appear in theories of adolescent psychology. Obvious examples include self-constructed ego identity, independence, and automony. All of these terms refer to the adolescents' abilities to reflect on experiences and to make sense of them so that reality is ordered as is the self within reality. Implied, but not necessarily stated, is that in becoming an individual, the adolescent has overcome dependence on other persons, in particular parents. To wit, the adolescent who employs formal reasoning need not look to parents for endorsement since the verification of reasoning requires only that logical procedures have been followed (see Sampson 1977; 1981; for critiques of this position).

Present results suggest that exaggerations of identity, autonomy, and independence need to be tempered. In the first place, the so-called "struggle for identity" hardly appears to be a lone journey into phenomenal experience or to be an inward battle of self-reflection. Parents appear to be part of the process in terms of communicative discussions. The fact that adolescents converse with their parents about themselves, their problems, and their uncertainties can be seen to testify to the social nature of the identity process. The point is not simply that "social experience" provides data for adolescents' self-reflection, but that the reflection itself is social as thoughts and feelings are talked out and sorted out with other persons. As was noted above, contemporary lives are so arranged that adolescents have considerable control over the information that pertains to themselves. It is significant that sons and daughters designate their mothers as persons with whom they seek discussion of their private concerns. While they still withhold some information, they disclose much about themselves and more than they have to, in order to satisfy objective demands.

Adolescents and Mothers

This finding becomes more interesting when it is coupled with adolescents' perceptions that their mothers are not judgmental but are supportive, not contentious but understanding. Seen in this light, adolescent-mother communications take on the character of social verification and represent a step beyond the child-like need for endorsement or approval. Adolescents view their mothers as persons who are willing to listen to them on topics that are personally self-revealing, even when the goal is not solely problem-solving but also includes consensual validation. These data supply a much needed correction to the notion that adolescents must construct their identities for themselves, by themselves. Current findings do not allow an estimate of the degree to which mothers are brought into the process. However, they show that mothers are brought in and that the process involves social construction with a tendency toward mutual procedures (e.g., Burke & Weir 1979; Wright & Keple 1981).

The closeness that adolescents feel toward their mothers deserves further elaboration. Adolescents express an unambiguous loyalty to their mothers that includes gratitude, respect, awareness of their roles, and feelings of reciprocal debt. Because this sense of debt is coupled with on-going communications on a person-to-person basis, one can moderate the excessive meaning of autonomy in some psychological theories. Undoubtedly, adolescents think for themselves. Undoubtedly, too, they think with the help of their mothers and solicit their mothers' input into their own reasoning. The attachment that adolescents feel is rather replete. They say that they want to act ''so that she knows you care,'' ''to make our relation better,'' ''so I don't hurt her feelings,'' ''make her feel better,'' ''so she has time for herself,'' ''so she won't feel unloved,'' '' 'cause she needs your help,'' and ''to keep our relation good.'' These statements seem to reflect a closeness in the relationship, a loyalty to the relationship that would modulate any exaggerated claim to autonomy.

Psychological notions that are predicated on any individualistic framework seem to fall short in giving adequate due to the importance of social solidarity. This connection has already been made in the historical-sociological literature referred to above (cf., Habermas 1979). It is important to bring this connection to the psychological literature as well. If one takes at face value what adolescents say they do and how they feel, then, part of their self-definition consists in social solidarity with their mothers. The relationship can be seen on the surface via continuing communication, and its strength can be gauged from the underpinnings of reciprocity.

Our studies were not directed to uncovering the origins of this bond, but there is plenty of evidence of its formation during infancy and childhood (e.g., Ainsworth 1969; Sroufe & Waters 1977). Given that parents divide family labor and that mothers acquire the duties of caring for and rearing the children, it follows that the mother-child bond continues to be reinforced during childhood. At the end of childhood, this relationship seems to have a definite structure of unilateral constraint and asymmetry. One can, therefore, question its future stability (Gouldner 1960). As was seen in the results of our studies, aspects of this structure are retained during adolescence, and this will bode ill for future severance of the relation when either the veil of all-knowing authority is pierced or adolescents discover their own competence. What may then sustain the relationship is its transformation into a new mode as mothers and adolescents begin to interact more cooperatively and mutually (Greenberg, Siegel, & Leitch 1983). This transformation is supported by mothers' taking seriously the expressive domain in which they meet adolescents on their own terms. For adolescents, social life, emotional fluctuations, and self-doubts are of central concern. When mothers show that they share these concerns, grounds for cooperation are laid.

Our speculation is that in dealing with the nonobjective side of adolescents' lives, mothers help establish new terms for their relationship with adolescents. These terms are enacted through interactive procedures that are appropriate for the content of the expressive area. What mothers can do is to enter discussions not to judge feelings or opinions but to empathize with them and to suggest strategies for dealing with them. The fact that adolescents report free-form, simple conversation as a frequent and preferred activity with mothers is significant. This seemingly bland finding may indicate that conversation for its own sake occurs regularly between mothers and adolescents, and that the defensiveness, which occurs because of mothers' ''authority'' roles, has been considerably reduced.

Daughters and Fathers

The data pertaining to the differences between mothers and fathers in their relations with their adolescent sons and daughters has been discussed in detail. What has not been presented are the data pertaining to the differences between sons and daughters with respect to their relations with each parent. While sons and daughters do not differ markedly with respect to their descriptions of relations with their mothers, there are several points on which they differ in these descriptions as they pertain to relations with their fathers. These points make up the general finding that while adolescents are in general more distant from their fathers than from their mothers, daughters are even more distant from fathers than are sons. This distance is exemplified in the lack of conversations or shared activities between fathers and daughters. For fathers and sons, sports activities may serve as a point where they can meet on equal grounds and exchange views, as well as share activities. In contrast, fathers and daughters do not have these shared experiences or interests. Thus the potential for free-form conversation and a cooperative exchange of ideas and views is limited between fathers and daughters.

With regard to topics of communication, daughters were far less likely than sons to select their fathers as persons they would be most likely to talk to about their *career goals* (17% daughters, 41% sons); their *problems with their mothers* (5% daughters, 34% sons); their *doubts about their abilities* (6% daughters, 29% sons); their *hopes and plans for the future* (10% daughters, 33% sons); their *feelings about their mothers* (11% daughters, 30% sons); their *fears about life* (2% daughters, 19% sons); and their *moral standards* (4% daughters, 18% sons). The differences between sons and daughters were similar with respect to their fathers as persons that adolescents were least likely to talk to. In particular, over 50% of the daughters said they would be least likely to talk to their fathers about their *feelings about close friends* (58% daughters, 32% sons); their *views about sex* (60% daughters, 30% sons); their *problems with an opposite-sex friend* (54% daughters, 35% sons); their *attitudes toward marriage* (61% daughters, 34% sons); their *fears about life* (54% daughters, 27% sons); and their *feelings about a same-sex friend* (58% daughters, 32% sons).

These differences between sons and daughters with respect to their fathers were also found in descriptions of the quality of their communications. Daughters were more likely than sons to select the father as the person who "does not admit doubts and fears to me" (58% daughters, 34% sons); and "does not talk openly to me" (56% daughters, 31% sons). They were less likely than sons to select the father as the person who "talks out differences with me" (6% daughters, 19% sons).

How do daughters perceive themselves in relations with their fathers? The results speak for themselves: 64% said *distant;* 65%, *uncomfortable;* 64%, *withdrawn;* 35%, *unwanted;* and 44%, *insensitive.* In addition, daughters were significantly more likely than sons to describe themselves as *dishonest* (33% daughters, 21% sons) and *phony* (38% daughters, 15% sons) when with their fathers. Finally, daughters were asked to describe how their relations with their fathers have changed over the past 5 years.

A 16-year-old said: "I used to listen to everything; thought he was always right. Now I have my own opinions. Now, I don't like him a lot. He's more strict. . . He gets worried. Doesn't like frivolity—always giving out advice."

A 15-year-old said: "We used to be really close. Now it's different. I've become more hostile. He doesn't understand me; doesn't know what I'm thinking, what I'm doing."

A 15-year-old said: "It was better 5 years ago. I get more defensive and more fresh. He's being more pushy. I am not afraid to say things now. Still I feel respect and look up to him. He's more pushy about school."

An 18-year-old said: "I used to ignore him. Now I'm angry. I still see him as my father. He gives me more freedom but demands a certain amount of respect from me."

An 18-year-old said: "We didn't get along at all at 15. Now we get along better. I don't show when I'm mad, but try to understand him. I know he won't change. He still treats me like I'm 13 and expects me to listen to him."

Thus, the general finding is that relations between fathers and daughters are more constrained and detached than are relations between fathers and sons. The main qualification to this general finding is that for some proportion of daughters, the distance begins to close during later adolescence. Eighteen-year-olds talk more with their fathers and feel that their fathers interact more personally with them, than 15-year-olds do. Older daughters also believe that their fathers are more concerned about them and watchful over them than are younger daughters. Older daughters also state their sense of obligation to fathers in terms of talking and doing things together while younger daughters are prone to state it in terms of obedience or meeting expectations. Finally, in describing changes in their relationship over the past 5 years, more older daughters than younger daughters perceived a shift in their fathers' respect for them and sensitivity to their interests. Here are a few of their statements: "He treats me more as an equal." "He appreciates me more; he treats me more seriously." "Father has become willing to bend a little, accept my views a little; he's easier to talk to—but still very protective." "We can relate to each better than before—I'm not as defensive; he treats me more maturely and relies on me to do well." And, "We're closer; I can be more open now." "He feels closer to me and will be open and say what he's feeling, if I initiate it." "He may be a little afraid because I'm growing up and now he can't have full authority."

Conclusions and Speculation

Contrary to our expectations, adolescents did not perceive a single relationship with their parents but described two relationships—one with fathers, the other with mothers. The modal relation with fathers appears to be an extension of the structure of unilateral constraint that was in place at the end of childhood. Children perceive fathers as persons who know best how children should act. Children look to fathers for approval that validates their actions and signifies that they are acquiring adult perspectives on reality. Fathers, in turn, perceive children's conformity as a sign that they are learning correct conduct and acquiring a broader understanding of the standards and norms that will serve them as they enter society.

Adolescents, in the main, continue to perceive their fathers as they did when they were children. This is true to the extent that adolescents still seek their fathers' approval and believe that fathers have insights into the society that they are about to enter. The perception, however, has become narrower in application to concrete performances that are instrumental for job and career preparation and for solving particular problems in which fathers have specialized competences. Fathers seem to have narrow views toward their sons and daughters, thinking of them as potential adults and caring most about their performances that indicate progress toward productive adulthood. As a consequence, fathers share only a small part of adolescents' here-and-now interests. As a further consequence, fathers and adolescents fall short of getting to know each other as individual personalities. Instead, they understand each other practically and through roles.

This relationship in itself seems not to promote psychological development of the self as a variegated and nondefensive individual (Piaget [1932] 1965; Sullivan 1953). The fathers' expectations of adolescents—what they want their sons or daughters to be—serves as a filter that bars coming face-to-face with another personality. The adolescents, in turn, wind up with a similarly constricted perception. This relationship is conducive to the maintenance of mystification. However, in the very distance between fathers and adolescents, there is opportunity for emancipation. Because fathers' demands are selective and because fathers do not intrude on most of what adolescents do, sons and daughters have room to think about reality with others from whom they can gain consensual validation.

One function of the paternal relationship can readily be seen as providing adolescents with long-range goals that, although administered indirectly, seem to be conveyed clearly. A simple version of the father-adolescent dynamic goes something like this: Fathers say that they want adolescents to be this kind of an adult, and to get there they must do this and not do that. Because adolescents perceive their fathers as experts on society, they can accept their fathers' expectations of them—although they may think the expectation is unrealistic and recognize that it fails to take into account their true competencies or personality. Another function of this dynamic may be to introduce adolescents to society, at least from the viewpoint of the stereotypic adult male role. In society, the individual will be judged impersonally through standards of performances and impersonally administered rules. There is little forgiveness in either standards or rules for the extenuating circumstances that individuals might feel keep them from meeting criteria.

Adolescents' relationships with their mothers have some of the characteristics that are found above. Mothers, no less than fathers, hold adolescents to performance standards that refer ultimately to impending adulthood. The message that mothers give is similar to that sent by fathers: My continued approval of you depends on meeting my expectations of the kind of adult I want you to be. But this aspect of the relationship is only one part of its full character, and it is communicated in a different style than is common in the paternal relationship.

First, mothers maintain regular contact with their sons and daughters. Second, their contact is not focused primarily on the children's future. Third, mothers engage themselves in adolescents' interests—whatever they might be. Fourth, mothers closely monitor their sons and daughters by acting both as disciplinarians and as advisors. Fifth, in their involvement in adolescents' daily experiential lives, mothers do not solely take the role as authorities, but serve as confidants who share experiences—with the end result being empathy. To this end, mutuality enters the relationship and the two parties come to be more like persons who see each other as they are, rather than as either is supposed to be. The mark of this achievement in mother-adolescent relationships is conversation for its own sake, the kind of conversation in which ideas and feelings are exchanged, not instructional episodes that are designed to influence or persuade.

There are limits to this closeness with mothers. Adolescents do not share all of their personal lives with their mothers, nor do mothers make total self-disclosures about themselves. The judgmental side tinges the relationship, as it must, given the mothers' orientation toward the future. Still, this relationship advances farther in cooperation than does the paternal relationship. Perhaps the key factor is mothers' concerns for adolescents' well-being in the here-and-now, coupled with their interest in what adolescents themselves care about. This give a tone to the relationship that permeates even moments of discipline and probably serves as a basis for the binding power of the maternal attachment.

Adolescents' perceptions clearly differentiate between these relationships. As observers from the outside, however, we may see the relationships as conjoined within the family context. The family is a system in which the two parents have different but reinforcing functions that are designed to help adolescents make the transition to adulthood, while maintaining the adolescents' allegiance to the family. Seen in this way, the paternal relationship is not so distant as it appears because it is mediated by the maternal relationship. In this system, mothers carry the brunt of the work and cover a multiplicity of tasks. The result is that the maternal relationship is a mixed structure of both unilateral authority and cooperation. This is not to say that this system is rational or conscious. Indeed, there seems to be a dynamic to the mother-adolescent relationship that, began in infancy, continues unrelentingly through childhood and adolescence. It is not clear when fathers begin to distance themselves from their children, but there is a hint in the data that fathers were more involved with their children during their childhood than they are during adolescence. Adolescent daughters recall their fathers' playfulness and emotional support, while sons recall doing chores with them and playing athletic games together.

The two central concepts found in the psychological theories of adolescence are emancipation and conformity. The former refers to the belief that in order to establish their own individuality, adolescents must free themselves from the parental bond. They must find self-definition outside the parental bond and learn to think for themselves without relying on their parents for validation. Conformity, on the other hand, refers to the parents' roles as mediators between the family and society. Parents are to instill standards and values that help to maintain society through properly forming society's incoming members.

Emancipation seems too strong a term for the present data. Rather, parents seem to grant adolescents considerable latitude by allowing them to have private lives apart from the family. However, the bond to parents is not severed so much as it is transformed. Fathers remain attached by proposing standards that they offer as means to adulthood. Mothers do this, and more, by remaining involved in adolescents' interests. Conformity also seems too strong a term for the results. Parents' demand for conformity is clear, but selective, as it is applied to a limited set of performances that keep adolescents on a path to productive adulthood and correct any deviations from that course. But conformity is not demanded in a total sense because adolescents are given freedom to have personal lives that parents monitor only loosely.

These exaggerations of emancipation and conformity seem to find a more balanced replacement in the dual process of separation and connection. Separation connotes emancipation but in a tempered sense. And connection includes conformity without emphasizing the duplication of the parent through the adolescent. It seems to be more clearly the case that the task of defining self occurs to some degree within the adolescents' relationship with their parents. Except for psychoanalytic thinkers (e.g., Blos 1967), theorists of emancipation speak only of severing the relationship without noting that the relationship continues and that it can be retained in some transformed structure. Socialization theorists, on the other hand, do not speak of the relationship at all—except through its functional effects. Consequently, they also miss the complex dynamics of parents helping adolescents become adults while seeking to retain the relationship.

What emancipation and socialization theorists do not adequately appreciate is the alliance that parents and adolescents make in a joint effort to combat society. Emancipation theorists propose that adolescents confront society on their own and master it, at least cognitively, by figuring out how society is ordered and ought to be ordered. This view may not give credit to society's real complexity or the need to have definite plans for action to succeed in it. Moreover, the view inadequately describes parents' involvement in helping their sons and daughters be successful. What socialization theorists do not appreciate is that parents do not necessarily want their children to have the same views of society that they had or to be in the same positions in society that they are.

Historians and sociologists have been more sensitive to the relationship between families with adolescents and society. Not all parents think of society as something to preserve as it is, or as something that their sons and daughters ought to perceive as benevolent. On the contrary, society is full of problems, and entrance into it presents difficulties. Parents take adolescents' parts in this and use their material and mental resources as well as their experiences for the purpose of giving their sons and daughters an edge. For parents to leave adolescents on their own would be irresponsible. For parents to seek to duplicate themselves in their sons and daughters would be equally dysfunctional.

What psychologists can contribute to this revised view, and what the present data begin to make clear, is how parents and adolescents co-construct an approach to society that will best serve the adolescents. In particular, psychologists might show how the alliance is worked out within the context of a continuing relationship that began in infancy and is likely to persist for several more decades. The strategies required for the overall task cannot be understood apart from the dynamics entailed in this relationship. The data give no evidence that parents and adolescents lack a commitment to their relationship or that they want it to be as it was during childhood.

If emancipation theories err toward individualism, then socialization theories sell short the place of relationships. Neither takes adequate account of the adolescent's membership in a family, loyalty to it, and commitments to specific relations. The findings of our studies help to show how these relationships are structured and possibly coupled in family systems. The goal in the next three chapters is to look at friendship as another important relationship both in itself and also as a further point of comparison that may help place adolescents' relations with their parents in a clearer context (cf., Douvan & Adelson 1966; Hunter & Youniss 1982; Wright & Keple 1981).

6

Activities and Communications of Close Friendships

As shown in the preceding chapters, several components of parent-adolescent relationships appear to have important implications for social development in adolescence. These relationships, however, are only two of a variety of inter-personal relationships that have the potential for affecting the processes of social development. Indeed, during the course of their everyday activities, most adolescents are involved in a number of relationships: among them teacher-student, boss-employee, coach–team member, and close friendship. Of these relationships, a close friendship has perhaps the greatest potential for contributing to social development simply because, during adolescence, it is marked by a high level of emotional involvement and importance. Some of the results of study 6 attest to the significance of this relationship for adolescents. In that study, a substantial majority of the adolescents sampled answered *true* to the statements: "I have at least one close friend who means a lot to me" (94%). "My close friend values my friendship" (92%). And, "Once I become friends with someone, we stay friends a long time" (92%). The importance of this relationship for understanding social development in adolescence is demonstrated by the finding that a substantial majority of these adolescents also answered *true* to the statements: "My close friend under-stands me better than my parents do" (70%). "I feel right now in my life I learn more from my close friend than I do from my parents" (70%). And, "I'm more 'myself' with my close friend than with my parents" (68%). In contrast, very few subjects answered *true* to the statements: "Friends are not really that important to me" (5%). "My friendships don't last very long" (9%). And, "I never had a really close friend" (7%).

The question we turn to now is how close friendships affect social develop-ment during adolescence. As noted in chapter 1, some theories of adolescence envision friendship as having a "negative" impact on social development.

Friends are seen as influencing one another in ways that serve to counteract the positive socializing influences of parents. In these views, however, the focus has not been on friendship, per se, but rather on the peer group or the peer culture as a general socializing force. When friendship has been investigated as a relationship in itself, apart from the general peer group, it has been found to embody those very principles which are conducive to social solidarity and prosocial values (cf. Berndt 1982; Wellman 1979; Youniss 1983).

In this chapter and in the following one, data will be presented that pertain to close friendship in adolescence. The goal is to delineate the features that characterize this relationship during adolescence. The issues of concern in this chapter are the kinds of activities that close friends engage in, the topics they discuss, and the quality of their communications. Data will also be presented pertaining to concepts of self in the context of a close-friendship and perceived changes in this relationship over time. The following chapter will focus on the kinds of conflicts that occur in close friendships, the ways these conflicts are resolved, and the perceptions of the obligations that two close friends have toward each other. Differences in responding as a function of the age or sex of the adolescents will be discussed where relevant. However, differences in responding as a function of "relationship" (i.e., mother-child, father-child, or close friend) will be reserved for presentation and discussion in chapter 9.

In all of the studies included in this section, *close friend* was defined for the subjects as a *person of the same sex as you who is not a brother or sister*. Although the relationship between opposite-sex friends was investigated in a few of the studies, the results pertaining to this relationship proved difficult to interpret. The confounding factor was that the term *opposite-sex friend* or even *boyfriend* or *girlfriend* did not mean the same thing to all the subjects. For some, the opposite-sex friend was someone with whom they were romantically or sexually involved, while for others the opposite-sex friend was seen as just a friend. As a result, responses to this kind of relationship actually pertained to two distinctly different relationships. Thus, although both of these opposite-sex friend relationships are of importance to an understanding of adolescent social development, they will not be discussed in this book given the limitations of our data base.

Typical and Enjoyed Activities

The general question, "What do close friends do together that they enjoy?" was investigated in studies 3 and 7. In study 3, adolescents were asked to describe 3 "enjoyable activities" that they do with their close friend while in study 7, the task was to describe 1 activity that was "most enjoyed." A slightly different question, "What kinds of activities are typical of close friendships?" was posed in an interview with the adolescents sampled in study 1. These adolescents were to describe 3 activities that they felt characterized their relationship with a close friend.

The results of study 3 virtually duplicated those of study 7. In order to avoid repetition, only the results of study 7 pertaining to the "most enjoyed" activity will be discussed. In this study, 64% of the females said they "most enjoyed" *going out together;* 28% reported that they "most enjoyed" *talking together;* 2% indicated that *recreational activities* were "most enjoyed"; and 1% said they "most enjoyed" activities related to *drug or alcohol use.* Three-percent of the activities were idiosyncratic, and 2% of the female adolescents did not answer the question. In general, then, female adolescents appear to most enjoy *going out together* and *talking together.* While these activities are obviously not mutually exclusive, the category *going out together* was restricted to specification of activities other than talking, such as "going to the movies," "going to parties," "going to the beach," "going to a game room," or just "going out." A few of these activities were opposite-sex related in that the purpose of going out together was "to pick up guys."

The responses of male adolescents provided a slightly different picture of enjoyed activities than that depicted by the females. While 36% of the males said they also "most enjoyed" *going out together;* 24% indicated that they "most enjoyed" *recreational or sports activities;* and 20% reported that they "most enjoyed" activities involving *drugs or alcohol use.* Only 10% of the males indicated that they "most enjoyed" *talking together;* 4% of the responses were idiosyncratic; and 6% of the males did not answer the question. The activities described as *recreational or sports* included team activities, such as baseball and hockey, as well as less structured activities, such as "riding bikes," "swimming," "board games," "motor cycle riding," "racing cars," and "playing cards." The category *drug and alcohol use* incorporates activities where use of an illicit substance was in itself the "enjoyed" activity—that is, "go out and get drunk," "get wasted," and "get high and drink." Use of these categories differed significantly between males and females ($p < .01$).

In summary, although both males and females clearly enjoy "going out" with their close friends, more females than males enjoy "just talking" while more males than females enjoy playing sports or engaging in "illicit" behavior. These findings are similar to the results of study 1 despite the fact that the task for study 1 was to describe "typical" rather than "enjoyed" activities. For the female adolescents in study 1, typical activities with close friends involved *intimate discussion* (60% of the activities), *going places and doing things* (25% of activities), *nonintimate discussions* (7% of the activities), and *showing friendship* (7% of the activities). Intimacy in discussion was considered to be reflected in statements such as: "We talk about our personal development." "We talk to each other about ourselves." "We talk about problems in our families." And, "We tell our most intimate feelings." Other topics included discussions of books, school, grades, or just "gossip" about others. The category, *showing friendship,* served as a "catch all" for activities that described the things close friends are expected to do for each other, for example, "stand-up for each other," "don't tell each others' secrets," "help each other," and "do favors for the other guy." Finally, the category *going places and doing things together* included for the most part statements that were no more specific than that: "We do lots of things together." "We go out places together." And, "We go out and do a lot of things." This lack of specificity may be due to the possibility that close friends typically do such a wide variety of "things" together or go to such a wide variety of places, that no single place or activity can be pointed out as more typical than any other.

The perspectives of the male adolescents as to the kinds of activities that typify their close-friendships again differ somewhat from those provided by the females. For the most part, the activities offered by males and females are the same, but their frequencies differ. For example, 30% of the activities provided by males involved *intimate discussions,* as compared to 60% for females; while 27% involved *nonintimate discussion,* as compared to 7% for females. Other activities noted as typical were *going places and doing things together* (23%), *showing friendship* (15%), and *competing* (2%). Three percent of the responses were not classified since they pertained to feelings, for example, "like each other a lot," instead of to activities.

The results of the studies discussed above suggest that, in their close friendships, male and female adolescents enjoy, and typically engage in, activities that take them out of their homes and allow them to interact with each other independent of parental involvement or even observation. They go to movies, parties, concerts, and sports events, or they just "drive around" or "hang around" together. Indeed, the nature of the activity does not seem to be important. Instead, what matters is that the friends are together and that they are "out," implying distance from parents and association with peers. A major difference between males and females is that apart from just going out together, close male friends most enjoy sports or "illicit" activities, while close female friends most enjoy just talking together. In addition, when close friends do talk together, the topic more typically involves personal issues and problems if the close friends are female, than if they are male. This is not meant to imply that friendships between males during adolescence lack personal or intimate communications, but rather that this aspect is more characteristic of a close friendship between females than of a close friendship between males.

Topics of Discussion

What do adolescents talk about with their close friends? This question was investigated in studies 6 and 7. In study 6, adolescents were presented with 7 general topic areas and asked to indicate whether or not each area was discussed with their close friend. The topic areas were the way you handle your *schoolwork* or what you should do to make better grades; the way you behave toward your *friends* or problems you may have with your friends; your *future plans* for school or jobs; what you should or should not do on *dates;* the way you behave toward your *family* or problems you may have with your family; your *religious beliefs* such as what you think about God and other religious teachings; and *social issues,* such as racial and sexual discrimination, draft for military service, and welfare programs. For all topic areas except *family,* males and females responded in almost identical fashion. With their close friends, 90% of the adolescents said that they discuss their *friendships,* 73% indicated that they have conversations about *dating,* 65% said that they discuss *social issues,* and 56% reported conversations about *religious beliefs.* In contrast to this similarity between the genders, 80% of the females, but only 54% of the males, reported that they discussed their *family* with their close friends. This male-female difference was significant ($p < .01$). In addition, with respect to the topic of *social issues,* 87% of the oldest adolescents (both males and females) reported discussion of this topic with close friends, while only 50% of the younger adolescents discussed this topic.

For the most part, then, most adolescents seem to talk to their close friends about their friendships, their future plans, their schoolwork, and their dating behavior. The majority of female adolescents also talk about their families with their close friends, and most 18–20-year-olds, of both sexes, discuss social issues with their close friends. These findings are supported and further elaborated by the results of study 7.

In study 7, adolescents were presented with a list of 22 topic areas and 4 potential discussion partners—father, mother, same-sex close friend, and opposite-sex close friend (see Appendix D). For each topic area, the task was to select the person with whom the subject was most likely and least likely to discuss the topic. The topics for which mothers and fathers were generally the most and least likely partners were discussed in chapters 3 and 4. In this chapter, the data pertain only to those topics for which the same-sex close friend was chosen more frequently than any of the other target persons, as the most likely and as the least likely discussion partner.

With respect to the most likely discussion partner, females chose the close friend more often than any of the other target persons for 10 of the 22 topics. Over 50% of the female adolescents selected the same-sex close friend as the most likely partner to discuss their *problems with mother* (63%), *feelings about mother* (61%), *problems with opposite-sex friend* (68%), *feelings about opposite-sex friend* (69%), and *views about sex* (53%). Female adolescents also chose the same-sex close friend more often than the other target persons when the topics involved their *problems at school* (44%), *fears about life* (43%), *doubts about abilities* (40%), *moral standards* (40%), and *views on society* (34%). Females, then, are more likely to talk to their close friends than to their fathers, mothers, or boyfriends about matters concerning their mothers; their boyfriends; their views about sex, morality, and society; their problems at school; and their doubts and fears about life and themselves. In fact, there was only one topic—*political beliefs*—for which females selected the close friend more often than they did the others as the least likely discussion partners (30%).

Communication between close male friends appears somewhat more restricted than that between close female friends. For most likely discussion partner, males selected the same-sex close friend more often than they did the other persons for 8 of the 22 topics. However, on only 2 of these topics was the selection of close friend made by over 50% of the males. These were *my problems with my opposite-sex friend* (54%) and *my feelings about my opposite-sex friend* (50%). Only 48% selected the same-sex friend for the topic *my views about sex*. Less than 40% selected the same-sex friend for the remaining 5 topics: *my feelings about mother* (34%), *my feelings about same-sex friend* (33%), *my views on society* (34%), *my moral standards* (31%), and *my fears about life* (29%). Males selected the close same-sex friend as the least likely discussion partner slightly more often than they did the other target persons on topics dealing with *my problems with same-sex friends* (31%) and *doubts about my abilities* (26%).

The data from studies 6 and 7 demonstrate that adolescents talk to their close friends about school, sex and dating, opposite-sex friends, friendship, family, and the future. More females than males, however, reported discussions of these topics with their close friends, and, regardless of the topic, more females than males selected the close friend as the preferred or most likely discussion partner. In study 7, for example, almost 70% of the females compared to about 50% of the males selected the same-sex close friend as the most likely partner in discussions concerning *problems with* and *feelings about* opposite-sex friends. A similar pattern emerged for other topics, particularly those pertaining to intimate feelings or problems. Thus, female adolescents showed more homogeneity than did males on the topics they discuss with their close friends. For most females, discussions of intimate issues, such as feelings and problems, appear to be as much an aspect of their close friendships as are discussions of nonintimate issues. While this description is valid for some of the close male friendships, for many others, the exchange of intimate information is apparently not an aspect of the relationship.

Quality of Communication

The preceding section focused on the content and range of topics covered by communications between close friends. This section presents data relevant to the form of communication between close friends. When two close friends have a discussion with each other, what qualities characterize this interaction?

This issue was investigated in studies 6 and 7. The general concern of study 6 was the nature of communication between close friends. The specific issues were whether or not adolescents perceive their close friend as *explaining his/her reasons for his/her ideas* in discussions of particular topics; whether or not adolescents perceive their close friend as *really trying to understand their ideas* in discussions of particular topics; and whether or not communications between close friends on particular topics are characterized by *symmetrical understanding, asymmetrical understanding,* or *nonunderstanding.*

As shown in the preceding section, 5 out of 7 topic areas were reported to be discussed with close friends by at least 67% of the adolescents. The topics were *schoolwork, friendships, family, future plans,* and *dating behavior.* For each topic, adolescents who indicated that they discussed that topic with a close friend were also asked to report how often (*often* or *not often*) their friend has explained his(her) reasons for ideas, and how often their close friend has really tried to understand the subjects' ideas. Responses to these items were combined in order to obtain a measure of the type of understanding characteristic of the relationship. For example, a discussion of a particular topic area was said to involve *symmetrical understanding* if the friend both often explained reasons and often really tried to understand the other's ideas. If the close friend was perceived as often performing one function but not often performing the other, communication on that topic was viewed as characterized by *asymmetrical understanding.* Finally, discussions were considered to be characterized by *nonunderstanding* if the close friend was described as not often performing either function.

The results demonstrated that for the majority of female adolescents, close friends were perceived as often really trying to understand them and often explaining their own reasons across all 5 topics. Over 70% of the females indicated that their close friend often really tried to understand their ideas in discussions about *schoolwork* (76%), *friendships* (80%), *future plans* (74%), *dating behavior* (80%), and *family* (82%). Correspondingly, over 60% of the females indicated that their close friend often explained his/her reasons for ideas in discussions of *friendships* (78%), *future plans* (62%), *dating behavior* (73%), and *family* (68%). Only 57% described their close friend as often explaining his/her reasons in discussions of *school work.* In addition, communications between close female friends were found to be characterized primarily by symmetrical understanding for all 5 topics with the order of frequency being *friendship* and *dating behavior* (71%), *family* (67%), *future plans* (59%), and *schoolwork* (57%). An analysis of the pattern of responding for adolescents across topics also revealed that symmetrical understanding was a major characteristic of communications between close female friends. For 21% of the females, all discussions with close friends, regardless of topic, involved symmetrical understanding; and for 45% of the females, symmetrical understanding characterized at least one-half of their discussions. Only 4% of the females indicated that none of their discussions with close friends involved symmetrical understanding.

The analyses of the responses of male adolescents resulted in significant contrasts between the genders. Males were less likely than were females to report that their close friend often really tried to understand their ideas, whether the discussions involved *schoolwork* (49%), *friendships* (51%), *future plans* (49%), *dating behavior* (56%), or *family* (35%). For each topic, the male-female difference was significant (*p* < .01). Similarly, males were less likely than were females to indicate that their close friend often explained his reasons for ideas, again, whether the discussion involved *friendships* (78% females, 51% males), *future plans* (62% females, 47% males), *dating behavior* (73% females, 50% males), *family* (68% females, 42% males), or *schoolwork* (57% females, 46% males). Gender differences were significant for *friendships* and for *family* (*p* < .05).

These results suggest that differences between males and females would also arise with respect to the type of understanding that charactered discussions between close friends. Indeed, chi-square tests of independence produced significant sex differences *(p* < *.05)* in the frequencies of the specific types of understanding for all 5 topic areas. Less than 50% of the males indicated that symmetrical understanding characterized discussions with their close friend when the topics were *friendships* (42%) and *dating behavior* (48%), and less than 40% reported symmetrical understanding in discussions of *schoolwork* (31%), *future plans* (37%), and *family* (29%). In contrast to the kinds of discussions between females, nonunderstanding was as characteristic of the communications between close male friends as was symmetrical understanding, particularly in discussions of *family* (48%), *future plans* (41%), and *friendships* (40%).

In summary, close female friends are significantly more likely than are close male friends to engage in discussions which involve symmetrical understanding—at least with respect to the 5 topics covered in study 6. Female friends explain their reasons for their ideas and really try to understand the ideas put forth by the other. Many male adolescents also seem to engage in this form of communication with close friends. However, many others clearly do not. Again, there appears to be greater homegeneity in the quality of communication between female close friends than between male close friends. These conclusions are both supported and further elaborated by the results of study 7, presented below.

In study 7 the focus was on the more general forms that interactions between close friends might take. The adolescents were presented with a list of 20 items that described particular forms of interacting, and with four target persons—father, mother, same-sex close friend, opposite-sex friend. Nine items pertained to the level of openness in communication, 8 items concerned behaviors in reaction to differences of opinion or to disagreements, and 3 items described interactions relevant to giving or seeking advice (see Appendix D). For each item, the adolescents were asked to select the person who best fit the form of interacting that was described in the item. A few adolescents, in response to this task, chose two persons for particular items. The data presented below concerning the results for each item include only those adolescents who selected one person—the same-sex close friend.

Female adolescents chose the close friend more often than they did any of the other target persons on 6 of the 20 items and less often than any of the other persons on 9 of the 20 items. Males selected the close friend more often than any of the other persons on 5 of the 20 items, but less often than any of the others on only one item. These items are presented in table 8 with the percentages of females and of males who selected the close friend for each item, and with the rank order of the males' selections of the close friend compared to the other target persons. As shown in table 8, females chose the same-sex close friend more often than any of the other target persons on all items that pertained to mutual openness and intimacy in communication, acceptance of differences of opinion, and mutual dependence. The close friend was chosen by females less often than were any of the other target persons on items that pertained to defensiveness or cautiousness in communication, rejection of advice, and refusal to accept differences of opinion or tolerate disagreements.

Although males selected the same-sex friend more frequently than any of the other persons on 5 of the 6 items describing mutual intimacy, advice seeking, and acceptance, the percentages were lower in most cases for the males than for the females—particularly with respect to *telling each other true feelings*. In addition, given the 4 target persons, many of the males selected the same-sex friend as the person who *does not admit doubts or fears to me* (19%), *does not express true feelings to me* (21%), and *does not talk openly to me* (19%). Some males also indicated that they were more likely to *hide true feelings from* (16%) and *not admit doubts and fears* (15%) to the close same-sex friend than to any of the other target persons.

An analysis of the response patterns of individual adolescents across items yielded results similar to those reported above. From this analysis, two groups of adolescents were identified. One group termed the mutual intimacy group, included adolescents who selected the same-sex close friend in response to at least 2 of the 3 mutual intimacy items (items 1, 2, 3 in table 8). The important issue here was whether or not intimacy was a factor in the adolescents' same-sex close friendships. Sixty-four percent of the females could be classified in the mutual intimacy group—indicating that intimacy was clearly an aspect of their interactions with same-sex close friends. Indeed, 44% of the females chose the same-sex close friend for all 3 mutual intimacy items. Mutual inti-

Table 8. Items Selected by Males and Females as Descriptive of Same-Sex Close Friendships

		Females Selecting Friend	Males Selecting Friend	Rank Order of Males' Selection of Friend
	Items for which females selected friend *more often than the other target persons (ranked 1st)*			
	1. This person and I talk openly to each other	54%	42%	1st
	2. This person and I are not afraid to talk about our doubts and fears	46	44	1st
a	3. This person and I always tell each other our true feelings	46	28	1st
	4. When we disagree, this person always listens to my side	32	25	1st
b	5. This person accepts my point of view, even if it is different from his/hers	47	27	2d
	6. This person and I depend on each other for advice	61	44	1st
	Items for which females selected friend *less often than target persons (ranked 4th)*			
	7. I am usually careful what I say to this person	7	4	4th
b	8. I hide my true feelings from this person	2	16	3d
b	9. This person has never admitted doubts and fears to me	7	19	3d
b	10. This person does not express true feelings to me	1	21	2d
	11. I would never admit doubts and fears to this person	5	15	3d
b	12. This person does not talk openly to me	4	19	3d
	13. When we disagree, this person gets upset if I don't change my opinion	12	15	3d
	14. When we disagree, this person says it is in my best interest to change my opinion	11	16	3d
	15. This person does not consider my advice worth seeking	10	15	2d

[a]$p < .05$
[b]$p < .01$

macy was also found to be an aspect of the close friendships of 45% of the males, with 30% choosing the same-sex friend for all 3 of the mutual intimacy items.

The second group, identified by an analysis of individual responses across items, was termed the nonintimacy group. Inclusion in this group was limited to adolescents who selected the same-sex close friend in response to at least 2 of the items pertaining to guardedness and lack of openness as a form of interacting (items 8–12 in table 8). While only 5% of the females met this criterion, 34% of the males were included in this group. Males included in the nonintimacy group were also found to respond fairly consistently to the other items in the questionnaire. For example, males in general selected the same-sex friend more often than they did any of the other persons for 2 items: *This person and I talk openly to each other.* And, *This person and I tell each other our true feelings.* None of the males in the nonintimacy group, however, selected the same-sex friend for these items; and only 4% of males in this group selected the same-sex friend for the item, *This person and I are not afraid to talk about our doubts and fears.*

In complement, 35% of the nonintimacy group (as compared to 15% of the total males) selected the same-sex friend as the *person who does not consider my advice worth seeking;* and 23% (as compared to 12% of the total males) indicated that they were *not interested in any advice* the same-sex friend had to offer. In addition, most of the males who selected the same-sex friend for items pertaining to intolerance of differences of opinion were from the nonintimacy group.

The results of the analysis of responses across items support the contention that close friendships are more homogeneous among female than among male adolescents. Close male friendships appear to take three forms. About 40% of the close male friendships appear to be differentiated from other relationships in the sense that they involve mutual intimacy. In contrast, about 33% of the close male friendships appear to be differentiated from other significant relationships in that they lack intimacy altogether and, in fact, entail a guardedness or defensiveness in communication. Finally, for about 25% of the close male friendships neither intimacy nor its absence seems to be a relevant factor. Again these findings for males are complemented by the results of study 7. In study 7, it was found that for 25% of the male adolescents none of their discussions with close friends were characterized by symmetrical understanding, while for 45% of the male adolescents, symmetrical understanding was involved in less than half of their discussions with close friends.

In summary then, about 66% of the females appear to have close friendships that involve symmetrical understanding and intimacy. Less than 50% of the males share this form of friendship, while almost 33% of the males may be viewed as having close friendships characterized by nonunderstanding, an absence of intimacy, and a sense of guardedness or defensiveness.

These conclusions are supported by the results of study 1 investigating the quality of interactions in close-friend relations. In one section of study 1, adolescents were asked to describe how their current friendships differed from those they had five years ago. The goal was to obtain descriptions of current close friendships by reflecting on the past. Although there were only 20 females (10, 14–16-year-olds, 10, 18–19-year-olds) and 20 males (10, 14–16-years-old, 10, 18–19-year-olds), the results are interesting because they correspond so closely to the findings of studies 6 and 7. Eighty-five percent of the females, with no age-related differences, said that their current close friendship was deeper than those they had experienced in the past and more focused on understanding one another.

Some of the females said of their close-friend relationships: "We're much more open, we just talk about ourselves now. It's not important to be popular anymore; just be able to talk. Friends can be different; they don't have to think alike." "Before, friendships were activity centered; not on persons. Now I try to really know someone. Now I will sacrifice for a friend." "Closer than when I was 10. I always express myself freely now. There's more caring and understanding. I can be friends with anyone now, just as long as they understand the way I am and that the relationship is equal." "Five years ago I was more concerned with social acceptance than I am now; more concerned with how I looked to peers. Now I want someone I can confide in." "My values have changed. I give more of myself now. When I was 13, I tried to be accepted by the popular group. Now I don't care. I value the person." "Now I look for people I can count on—not just an acquaintance. I used to look for popularity or people who are like me. Now they don't have to be the same as me anymore." And, "The relation is deeper, less superficial. When you're younger, you look for good times. Now you want someone who can share the bad times as well as the good."

While the females were nearly unanimous in their depictions of friendship, the males were diverse in their definitions. Of the 10, 14–16-year-olds, 6 emphasized that friends were persons with whom one shared activities. For example, a 14-year-old said: "I'm in the 'in crowd' now, before I wasn't." Another 14-year-old said: "I can do more things now—go to dances, stay over at his house. I treat them nicer now." A 15-year-old boy said: "I have more friends now. We compromise more. Friendship is the same in that I still want someone I can play sports with." Of the four remaining 14–16-year-old males, all focused on the change in terms of talking, discussion, or personal interest. They said "We're closer; we talk more now." "Five years ago we just played; now we talk over things and discuss problems. Then it was just a good time. Now you have to be open and able to talk." "Five years ago, friendship was superficial and I had to be dominant. Before I was friends because they had something I wanted. Now I look for whether someone is interesting and has depth of character." And, "I'm a deeper friend now, someone you can talk to. When I was 11, I looked for someone to play with. Now I look for a deeper friend."

Of the 10, 18–19-year-old males, 4 predicated friendship on shared activities and judged that their friendships today had not changed in form over the past 5 years. The 6 males who said that their close friendships had changed emphasized discussion and depth of personal sharing. One said: "We talk more about problems. Look for a broader scope of interests; not just sports." Another said: "At 14, friends were playmates. Now a friend is an advisor. He's someone you go to when you need help; not just for a good time." Still another said: "Now we talk more; not just play. I'm more concerned about them than I was. More interested and look for more serious things." Finally, one said: "Friendship is now based on the kind of people we are rather than interests. I'm more honest and giving."

These results show that females were homogeneous in describing their current close friendships in terms of mutual understanding through open discussion. While this same concern was shared by 10 of the 20 males, the remainder emphasized similarities in activities and interests, or popularity. This suggests that for those adolescent males and females for whom friendship does not involve mutual intimacy and understanding, the basis for the relationship may simply be shared interests, combined with similarity of thought and position with respect to other peers (i.e., popularity). If this suggestion is valid, then it may be assumed that there is a group of adolescents whose friendships are similar to those of young children and preadolescents.

Conceptions of Self in Close Friendships

In this section data will be presented about how adolescents perceive themselves in their close riendships. In a pilot study, adolescent subjects were asked to provide 3 descriptions of the way they felt or acted when they were with their mother, father, and same-sex close friend. Thirty of these self-descriptions were then presented in study 7 to a different set of adolescents, along with 4 target persons—mother, father, same-sex friend, and opposite-sex friend. For each self-description, the adolescents were to select the person with whom they were most likely to feel or to act in that manner. For example, when presented with the self-description *relaxed,* adolescents were to select from among the 4 target persons, the one with whom they felt most relaxed (see Appendix D).

Female adolescents chose the same-sex friend more often than any of the other target persons for 8 of the 30 self-descriptions. These were, in order of decreasing frequency, *outgoing* (70%), *myself* (55%), *relaxed* (50%), *open* (45%), *accepted* (43%), *accepting* (41%), *honest* (38%), and *trusting* (35%). The same-sex close friend was selected less often than any of the other target persons for 7 items—*uncomfortable* (2%), *distant* (4%), *unwanted* (5%), *serious* (5%), *argumentative* (6%), *careful what I say* (9%), and *insecure* (11%). Over 50% of the males selected the same-sex close friend for the descriptions *outgoing* (65%), *relaxed* (60%), and *myself* (53%); and over 40% described themselves as *open* (41%), *playful* (42%), and *accepted* (41%) when with the same-sex friend. Males chose the close friend less often than any of the other target persons for the descriptions *loved* (0), *sensitive* (1%), *careful what I say* (2%), *uncomfortable* (7%), *serious* (10%), *unwanted* (10%), and *withdrawn* (12.5%).

Overall, the majority of females seemed to feel that they were more outgoing, more themselves, and more relaxed when they were with their close same-sex friends than when they were with any of the other target persons. A substantial percentage also described themselves as most likely to feel accepted by their same-sex friend and to be accepting of their same-sex friend. For the most part, males produced similar patterns. They were most likely to be outgoing, relaxed and themselves with same-sex friends, while a substantial percentage also said they were likely to be open, playful, and accepted.

There were important differences, however, between the response patterns of males and females. A substantial number of males, for example, reported that they were most likely to be *selfish* (32%), dishonest (26%), *insensitive* (30%), *distrustful* (28%), and *criticized* (25%) when with their close male friend. In contrast, no more than 15% of the females selected the close friend for any of these self-descriptions. Male-female differences were significant for the first 3 items ($p < .05$). This finding supports the contention that close female friendships in adolescence are more homogeneous than are close male friendships, and that a substantial percentage of close male friendships (30%) may involve factors of guardedness and defensiveness.

Nonintimate Male Friendships

A persistent finding across a variety of studies and samples was that roughly 30% of the males appeared to be involved in close friendships that differed markedly in form from close friendships manifested by the majority of female adolescents sampled and from about 40 to 50% of the males sampled. For example, in one study, roughly 30% of the males did not engage in intimate discussions with same-sex friends. In another study, approximately 30% of the males had discussions with same-sex friends that were rarely characterized by symmetrical understanding. In yet another study, roughly 30% of the males indicated that they were unlikely to be open with or to tell their true feelings to their close friends. Finally, in the study just reported, about 30% of the males described themselves as distrustful, dishonest, or insensitive when with their close same-sex friends. In order to determine whether these findings might be related, a different analysis was performed on the data from study 7. The responses of the male adolescents previously classified as the nonintimacy group with respect to the quality of interacting were compared to the responses for males in general with respect to the topics of communication, the conceptions of self, and the views about friendship.

As reported previously, male subjects having nonintimate same-sex friendships also tended to reject same-sex friends as advisors and to perceive same-sex friends as intolerant of differences of opinion. With respect to topics of communication, males in the nonintimate group rarely chose the same-sex friend as the most likely partner for any of the topics. In fact, 23% of this group did not select the same-sex friend as the most likely discussion partner for any topic; and 15% selected the same-sex friend for no more than 3 topics. In addition, while over 50% of the males in general selected the same-sex friend as the most likely discussion partner for the topics *problems with opposite-sex friends* and *feelings about opposite-sex friends,* only 26% of the nonintimacy group selected the same-sex friend as the most likely discussion partner for these topics. In fact, 38% of the subjects in the nonintimacy group selected the close friend as the least likely discussion partner for these same topics.

Similar patterns were found for other topics. For example, while 34% of the total males selected close same-sex friend as the most likely partner with whom to discuss their *feelings about mother,* only 11% of the nonintimacy group selected same-sex friends as the most preferred partner on this item, and 38% of the nonintimacy group selected the same-sex friend as the least preferred partner. Male subjects in the nonintimacy group were more likely to select close friend as the least likely discussion partner (average number of topics selected = 9) than as the most likely partner (average number of topics = 3). For 27% of this group, the same-sex friend was selected as the least likely discussion partner on at least 11 of the 22 items. In addition, concerning many of the items for which close friends were selected as the least likely discussion partners by the males, most of the numbers can be accounted for by the nonintimacy group. For example, of 21 males who indicated they would be least likely to talk to their close friends about *doubts about abilities,* 12 were from the nonintimacy group. Similarly of the 15 males who selected close friend as the least likely partner to talk about their *feelings about mother,* 10 were from the nonintimacy group; and of the 19 males who selected close friend as the least likely partner to talk with about their *fears about life,* 16 were from the nonintimacy group.

These findings suggest that subjects in the nonintimacy group not only responded consistently with respect to the other items assessing quality of interaction, but also responded consistently with respect to topics of communication. Similar results were found for conceptions of self. Over 50% of the subjects in the nonintimacy group described themselves as *insensitive* (as compared to 30% of total males), *selfish* (32% of total males), and *criticized* (25% of total males) when they were with their same-sex friend. In addition, in the same-sex friend relationship, over 40% described themselves as *phony* (22% of total males) and *distrustful* (28% of total males); and less than 8% described themselves as *open* (41% of total males), *trusting* (26% of total males), or *honest* (25% of total males).

Infrequently selected self-descriptions could also be accounted for almost entirely by the subjects in the nonintimacy group. For example, of the 10 male subjects who described themselves as *withdrawn,* 8 were from the nonintimacy group; of the 8 who described themselves as *unwanted,* 6 were from the nonintimacy group; and of the 9 who described themselves as *distant,* 8 were from the nonintimacy group. In fact, the only positive description for same-sex friend that occurred with any frequency for this group was *outgoing* (54%).

In general, then, the nonintimacy group tended to have same-sex friendships that were not only less open and more guarded than were their other relationships, but that also involved an intolerance for differences of opinion, a rejection of each other as advisors, and a reluctance to discuss many issues with each other—particularly those issues that touched on personal feelings or problems. In complement, members of this group also tended to see themselves as likely to be insensitive, selfish, criticized, phony, and distrustful when they were with their same-sex friends. It is interesting to note, however, that the general view of friendship provided by the nonintimacy group did not differ from that provided by the total sample of males. Members of the nonintimacy group still answered *true* to these items: "I have one close friend who means a lot to me" (92%). "My friends value my friendships" (81%). "Once I make friends with someone we stay friends a long time" (92%). "Close friends understand me better than parents" (54%). And, "I am more 'myself' with my close friends than with my parents" (69%). They also answered *false* to these items: "Friends are really not that important to me" (92%). "I spend more free time with parents than with friends" (81%). And, "I don't like to get too close to my friends" (85%). It appears, then, that while nonintimacy male subjects have friendships that are characterized by many immature elements, they still value these relationships and view them as important to their lives.

Summary

The data presented in this chapter suggest that for the majority of females close friendships in adolescence may be characterized by shared activities; mutual intimacy; mutual understanding; acceptance of and respect for differences of opinions; a wide range of topics for discussion; and a perception of self as relaxed, open, natural, outgoing, accepted, and accepting. It appears that for roughly 40% to 45% of male adolescents, this characterization also applies to their close friendships. For about 30% of the males, however, this characterization does not apply. For this group, close friendships are characterized by shared activity, but also involve guardedness in communication rather than intimacy, intolerance rather than acceptance and respect, nonunderstanding rather than mutual understanding, and a limited range of topics for discussion. These males are more likely to see themselves in close friendship as criticized, distrustful, insensitive, and selfish, than as open, relaxed, and accepting. Finally, for the remaining males and females neither characterization of friendship seems to fit well. For these adolescents, the issues of mutual intimacy and understanding may simply not be relevant to their friendships.

7

Problems and Obligations of Close Friendships

This chapter focuses on adolescents' conceptions of the behaviors that cause problems in close-friend relationships, on the ways of resolving these problems, and on the kinds of obligations that close friends have toward one another. As noted in chapter 2, conceptions about relational problems and obligations are assumed to reveal information about the rules of behavior that govern specific relationships. The study of obligations focuses on the issue of what friends should do to, or for, one another, while the study of problem-causing behavior examines the issue of what friends should not do to, or for, one another. Problem-causing behaviors serve to identify relational rules by specifying the events that may be viewed as violations of these rules—with rule defined as a form of interacting that participants feel is essential for maintaining a relationship in a positive form.

The goal of this chapter, then, is to present data regarding the rules of behavior that govern close friendships. These rules can be known to an observer to the extent that they represent expected forms of interacting within the context of a close-friend relationship. To this end, the chapter will include data concerning adolescents' conceptions of (1) actions that cause problems in close friendships, (2) actions that may be taken to resolve problems, (3) obligations that close friends have toward one another, and (4) the qualities that characterize close friendships. For the most part, as in chapter 6, data for males and females will be discussed separately, and age differences will be noted where relevant.

Problems in Close Friendships

Two questions addressed the issue of problems in close friendships. The first question was: What kinds of events cause problems in a close friendship? The second question was: How frequently do these events occur in this type of relationship? The first question was examined in studies 3 and 7. In these studies, adolescents generated their own descriptions of problem-causing behaviors. Several of these were then selected for inclusion in study 4—where the task was to report the frequency of occurrence of each situation in close friendships.

Problem-causing situations were elicited in study 3 by having adolescents describe an action that they felt caused the "most serious conflict" in their relationship with a close friend. A content analysis of responses resulted in a classification of actions into four major categories. These are presented in table 9, along with the numbers of males and of females providing responses in each category. As shown in the table, serious conflicts in close friendships are caused by *untrustworthy acts, lack of sufficient attention, disrespectful acts* (to both person and property), or *unacceptable behaviors.*

Examples of specific events categorized as *untrustworthy acts* are: "She did not keep my secret"; "She tried to pick-up a guy I like"; "He told things about me that are false"; "I told his mother about his relationship with a certain girl"; "He tried to take my job over"; "I told him to meet me but he didn't show"; and "He took my girlfriend." The category, *lack of sufficient attention,* included the following events: "She ignores me"; "She went with other friends instead of me"; "She made me feel leftout"; "She went to a

Table 9. Issues Described as Causing the Most Serious Conflict in a Close Friendship

Issues	Frequencies per Category Sex of Subjects[a]	
	Females	Males
1. *Untrustworthy acts* (doesn't keep secrets, talks behind back, gets other into trouble, breaks promises, lies, takes a job away, takes opposite-sex friend away, goes out with other's opposite-sex friend)	59	43
2. *Lack of sufficient attention* (leaves other out, ignores other, doesn't come to party, doesn't call, spends time with others, doesn't include in plans, wants to be with opposite-sex friend, ignores when opposite-sex friend is around)	28	13
3. *Disrespectful acts* (is snotty, is rude, calls names, puts down, makes fun of, bossy, uses other, hits, argues with, fights with, breaks something of others, steals something from other)	17	39
4. *Unacceptable behaviors* (talks too much, too moody, drinks too much, has a bad temper, is conceited, lies, quit school, is stubborn, is spoiled, brags, acts stupid, smokes pot)	18	14
5. *Miscellaneous*	6	5
6. *No answer*	30	40

[a]Sex difference: $\chi^2(3) = 16.45$; $p < .01$ with categories 5 and 6 excluded.

party with another friend''; ''I spend more time with my boyfriend''; ''She didn't talk to me at a party''; ''He didn't call me to go out and play hockey''; and ''He left me hanging at a party.'' Examples of *disrespectful acts* that referred to acts against property were: ''He stole something from me'' and ''He broke my bong.'' Some *disrespectful acts* against persons were: ''He tried to hurt me when he was mad''; ''I called him a 'dip' ''; ''He made fun of me''; ''I hit her''; ''She orders me around, bossy''; ''I always put her down''; and, ''She told me to 'shut-up' for nothing.'' Finally, the term *unacceptable behavior* was applied to the following statements such as: ''She got mixed up in a bad crowd''; ''She's too self-centered''; ''Thought she was 'God's gift' ''; ''She goes out with older men''; ''He steals things''; ''He always has to get his way''; ''He embarassed me with his foolishness''; and ''He drinks too much.''

The frequency of reporting across these categories was found to vary significantly depending upon the sex of the subjects ($p < .01$), with males more likely than females to report serious conflicts resulting from *disrespectful acts* (25% males, 11% females) ($p < .01$), and with females more often than males reporting serious conflicts due to *lack of sufficient attention* (18% females, 8% males) ($p < .01$). For both males and females, however, the most frequently generated cause of serious conflict in close friendships was the failure of one of the participants to act in a trustworthy manner (38% of females, 28% of males).

The data from study 7 are consistent with these results. In study 7, however, problem-causing events were elicited by asking adolescents to name one thing that they do that hurts their relationship with their close friend of the same sex and to name one thing that their close friend of the same sex does that hurts their friendship. The content analysis of these data yielded 5 categories of ''harmful behaviors.'' Four of these were identical to those presented in Table 9. The fifth category, *inadequate communication,* included responses such as these: ''I keep stuff from him.'' ''I don't always listen when she has a problem.'' And, ''I'm not open always.''

In study 7, variations in the response patterns across categories occurred as a function of the offender being described as either the subject or their best friend. When the best friend was described as the offender, variations also occurred as a function of the sex of the subjects ($p < .05$). In general, females were more likely than males to report that *inadequate communication* harmed their close friendship, while males, more often than females, noted that their close friendship was harmed by *disrespectful acts*. When the close friend was the offender, the order of frequency for harmful events generated by females was *untrustworthy acts* (25%), *lack of sufficient attention* (21%), *unacceptable behavior* (16%), *inadequte communication* (13%), and *disrespectful acts* (9%). One percent of the responses could not be classified and 15% of the girls said *nothing* or did not answer the question. For males in this analysis, (best friend hurts) the order of frequency was *disrespectful acts* (20%), *unacceptable behavior* (20%), *untrustworthy acts* (15%), and *lack of sufficient attention* (11%). Twenty-nine percent of the males did not complete this task or wrote *nothing,* and 5% of the responses were idiosyncratic.

When the offender was described as "you," the order of frequency for females was *lack of sufficient attention* (24%), *disrespectful acts* (16%), *inadequate communication* (14%), *unacceptable behavior* (13%), and *untrustworthy acts* (10%). For this task, 20% of the girls said *nothing* or did not respond, and 4% of the responses were idiosyncratic. Females, then, tended to see their close friend, more often than themselves, as acting untrustworthily and themselves as more often acting disrespectfully. For males in this task, the most frequently chosen category was still *disrespectful acts* (19%); but the following frequencies varied with *unacceptable behavior* being the least frequently generated category (6%), followed by *lack of sufficient attention* (8%), *poor communication* (10%), and *untrustworthy acts* (13%). Here 40% of the males said *nothing* or did not answer the question, and 5% of the answers were idiosyncratic.

The data from studies 3 and 4 provide a fairly consistent picture of the kinds of behavior that cause problems in close friendships. If these problem-causing events may be viewed as violations of the rules that serve to maintain these relations, it is plausible to assume that some requirements for the continuance of a close friendship are that participants (1) act trustworthily, (2) pay attention to each other, (3) treat each other with respect, and (4) exhibit acceptable behavior. For a few subjects—mostly female—it also appears important that participants in a close friendship communicate well. This includes being open and listening to the other person. The results of these studies suggest further that while violations of the expectancy to act trustworthily are perceived as serious by a large percentage of both males and females, the perceived seriousness of violations of the other rules varies in frequency depending upon the sex of the subjects. Females, in general, were less likely than males to report that they treated each other disrespectfully. In contrast, males were less likely than females to report that they failed to pay sufficient attention to each other. This issue regarding possible sex differences in the frequency of occurrence of particular conflicts is dealt with more directly in study 4.

In study 4, adolescents were presented with a list of 22 possible problem-causing situations and asked to indicate if each situation had *happened at least once* or had *never happened* in their own close friendship with a person of the same sex. If the situation had happened, subjects were also to indicate whether or not it had caused a conflict in the friendship. Half of the items described the offender as "I" (e.g., "I have a boyfriend/girlfriend and just don't have time for my close friend anymore."), and half described the offender as "my close friend" (e.g., "My close friend would not talk to me about a personal problem.''). The 22 items were distributed across the 5 categories found in studies 3 and 7. These were *untrustworthy acts* (5 items), *disrespectful acts* (5 items), *insufficient attention* (5 items), *unacceptable behavior patterns* (2 items), and, *inadequate communication* (2 items). Also included were items pertaining to *failures to reciprocate* or to *help when asked* (see Appendix B).

Items pertaining to untrustworthy behavior involved failing to keep to plans, telling a lie, telling a secret, talking behind the other's back, and ''fooling-around'' with the other's opposite-sex friend. At least 40% of the females reported that telling secrets (43%), lying (42%), and talking behind the other's back (40%) were situations that had ''happened at least once'' in their close friendships. Only 30%, however, said that their close friend had ever failed to keep to plans, and as few as 17% indicated that they had ever fooled around with their close friend's boyfriend. This frequency pattern for untrustworthy acts was similar for males, except that more males than females reported the occurrence of all 5 situations in their close friendships. The differences, however, were not statistically significant. For example, over 50% of the males indicated that they had told a close friend's secret (55%) and that they had lied to a close friend about something important (52%). Also, over 50% reported that their close friend had talked about them behind their backs (57%). In addition, as many as 47% of the males acknowledged that their close friend had failed to keep to plans, and as many as 28% admitted that they had fooled around with their close friend's girlfriend. For both males and females, the majority of subjects who reported the occurrence of a situation also reported that it caused a conflict in their relationship.

The items pertaining to *disrespectful acts* included 3 situations in which lack of respect was reflected in one friend's actions toward the other (argue over a difference of opinion instead of accepting it, fight over a disagreement instead of trying to compromise, criticize the other), and 2 situations in which lack of respect was reflected in the treatment of the friend's property (break something or damage something). Situations reflecting person-to-person disrespect were frequently reported to have ''happened at least once'' in the close friendships of the female adolescents. Many of the females indicated that they had, at least once, argued with their close friend over a difference of opinion (68%), fought with their close friend instead of compromising (58%), or been criticized by their close friend (40%). In contrast, only 22% of the girls said they had broken something that belonged to their close friend, while 35% reported that their close friend had damaged something that belonged to them. Overall, more males than females reported the occurrence of *disrespectful acts* in their close friendships. Sixty-eight percent of the males indicated that they had argued with a close friend; 60% reported fighting with a close friend; 50% acknowledged that their close friend criticized them; 52% said that their close friend damaged something that belonged to them; and

38% admitted that they had broken something that belonged to their close friend. For this latter action, differences between males and females were significant ($p < .05$). Again, for both males and females, the occurrence of any of these situations was reported to have caused a conflict in the relationship. The one exception to this was that breaking something that belonged to a close friend was seen as causing a conflict in the relationship by only 18% of the females.

The data above suggest that *untrustworthy* and *disrespectful acts* do occur in the close friendships of many adolescents. In our sample, the frequency of occurrence is generally higher for males than for females, particularly for *disrespectful acts* directed at property rather than at persons. For behaviors pertaining to *lack of sufficient attention,* however, the response patterns for males and females were, for the most part, quite similar. The items that were incorporated into this category concerned one friend (1) spending more time with someone else, (2) ignoring the other, (3) spending more time with an opposite-sex friend, (4) making new friends whom the other doesn't like, and (5) going out with the friend but then spending more time with other people. For both males and females, the situation that was most frequently reported to have "happened at least once" in their close friendships was: "I made new friends that my close friend didn't like" (58% of males and females). In contrast, few males and females indicated that their close friend had ever ignored them for a week (25% of females, 18% of the males). In general, over 50% of the males and females acknowledged that their close friend had spent more time with another person than with them (52% of females, 53% of males) and that they had an opposite-sex friend and didn't have time for their close friend (55% of females, 57% of males). The only difference in responding occurred with this item: "I went somewhere with my close friend but he(she) spent all his(her) time with other people." Here, 40% of the females compared to only 25% of the males, reported that this situation had occurred. Again, as with *untrustworthy* and *disrespectful acts,* if a situation was reported to have occurred, it was also reported to have caused a conflict in the relationship.

With regard to the category of *unacceptable behavior patterns,* few males (28%), or females (23%), reported that their close friend had a drinking problem, but many males (65%) and females (72%) noted that their close friend had been, at least once in their relationship, unduly critical of other people. Poor communication in the relationship was reflected in the finding that more than 50% of the males and females acknowledged that their close friend had failed to talk to them about a personal problem. Many of these adolescents said that they had given their close friend a lecture when he or she did talk to them about personal problems.

Overall, the situations pertaining to failures to reciprocate or to help when asked were not frequently reported as occurring in close friendships. However, the frequency of reporting was usually significantly higher for males than for females. Males were more likely than females to report that their close friend had (1) refused to loan them money (25% males, 7% females) ($p < .01$); (2) helped them but that they had not returned the favor (25% of males, 7% of females) ($p < .01$); and (3) said that he(she) did not have time to help them with schoolwork (22% males, 10% of females).

The data from study 4 demonstrate that the problem-causing situations that were generated in studies 3 and 7 are not rare occurrences in adolescent friendships. For example, over 50% of the females in study 4 acknowledged that in their friendships they had experienced, at least once, 7 of the conflict-causing situations, and 6 more of these situations were reported by at least 40% of the females to have occurred. For males, the rate is even higher. Over 50% reported the occurrence of 12 of the conflict-causing situations, and 2 others were indicated by at least 40% of the males. The conflicts that occurred most frequently involved the *disrespectful acts* of arguing and fighting and the exhibition of *unacceptable behavior,* such as being "overly critical of others." Also frequently occurring were instances of *lack of sufficient attention,* particularly where one friend spent more time with someone else. The situations least frequently reported to have occurred involved failures to reciprocate or to help when asked. Perhaps these last two situations deal with issues that are so basic to friendships that they are rarely violated.

From the combined results of studies 3, 4, and 7, it is possible to draw two major conclusions. One is that within a close friendship the participants are expected to act trustworthily and respectfully, to pay sufficient attention to each other, to exhibit acceptable behavior patterns, and, to a lesser extent, to communicate openly. Any failure to meet these expectations causes harm to the relationship. Thus these expectations may be viewed as representing the rules that govern a close friendship. The second conclusion is that these rules are often violated and that these violations often cause conflict in the relationship. It seems implausible to assume, however, that, for adolescents, a violation of a behavioral rule would result in the termination of the relationship—as it often does in relationships between young children (cf. Youniss 1980). Instead, as in adult relationships, close-friend relationships of adolescents are more likely to continue. However, the question remains as to what actions are required for the relationship to continue after a violation has occurred.

Resolving Problems in Close Friendships

Resolving problems in close friendships was dealt with in studies 3 and 5. In study 3, adolescents who were asked to describe a situation that caused the most serious conflict in their close-friend relationship were also asked to describe how the conflict was resolved so that the friendship was once again close. Of the 128 females and 114 males who described conflict-causing situations, 115 females and 106 males also provided descriptions of resolutions. A content analysis of these descriptions resulted in the categories shown in Table 10.

Category 1, *offender apologizes,* included all responses where an apology was either given immediately after the offense or was the final resolving action—for example, "I told her the truth and apologized," "Didn't talk for two weeks, then she apologized," and "I told him off, he apologized." Statements indicating that resolution occurred after the participants had talked over the problem were classified in category 2, *talk it over.* Category 3, *offense ceases/offender makes reparation,* incorporated resolutions that involved the cessation of the conflict-causing behavior (e.g., "She doesn't ball me out anymore." "I realized I was wrong and stopped acting that way." "He gave back the bike."), or that involved some kind of reparation by the offender (e.g., "I bought him a new window." "He got me a new hoop."). Statements included in category 4 indicated that the conflict was not resolved through any overt actions but that the offense was simply *forgotten* or *accepted* by the other. Examples of these kinds of resolutions are: "I just put up with it." "We just forgot about it." "We didn't talk about it, just forgot it." And, "I just accepted it." Finally category 5 included responses stating that the problem was either *not resolved* (47 of the 56 responses) or that the friendship had ended as a result of the conflict (9 out of the 56 responses). It was unclear from the subjects' statements whether *not resolved* answers meant that the relationship had ended of that the relationship had simply continued in spite of the problem.

As shown in table 10, the major resolution provided by females (43%) was to talk over the problem. This resolution was given most frequently by females regardless of the particular type of offense. For example, of the 59 females who described the conflict-causing situation as involving *untrustworthy acts,* 32% said it was resolved through *talking it over,* 22% said it was *not*

Table 10. Resolutions to the Most Serious Conflicts in Close Friendships

	Sex of Subjects[a]	
Procedures of Resolution	Females (N = 115)	Males (N = 106)
1. Offender apologizes	14	16
2. Talked it over	49[b]	16
3. Offense ceases/Offender makes reparations	11	20
4. Offense forgotten or accepted	15	24
5. Situation not resolved	26	30

[a]$\chi^2(4) = 21.53; p < .01$
[b]$\chi^2(1) = 16.75; p < .01$, pair comparison

resolved, 17% said it was resolved through *apology,* 12% said it was *forgotten or accepted,* and the remainder indicated that resolution occurred because the *offense ceased* or the *offender made reparations.* Overall, 64% of the females indicated that the conflict that was caused by the violation was resolved through the utilization of overt procedures (categories 1, 2, and 3 in Table 10) that were designed to repair the relationship; 13% reported that the conflict was resolved by indirect means whereby the offended person simply accepted or disregarded the violation; and 23% said the situation was not resolved at all.

In contrast to the females, only 45% of the males indicated that conflicts in their close friendships were resolved through overt means; 23% reported that they were simply forgotten or that the violation was accepted; and as many as 28% said that the conflict was not resolved at all. In addition, for males, the most frequently described overt resolution was to have the *offense cease* or to have the *offender make reparation* (19%). *Apology* and *talking it over* accounted for only 15% of the responses. Resolutions involving *apology* and *talking it over* were described almost exclusively when the particular violation involved an *untrustworthy* or *disrespectful* act. *Forgetting or accepting* the offense was also associated with these violations. In fact, of the 43 males who indicated that *untrustworthy acts* were the cause of serious conflict, 23% said that they *forgot about it* or *accepted it,* 23% said that it was not resolved, 16% reported that the offense ceased, and 6% said that they *apologized* or *talked it out.* This pattern was similar for *disrespectful acts.* Twenty-six percent of the 39 males resolved the conflict by *forgetting about it,* 23% resolved it through *apology,* and the remainder described other resolutions or stated that the conflict was not resolved.

In general, when confronted with a conflict-causing situation, females appear to resolve the conflict by using specific procedures designed to attain this end, the most common being *talk it over* or *talk it out.* Exactly what this procedure involves may be estimated from the responses given by a few articulate adolescents. One female explained *talking-it-out* in this way: "I explained and then she did, and then I asked her some things, and then it was okay." And one male subject said: "I told him I was angry, he explained why he did it, I told him how I felt, then we sort of talked it out some more." In comparison to females, males were less likely to resolve their conflicts with friends through overt procedures ($p < .05$). Instead, conflicts in male friendships tended either not to be resolved at all or to be resolved because the offended person simply forgets about the violation or accepts it as part of the offender's personality.

The use of procedures to resolve problems in relations was also examined in study 5. In this study, the adolescents were interviewed and presented with the following hypothetical situation:

Bob(Jane) and Charles(Mary) are very good friends but Bob(Jane) has a girlfriend(boyfriend) who he(she) spends a lot of time with. Charlie(Mary) is very upset about this and feels that Bob(Jane) doesn't want to be friends with him(her) anymore. He(She) feels that Bob(Jane) wanting to be with his(her) girlfriend(boyfriend) so much causes problems for their friendship.

They were then asked: Do you think this situation would cause a problem in the close friendship? If so, what do you think would have to happen to resolve the problem? Has a similar type of situation ever happened in your relationship with a close friend? If so, how did you and your close friend resolve the problem?

Seventy-seven percent of the females indicated that they felt the situation would cause a problem for the relationship. Of the hypothetical resolutions to the problem, 60% involved *talking about it* ("tell her feelings," "explain why she wants to be with her boyfriend," "tell her she feels left-out"), 38% described a *cessation of the offense* without discussion ("spend more time with her friend," "divide her time more equally"), and 2% maintained that the offended person should simply *accept the situation*. The responses of males were similar to those of females for the hypothetical situation. Seventy-five percent of the males agreed that the situation would cause a problem for the relationship. In addition, 58% of the males provided hypothetical resolutions that involved *talking it over,* only 38% gave *cessation of offense without discussion* as a resolution, and 2% reported that the problem would be resolved through *apology* or *acceptance of the offense.*

In contrast to the results for study 3, then, both males and females in study 5, when confronted with a hypothetical conflict-causing situation, provided resolutions in which at least one of the participants was required to take some overt action. When asked to describe actual resolutions for real-life situations, however, the subjects in study 5 responded quite similarly to the subjects in study 3. Of the 33 females who reported that they had experienced this situation in their own close friendships, 78% reported resolutions that involved overt actions—primarily *talking it over* or making arrangements to *spend more time with the same-sex friend.* In contrast, only 42% of the males who reported the occurrence of this situation in their own friendships indicated that the problem had been resolved through *overt action.* Instead, the majority acknowledged that the problem had *not been resolved* or that the offended person simply came to *accept* the situation.

The hypothetical resolutions given in this study were also content analyzed with respect to the end result of the resolution. If the resolution resulted in a maintenance of the situation with the offended person ceasing to see the behavior as a violation, the resolution was classified as a *status quo solution.* A resolution that resulted in a change in the situation was categorized as a *com-*

promise solution. In this type of solution, the offender continued to spend time with his(her) opposite-sex friend but also made a concerted effort to spend more time with his(her) same-sex friend. These efforts ranged from "splitting up his time 50–50" to "all going out together." The analysis of the data according to types of solutions resulted in the finding that while the majority of both males and females provided *compromise solutions,* this type of solution was given significantly more often by females (88%) than by males (67%) (*p* < .01).

As in study 3, the females in study 5 appeared more likely than the males to deal with problems in close friendships through overt procedures designed to maintain a friendship in spite of the violation. Although many of the males did deal with relational problems in this manner, many others appeared either to ignore the problem or to utilize internal procedures (i.e., defense mechanisms) designed to resolve the conflict by *forgetting* or *accepting* the offense. The difference between males and females concerning the resolution of problems in close-friend relationships followed a pattern similar to that found in the studies reported in Chapter 6. About 66% of the females and 45% of the males shared the same perspective; however, about 33% of the males provided a distinctly different perspective that was not shared by the females. In this instance, approximately 66% of the females reported that problems in their close friendships were resolved through overt procedures, with only a small percentage indicating that the resolution involved *acceptance, forgetting,* or some other internal process or defense. In contrast, about 45% of the males suggested overt procedures for resolving problems, and 25–30% offered internal procedures for resolving problems. It is interesting to note that these differences held when the adolescents were asked to describe resolutions of actual problems. However, when they were confronted with a hypothetical problem and asked to give a hypothetical (i.e., ideal) solution, 98% of both the males and the females provided clear examples of overt procedures. This suggests that the majority of males and females are similar to one another in their knowledge about how problems in relationships can be dealt with so that the relationships can be maintained. The difference between males and females appears to arise when they are confronted with actual situations. Then, a substantial percentage of the males use internal rather than overt procedures to resolve problems.

The Quality of Close Friendships

The attempts to maintain a close friendship even in the face of serious violations of the rules, suggest that there are qualities inherent in this relationship that make it desirable to preserve.

The aspects of close friendships that make them particularly desirable to maintain were examined in studies 2, 3, 6, and 7. Study 3 dealt with the aspects of fairness, reciprocity, and mutual intimacy. Study 6 focused on how close friends might deal with disagreements about what to do or where to go. Study 7 concerned the types of needs that are met in close friendships. And study 2 examined the idea of meeting needs by focusing on the obligations inherent in these relationships.

In study 6, adolescents were presented with the following situation:

> Think of the times when your best or good friend (same-sex) wants you to do something when you want to do something else. How often (*hardly ever, not often, often, very often*) does your friend do the following things when he(she) wants you to do something you don't want to do?

This situation was followed by 8 possible procedures. In 4 of these, the best or good friend was described as utilizing his(her) authority or making demands to get his(her) way. In the other 4, the friend was portrayed as utilizing mutual procedures or procedures of compromise.

It was found that procedures based on authority or demand were rarely, if ever, utilized in the close-friend relationship in response to such a situation. Over 80% of the adolescent males and females reported that their close friend hardly ever "says I'm supposed to do what he(she) tells me to do" (84%), "simply tells me to do it" (85%), or "says he(she) expects me to do it" (89%). Most of the remaining adolescents indicated that their close friend did not often utilize these procedures. In addition, 68% of the subjects said their close friend hardly ever "keeps telling me to do it until I do it." Thirty percent indicated that their close friend does not often use this procedure.

Close friends were also rarely found to utilize some of the more mutual procedures or compromise-based procedures that were listed in response to this situation. For example, procedures involving attempts to change the other's point of view, such as "keeps talking to me about it hoping I would start wanting to do it" and "says I would enjoy doing what he(she) wants to do" were reported by over 60% of the subjects to be not often, or hardly ever, utilized by their close friends. In addition, the quid pro quo response—"tells me he(she) will do favors for me at another time if I do it"—was said to rarely occur in close friendships by over 70% of the subjects. In fact, the only procedure that was reported to be used often, or very often, by the subjects' close friend in response to the hypothetical situation was "asks me if I would be willing to do it" (81%).

Thus, when two close friends disagree about what they want to do, they rarely resolve the disagreement through unilateral means, nor do they appear to attempt to change each other's point of view or to offer rewards. Instead, one friend simply asks the other if he(she) would be willing to do what the first one wants. It would appear then that close friends expect each other to be willing to do things that they may not really want to do (i.e., make a sacrifice) simply because they are close friends. It is assumed that this is a reciprocal process and that the friends have some way of balancing the process so that one does not concede more often than the other. This fairness or reciprocity between close friends is examined further in study 3.

In study 3, subjects were presented with the following statements, to be answered *true* or *false* about their close friend of the same sex: (1) My close friend of the same sex usually expects more from me than he(she) is willing to give back. (2) My close friend usually acts as if I am as important as he(she) is in our relation. (3) I usually feel comfortable telling my close friend of the same sex just about everything about myself. An analysis of the frequency of the responses indicated that for the vast majority of subjects, both males and females, close friends were perceived both as being fair (66% of the subjects answered *false* to number 1) and as being equals in the relationship (78% of the subjects answered *true* to number 2). On self-disclosure, however, only about 50% of the males indicated that they felt comfortable disclosing ''just about everything'' to their close friends, while 76% of the females answered *true* to this item ($p < .01$). These data suggest that close friendships for both males and females involve the qualities of *fairness* and *respect*, but the quality of *intimacy* appears to be found more often in close friendships between females than between males.

In study 7, the adolescents were given the following statements to be answered *true* or *false:* (1) My close friend usually sees to it that I have something if I need it. For example, if I need to borrow money or a book for school, my friend will give it to me. (2) My close friend is usually sensitive to my feelings. For example, when I have a problem she(he) listens to me. These adolescents were also asked to describe what they do in return for their close friend if he or she meets these needs. A frequency analysis of these data demonstrated that for almost all the subjects, close friends were described as meeting both material (94%) and emotional (92%) needs. A content analysis of what was done in return for the friend when the subjects' needs were met resulted in the finding that 94% of the subjects reciprocated symmetrically when both material and emotional needs were met. Almost all the subjects said: ''I do the same for him.'' ''I lend her money, too.'' Or, ''I listen to his problems, too.'' The data from this study are problematical, however—because of a clerical error, the items in this section of study 7 did not identify the close friend as a ''person of the same sex as you.'' With respect to meeting material needs, this omission was not a problem. All of the subjects responded as if the subject was of the same sex. For emotional needs, however, 30% of the males were clearly responding to a close female friend—''I listen to her problems and help''; ''I do the same for her''; or ''I listen when she has a problem.'' In contrast, only 2% of the females responded to a close male friend for this item.

In summary, for the majority of adolescents of both sexes, close friendships with persons of the same sex appear to incorporate the qualities of fairness and mutual respect and serve to meet the material needs of the individuals. For most females, this type of relationship also involves mutual intimacy and meets their emotional needs. For many of the males, these aspects are also present; yet for many males, mutual self-disclosure is clearly not an aspect of this relationships. For about 33% of the males, it appears that emotional needs are more likely to be met by a friend of the opposite sex than by a friend of the same sex.

The kinds of needs that might be met in a close-friend relationship were also examined in study 2 by asking this question: What should one friend do for the other? Here adolescents were asked to describe the most important thing they felt they should do for their close friend and to explain why they felt this obligation was important. As in the other studies, the friend was described as a close friend of the same sex.

A content analysis of these obligations resulted in the identification of the 3 categories shown in table 11. As is apparent from the table, the majority of females indicated that close friends were required to *be there when needed* (70%). Obligations involving *trustworthiness* or *consideration* were less frequently provided by females (22%), and obligations pertaining to *loyalty* or *protectiveness* were rarely given (4%). For most of the female subjects, helping a friend with problems and, less frequently, being trustworthy or considerate were considered important because these actions served as the *basis for friendships* (44%). In this vein, the females said: "It's what you do if you're a friend." "That's what friends are for." "If you're a friend that's what's expected." And, "It's what makes a friendship." A substantial percentage of the females, however, suggested that helping with problems was important because it *showed caring* for the other person (36%). One friend was obliged to help the other with her problems "so the friend feels wanted," "so I don't hurt her," "she'd feel down if I didn't," and "makes her feel cared about." Finally, only 16% of the females indicated that obligations were important because they *keep the friendship running smoothly*.

The results were somewhat different for males. As shown in table 11, most of the males indicated that important obligations to friends involved either *being there when needed* (36%) or *being loyal and protective* (40%). Thus males made statements such as these: "Protection is important, if you're a good friend you want to protect him, warn him if you forsee something coming up." And, "Give him support. That's what friends are for. Sometimes kids can't go to parents, they go somewhere else—to friends." These obligations were, for the most part, perceived as important because they served as the *basis for friendship* (62%). Only 12% of the males provided reasons that involved the *feelings of the other person,* and 24% suggested that obligations were important because they *kept the relation running smoothly*—that is, prevented conflicts.

Table 11. Obligations to Close Friend

| | Sex of Subjects[a] | |
| | Females N = 50 | Males N = 42 |
Types of Obligations		
1. *Be trustworthy or considerate* (don't lie, don't tell secrets, keep to plans, be nice, be friendly, don't cut down)	11	9
2. *Be there when needed* (help out when she has a problem, talk to her when she has a problem, be there to lend moral support, be there when you're needed)	35[b]	15
3. *Be loyal/protective* (stick up for her in a fight, keep him out of trouble, stick together, be loyal, don't tell on him, stand by him if he's in trouble, be faithful and loyal)	2[b]	17
4. *Miscellaneous*	2	1

[a]$\chi^2(2) = 19.67; p < .001$
[b]Pair comparisons; $p < .01$

Summary

The data provided in chapter 6 provide information about close friendships with respect to the quality of communications and interactions in them. Chapter 7 expands on this picture of close friend relations by providing data pertaining to the qualities of the relation, the conflicts in the relation, and the procedures of conflict resolution. In chapter 8 these data are summarized and discussed with respect to their implications for understanding of friendship.

8

Cooperation, Consensus, and Co-construction

The data presented in chapters 6 and 7 are descriptive of adolescents' conceptions of their relationships with close friends. In this chapter, these conceptions will be summarized and discussed with respect to their implications for an understanding of the structure of friendship and of the process of individuation. Differences found between close friendships of male adolescents and of female adolescents will also be summarized and related to other findings that are relevant to this issue. Finally, our perspective on adolescent friendships that resulted from an analysis and interpretation of our data will be compared and contrasted with the prevailing theoretical perspectives that were reviewed in Chapter 1.

Summary of Results

Close friendships are clearly important relationships to adolescents. The vast majority of teenagers who were sampled reported that they "have a close friend who means a lot to me" and "who values my friendship." The relationship itself is depicted as enduring over time and as being relatively problem free. Most adolescents also felt that close friends are persons who "understand" each other and "learn new things" from each other.

When close friends are together, they appear most likely to engage in unstructured activities that are usually described as "going out together" or "hanging around together." The specific places that friends "go out" to or "hang around" in, do not seem to be important. What seems to matter in these situations is that the friends are together—away from parental supervision or observation, and outside the structured environments represented by home and school. Thus, friends go to movies, concerts, bars, parties, shopping malls, or parks. They play games, ride around in cars, and talk. When they talk, close friends are as likely to talk about their feelings, problems, fears and doubts, as about T.V. shows, school, grades, or sports. In addition, conversations between close friends appear to be characterized by mutual understanding. Each friend takes measures designed both to understand the other and to be understood by the other. The process of mutual understanding takes place in an atmosphere of openness, trust, and acceptance of the other's point of view, even if it differs from their own. In complement, within the context of this relationship, adolescents perceive themselves as outgoing, open, accepted, and accepting.

Given this view of close friendships, it is not surprising that adolescents also perceive close friends as meeting each other's emotional needs. In fact, this function is seen by many adolescents as the major obligation that close friends have toward each other—to help each other or just to listen when there is a problem. Close friends are described as "taking the place of a psychologist" or as "more likely to understand how you feel" than anyone else is. As one 17-year-old girl put it: "If you didn't listen to your friend's problems, she wouldn't have anyone to talk to and everything would build up. You're her only hope!" For most adolescents, "this is what friendship is all about."

In addition to providing emotional support, adolescents also indicated that close friends should be trustworthy, loyal, and considerate. For most of the adolescents in our sample, a failure to act in this manner was viewed as harmful for the relationship or as bringing the friends into conflict with each other. In adolescence, although such harmful behavior did occur, it did not necessarily result in a termination of the relationship, as it might for younger children. Instead, harmful actions were more likely to be met with conciliatory actions that were designed to restore the relationship to its previous form, or in some way to undo the harm. Conciliatory actions most commonly involved apologies, discussion, or simply behavioral changes.

Differences in the Close Friendships of Males and Females

The analyses of specific sets of data resulted in a variety of different responses according to the sex of the subjects. When combined, two general differences emerged that corresponded to the findings of several other research efforts. The most general finding was that female adolescents tended to disclose more, and to talk more, about their personal problems than do male adolescents (cf. Sharabany, Gershoni, & Hofman 1981; Fischer 1981; Jourard 1971; Jourard & Richman 1963; Rivenbark 1971). A second finding was that female adolescents, in general, appeared to be more oriented toward meeting emotional needs than were male adolescents (cf. Bernard 1981; Fischer 1981; Kanter 1977).

Despite these general differences, however, the descriptions of relationships with close friends, which were presented in the summary of our results, were provided by at least 40%–45% of the males sampled in each study, as well as at least 66% of the females. Thus, almost half of the males in any given study responded in identical fashion to the majority of the females. This finding argues against the notion that during adolescence, males and females necessarily conceptualize relationships with close friends in distinctly different ways.

In many of the studies, however, there was a group—representing about 33% of the male adolescents—that did provide responses that were clearly different from those given by the majority of all the subjects. For example, for 33% of the males in study 7 (as compared to 4% of the females), relationships with close friends were characterized by an absence of intimacy and trust. Close friends were seen as persons from whom true feelings and self-doubts were to be withheld. Members of this group of males were also found to avoid discussion of personal matters with their close friends and to describe themselves as "distant" and "distrustful" when with their close friends. In study 6, 30% of the males in the sample indicated that discussions with their close friends were characterized by mutual nonunderstanding instead of mutual understanding. For these subjects, close friends were viewed as rarely taking measures that were designed either to understand the other or to be understood by the other. In addition, in 2 studies on resolving conflicts, approximately 30% of the males did not respond to harmful acts with counteractions intended to undo the harm. Instead, members of this group indicated that they "just accepted" the harmful behavior or "forgot it."

To summarize the results with regard to sex differences, it was found that, across a variety of research methods and samples, at least 66% of the females and 40%–45% of the males responded similarly. However, 33% of the male adolescents provided distinctly different response patterns. Whether or not this 33% represents a consistent conception of friendship for some of the male adolescents is a question for future research. At this point, it is only possible to speculate about differences in responses about relationships with close friends according to the sex of the subjects—both in our studies and in many other studies. While many males and females share similar conceptions about friendship, there is a substantial group of males who deviate considerably from this conception. How this group of males might look with respect to the structure of friendship and to the process of individuation is discussed in the following sections.

The Structure of Friendship

Descriptions by adolescents of their close friendships, as presented above, clearly demonstrate that whatever does go on within the context of these relationships is co-constructed by the participants and not guided or directed by outside intervention. It is the friends themselves who determine not only the kinds of activities they engage in but also the form of their interactions and the kinds of behaviors expected in, or required to maintain, the relationship. Support for the notion that friendships in adolescence are relatively independent of outside influence lies first in the finding that the majority of activities that close friends engage in are almost completely unstructured. These activities are not characterized by any formal rules or regulations designed to guide behavior, and they often have no more specific goal or content than merely being "out together." Second, these unstructured activities take place, for the most part, outside the purview of parents, and, thus, their content is not subject to direct parental review or evaluation. Finally, problems arising in the close friendships of adolescents are apparently dealt with by the friends themselves without recourse to an outside arbiter. In fact, of the 328 adolescents who provided information about resolving problems in their close friendships, only one suggested that parental involvement might be sought. These findings serve to differentiate the close friendships of adolescents from those of younger children. For younger children, interactions between friends are often observed by parents or other adults and are sometimes directly guided or influenced by them. In addition, conflicts arising in friendships between younger children are frequently settled by seeking the advice or guidance of an outside arbiter, usually an adult.

In summary, then, although the social forces of any society may make the general form of friendship inevitable, the more specific form and structure of close friendships in adolescence appear to be determined by the friends themselves. Among the many features of close friendships that are constructed by the participants, there are 2 that have particular significance because of their implications for a more general understanding of social development. These are the process of consensual validation and the principles of the relationship.

Consensual Validation

Technically, consensual validation refers to a reciprocal process whereby two persons seek to understand their world through a mutual exchange of ideas, feelings, and thoughts that are offered to each other for comment, discussion, or evaluation. This process involves a continued give-and-take, so that the final criteria for validation come from both persons rather than from only one. Within the context of a close friendship, then, if A offers B his or her perspective, B is free to comment on it or evaluate it; but A is then also free to evaluate B's comments and evaluations; and so on until agreement is reached. The fact that reaching agreement requires equal input from both persons is what serves to distinguish consensual validation from a process that may be termed unilateral validation. In this latter process, A presents a perspective to B, and B evaluates this perspective using his or her own criteria for validation. A is not free to evaluate B's evaluations or comments without risking conflict with B. This process is found to be more characteristic of parent-adolescent relationships than of close friendships.

Consensual validation, then, results in an understanding of the world that is constructed by the self in a relationship with another person and through a cooperative process with that other person. Thus, it leads not only to an understanding of experiences and events but also to an understanding of the self and of the other. It can be contrasted with a process often called "self-reflective reasoning." In this process, individuals gain understanding of the world by drawing back from their experiences, reflecting on them, and submitting them to reasoning processes. The goal is to place each experience within some broader cognitive scheme in which the individual's understanding of the experience would gain validity from its consistency within the scheme.

Several findings from our studies indicate that in the context of relationships with close friends, adolescents sought understanding through the process of mutual reflection. They talked to close friends about their feelings, problems, and thoughts; and they depended on close friends for advice and help. Differences in opinions are not only accepted by close friends but they are also accorded serious consideration as potentially valid perspectives. Adolescents also indicated that they learned new things from their close friends and were under an obligation to listen to close friends when they had a problem or a point of view they wanted to express. To underscore this point, one 17-year-old boy said: "You have to give your friend advice when he has a problem. . . . The advice coming from a friend would be better than that from just anyone, like Ann Landers or Dear Abby." An additional point was made by a 13-year-old girl: "If your friend does something wrong, you don't tell them that, you just try to help out." Another 13-year-old female took a slightly different approach: "You have to talk to your friends, you can't always go to parents. A friend can keep the other from doing something wrong." Finally, a 16-year-old girl summed up the situation by reporting: "Most people need a close friend to talk to. Can't always decide what you want to do yourself. Need a second opinion."

From the perspective of most of the adolescents in our studies, close friends appear to provide an important service to each other. They are the sounding boards for ideas, feelings, and problems. Sometimes they provide critical feedback, sometimes they just listen, and sometimes they give advice. Whatever the specific content, the process is always mutual, and the goal is to have their understanding of the world validated. Thus, for these adolescents the major function of friendship appears to extend beyond the "fun-times" offered by friendship between younger children. Instead, as one 18-year-old male stated quite straightforwardly, "A friend is an advisor. Someone to go to when you need help, not just a good time."

This description of friendship, however, does not appear applicable to all male adolescents. In particular, about 33% of the male adolescents appeared still to view friendship in terms of pleasurable association or shared activity and nothing more. Some adolescents indicated this view when asked to describe changes in their relationships with close friends over the past five years. A 16-year-old said: "I still mainly want someone I can play sports with." "We do more things now, go to dances, go over to his house," said a 15-year-old. Another 15-year-old said: "When I was younger, we couldn't go as many places. Now we go to more places." "I now have more friends. My interests are different," stated an 18-year-old. And a 19-year-old said: "I look for dependability. Still up for a good time." Also, for approximately 33% of the males, the process of consensual validation does not appear to be an aspect of their relationships with close friends. They are not open with each other, they are not interested in each other's advice, they do not seek mutual understanding in their discussions, and their discussions do not include personal matters. Instead, they seek to "keep it light." In spite of these findings, however, almost all male adolescents did indicate that they had a close friendship, that this relationship was important to them, that it endured over time, and that it was relatively problem free. Thus, even for this group, friendship is still valued as an important relation, even it its main function is to have fun.

The Principles of Close Friendships

The overall pattern of our results is consistent in advancing the conclusion that adolescents' close friendships are indeed principled relationships. As noted above, one of the major principles is that of equality. This was stated succinctly by one male adolescent: "Friendship is something that has to be shared equally. It should be mutual. If it isn't mutual then you just let it flop." But equality cannot be the only principle governing friendship since this principle could be applied to strangers or acquaintances as well as to close friends. From our data, it is clear that there are other principles governing this relationship, and one of the most important is the principle of *mutual caring*. One of the reasons that close friendships in adolescence are fairly long-lasting and have relatively few problems is probably that the participants have a vested interest in each other's well-being. As one 14-year-old female said, "Friends care about each other and about what has happened to each other and how the other turns out." For adolescents, close friends are obligated to "be there when needed," "to listen," "to help with problems" because "it shows you care." And, as one 16-year-old female noted, "It is important for a person to know she's cared about." The importance of mutual caring is also evident in the finding that failures to show concern—as exemplified by statements such as "doesn't pay attention to me," "ignores me," "doesn't listen to me," and "leaves me hanging at a party,"—are viewed as bringing the friends into conflict with each other or, in general, as harming the relation.

A second principle that emerged from our data as critical to the functioning and maintenance of relationships between close friends was that of *mutual respect*. This principle was evident in several findings. For one, the majority of adolescents reported that the close friend "acts as if I am as important in the relation as he(she) is" and "does not expect more from me in the relation than he(she) is willing to give in return." In addition, it was found that close friends accept each other's points of view, even if they differ from their own, and give careful and serious consideration to each other's opinions whenever differences do arise. Failure to be fair, to be accepting, to listen, or to treat each other with consideration was seen as being harmful to the relationship and as requiring some sort of actions to repair the harm so that the relationship can continue. The principle of mutual respect, however, appears to refer to the expectation that friends not only will not hurt or demean each other, but that they will also not hurt or demean themselves. Under this principle, close friends are required to behave in ways that allow them to respect each other not only as friends, but also as self respecting individuals apart from the relationship. Behavior that demonstrates a lack of self-respect, at least from the perspective of the friend, violates the principle of mutual respect and, therefore, threatens the continuance of the relationship. This "unacceptable behavior" can range from "drinking too much" and "lying to people" to "acting like a jerk" and being "too moody."

A third principle governing close friendships appears to involve *mutual trust*—trust that the other cares for them, accepts them, and respects them. In its specific sense, this principle applies to the expectation that friends will not commit any untrustworthy acts, such as revealing information shared in confidence, failing to keep promises or keep to plans, intruding in boyfriend or girlfriend relations, or telling lies. In its more general sense, mutual trust is reflected in the belief that the principles of caring and of respect are valued equally by both participants in the relationship. This allows close friends to seek advice from each other, to take personal problems to each other, and to reveal self-doubts and fears about life—all in an atmosphere of trust.

The fourth principle, *symmetrical reciprocity,* may be viewed as the principle that underlies all friendships since it is what orients people toward one another in a positive fashion. This means, simply, that if *A* does something for *B, B* is required to do the same for *A,* and vice versa. The return does not have to be immediate, and, indeed, in the case of friendship, it rarely is. The expectation is, however, that the action will be reciprocated in a symmetrical manner. Thus, if one friend lends the other money, the expectation is that the other will at sometime return the favor. In the same vein, if one friend helps the other with a problem, the other is obligated to do the same. Our data indicate that adolescents take this principle seriously. Over 90% of them reported that when a close friend met their material or emotional needs, they reciprocated in kind. This principle is important because, while the principles of *caring, trust,* and *respect* serve to enhance the meaning and function of close friendships for adolescents, the principle of symmetrical reciprocity provides the very basis for the relationship's existence.

While it is clear from the data that the principles of *caring, trust* and *respect* are critical aspects of close friendships in adolescence, it is equally clear that these principles are frequently violated. Yet, these violations do not necessarily terminate the relationship. Instead, they are like momentary denials or breaches that admit of reaffirmation and repair. The question then, is, if these principles are so critical to the relationship, why would repair be sought when the principles have been violated. The dynamics of friendship cannot be discounted here. The overall picture is that of a considerable investment of self in a close friendship. The amount of time spent in friendship, the extent of self-disclosure, and the degree of dependence for help demonstrate the depth of involvement. It is not surprising that adolescents do not give up such relationships easily and that when violations occur, adolescents will usually seek to resolve any conflict rather than ignore it or let it destroy the relationship.

This discussion of the principles governing relationships with a close friend serves to underscore the point that this is a significant relationship to most adolescents and is not to be taken lightly. Close friendships provide not only a context for learning and self-validation but also a safe place in which one can feel cared about, respected, and trusted. To offset this ideal picture, however, close friendships are also relationships in which participants hurt each other, lie to each other, betray each other, and demean each other. As troublesome as these acts are, they need not end the relationship. Instead, they are discussed, an apology is made, or some sort of reparations are offered in an effort to restore to the relationship the principle that was violated.

Again, while this description applied to most of the adolescents in our studies, there still remained approximately 30% of the males for whom it was questionable whether their friendships could be characterized by all of the principles discussed above. From our data, it appears that most close friendships in adolescence, both male and female, involve mutual respect and are grounded on the principle of reciprocity. In the issues pertaining to *mutual caring* and *mutual trust*, however, approximately 33% of the males provided response patterns that differed from the majority of the adolescents.

Individuation

In the context of the parent-adolescent relationship, the concept of individuation pertains to the notion that during adolescence, individuals not only seek to separate themselves from their parents and to assert their individuality, but also seek to remain connected to their parents. This process serves as a balance between enmeshment, where there is no individuality, and total detachment from their parents, where there is no connectedness. The concept of individuation, then, can be contrasted against the proposition that during adolescence, individuals seek to become autonomous from parents so that they may eventually function as adults—independent of parental influence or advice. For the parent-adolescent relationship, the discussion of individuation (see Chapter 5) focused on demonstrating that adolescents seek to remain connected to parents and that this goal is not incompatible with their simultaneous attempt to assert their own individuality. For the close-friend relationship, it may be more appropriate to focus on the evidence indicating that adolescents seek to maintain their individuality despite their strong connections to their close friends.

The discussion concerning the structure of friendship reviewed the evidence indicating that during adolescence close friends clearly are closely connected to one another. In review, close friends rely on each other for self-validation, as well as for validation of their ideas about the world. Close friends are also connected by an emotional bond in that they care about each other and feel obligated to help when they are needed. The evidence from our studies also indicates, however, that this relationship does not involve total dependence nor preclude separateness in thinking and acting. In fact, the essence of this relationship seems to be that one is accepted even though he or she may think or act differently than the other. Close friends were described as people "you can tell anything to and they won't be shocked" or "you can talk to and not be embarrassed about the way you feel." And, it is in the context of this relationship that adolescents report they are most likely to be "themselves."

Recognition and acceptance of individuality was also expressed in adolescents' descriptions of how their friendships have changed over time. They said, "Friends can be different now. We don't have to think the same." "I can be friends with anyone now, just as long as they understand the way I am. . . ." "I used to look for people who are like me. Now they don't have to be the same as me anymore." "Now I try and really know the person." And, "Now if we don't agree, I keep an open mind." These quotes suggest that prior to adolescence, the individuality of close friends was not frequently valued or sought. In fact, data from younger children indicate that similarity of personalities, or at least perceived similarity, is a major aspect of a close friendship. The present data, however, clearly demonstrate that by adolescence the personhood of the close friend is not only tolerated but often appreciated.

In summary, the attachment between friends has a positive value that counters existential aloneness and self-reliance on personal reflection. Simultaneously, the demands of friendship need not stifle the individual's search for identity and the self-exploration it entails. Friends prize each other's individuality, and for them connectedness is not incompatible with separateness. One may infringe upon the other but, for the most part, adolescents testify that friendship includes both connectedness and separateness as essential elements.

Theoretical Positions

One of the strongest views on adolescent friendship comes from socialization theory. According to this position, individuals acquire behavior patterns from exposure to other persons and to these other persons' reinforcing or nonrein-forcing responses to the individual's actions. When this position is applied to adolescence, an interesting picture results. Adolescents who affect one an-other are presumed to be equally naive and not yet committed to behavior patterns that form the common heritage of a culture. The likelihood, then, is that adolescent friends can lead one another away from those patterns that adults understand to be important for the culture's preservation.

This view had led to a body of studies designed to assess peer influence (cf. Hartup 1970; Bengtson & Troll 1978). The results have given credence to the popular view that peer pressure to conform is an important force in leading adolescents to deviant patterns regarding alcohol and drug use, sexual explo-ration, and preferences for clothes, music, and food. Our data show that friends do, in fact, influence one another. Adolescents regularly seek advice from friends and are open to criticisms, as well as suggestions for solutions to their problems. Yet, the same results suggest that it would be incautious to identify friendship with peer pressure. Undoubtedly, friends can encourage each other toward deviant actions; for example, smoking pot and using alco-hol appeared as activities that some adolescents enjoy in friendships.

There is, however, a different kind of conformity that is typical of friend-ship. It is a conformity to loyalty, to trustworthiness, and to those principles that adolescents say operate within the relationship. These principles appear quite traditional in substance. They represent a set of basic values that pertain to social cohesion since they call for tempering of the self in concern for the other person. An obvious example comes from adolescents' statements that they would sacrifice personal desires to help friends whose problems they voluntarily share from a sense of obligation. If one prefers to view friendship within the socialization framework, such principles cannot be overlooked. They are integral to the relationship and are co-constructed by the partners who begin with the primitives of reciprocity and fairness.

This side of friendship has tended to be neglected by theorists who have focused on particular behaviors that occur within peer associations. An excep-tion is Hirschi (1969) who views friendship as a case of social control that keeps the individual from acting solely for self. The aspect of control enters into friendships because individuals understand that their actions affect other persons about whom they care and who care about them. This adds social responsibility to their actions by way of constraining the self and keeping it in correspondence with other persons. This is not to say that friendship, or any other relationship, guarantees the absence of deviancy. It does, however, highlight the positive socialization that follows from the inherent demands of friendship.

An overlooked aspect of adolescent friendship is mutual respect for per-sons. Piaget ([1932] 1965) and Sullivan (1953) have been particularly clear on this point. The respect that friends have for each other is founded on the rules of the relationship that the parties have constructed and follow. The expectations that one has for the other are no more than the expectations for oneself. The self and the other are evaluated by common standards to which both are known to adhere. The result is that friends interact within definite boundaries. Each knows when a violation has occurred. Both feel responsible to justify their own actions that constitute violations. And each respects the other for acting according to the rules that apply equally to the self as to the other.

There is no need to exaggerate the possibilities for positive socialization. The acquisitions that are made in friendship can be seen from the adolescents' own descriptions of interactions with friends. The rules we have summarized are restatements of the adolescents' responses put into more abstract terminology. In this regard, it is important to note that the adolescents whom we interviewed should not be accused of being idealistic or romantic. For any principle they expressed, they also described a violation. For any violation manifested by the other, there was also a violation by the self. But the same was true of ways to resolve conflicts. Resolutions were effected to repair a breach so that the friends could attest to the principle at stake and resume their relationship.

One of the difficulties in socialization theory is the static characterization of friendship in terms of general considerations, mainly that adolescents are not adult members of society. By looking more closely at what adolescents do and think, we see our data as a step in the direction of breaking this characterization. The data are not first-hand observations of on-line interactions per se, but come closer to the practices of friendship than the data usually found in socialization theories. It is worthwhile to note that adolescent friendships are particularly difficult to observe directly. Much of what occurs within these relationships takes place outside the view of adult would-be-observers—for example, mutual disclosure and solving personal problems. Still, it should be noted that when clever techniques have been used to capture some of the communication details that occur within friendships, the results have confirmed our interview data by demonstrating to similar procedures of communication that we have found (cf. Gottman 1983).

Cognitive Theory

As was noted in chapter 1, psychological theorists have recently begun to emphasize the cognitive powers that adolescents can apply to such issues as identity formation, perspective taking, and moral judgment. The general theme is that adolescents have capacities to employ reason, which younger children do not possess. While children are, therefore, dependent on adults for confirmation of their ideas, adolescents are more self-reliant. These theories , then, focus on the achievements that adolescents can make through their own self-reflections. Because adolescents can reason rationally, it is presumed that they can find ways of ordering reality by operating on their experiences and by transforming them into conceptually consistent versions of persons, moral thoughts, and things.

Historically, cognitive theory served the purpose of correcting the socialization model that failed to credit the individual with sufficient initiative. This correction was needed especially in the moral domain, if adolescents were to have freedom, responsibility, and commitment. This was no small correction; however, its significance need not be reviewed here (see, Kohlberg 1969). There is, however, a potential problem with this position because it has led to the view that adolescents manage their development pretty much on their own. Experience per se is not seen as a determinant but as only an occasion for self-reflection. Self-reflection is seen by the cognitive theorists as transforming experience and as the means to logical conclusions of what is and what ought to be.

A telling example is found in the description that cognitive theory gives to role taking. The problem is that of informing the self that another person may perceive a situation differently than the self. The problem is said to be mediated by the self's use of role-taking skills in which the one individual analyzes cues that are signified through the other person's action. The self, then, constructs a logical version of the other person's position—what the other is perceiving, feeling, or thinking. The construction, in turn, affects the self by stemming egocentrism and by bringing the other person's position to bear on the self's position.

This process epitomizes self-contained cognition because it virtually discounts social interaction between the self and the other. It comes close to freezing the other person as the self probes the other person's surface behavior in an attempt to get inside. Our data suggest that a different kind of role taking applies to friendship. The self and the other are equally active in a process that includes exchanging personal "inside" data so that each friend can be understood as well as can understand. Friends communicate what they are feeling or thinking. They talk over differences. And they confront disagreements by asking each other for accounts of their reasoning. This is not role taking from a distance, but is role making in consort where the objective is mutual understanding and the means is symmetrical, open communication.

This example testifies to two broader points that were found through our studies. The first point is that adolescent development occurs through social construction. This is neither self-construction that proceeds through the privacy of self-reflection, nor is it socialization in which the other person controls the self through reinforcing techniques. The second point is that within friendship social construction is more cooperative than unilateral. As was seen in our findings, friends work together to help one another. They work to form views that they can share through techniques such as discussion, compromise, and argument. They criticize each other, as well as exchange advice.

Our results should help to correct a tendency to excess in cognitive theory that depicts the adolescent as a lone agent struggling to comprehend the surrounding world. While adolescence may involve a sense of existential aloneness, friendship provides an alternative in which someone else is engaged in the self's concerns and vice versa. Friendship allows reflection to be brought to a public forum so that the uncertainty of self-rumination can be clarified through social reflection to which each friend contributes.

A special note may be added here. Major theories of moral development have not begun to explore an insight that was suggested by Piaget ([1932] 1965) some years ago: the principles that friends co-construct to form and maintain friendship may, in fact, provide the substance of moral principles. According to Piaget, the rules are probably initially constructed for pragmatic reasons. However, once practiced, they may be reconstituted into principles and subsequently be generalized as norms that apply beyond friendship to persons in general (Youniss 1981). Our data cannot explicate this argument except to demonstrate that the rules which adolescents describe for friendship are particular cases of the moral principles that cognitive theorists have previously attributed to the fruits of self-reflection. The data are thus in keeping with Piaget's definitions of morality as mutual respect and of moral autonomy as the willingness of individuals to abide by the norms of reciprocity and fairness so that they may be understood by as well as understand others.

Psychoanalytic Theory

It is difficult to apply our data to this theoretical position that actually includes a pluralism of views. One point, however, merits elaboration. Psychoanalytic scholars have viewed adolescence as a time to revise the self of childhood in relation to parents (Blos 1967). A minimum achievement is to clarify the debt adolescents owe to parents for thoughts and feelings. It is relevant that most female and some male subjects cited close friends as the persons with whom they discussed problems and feelings about their mothers and siblings. We have seen what this communication involved by way of disclosure and exchanging advice.

Taking these results together, friendship can be seen as providing a means to facilitate coming to grips with the parental relationship. In talking about the parental relationship, it is possible that friends begin to clarify the source of their thoughts and feelings. Sullivan (1953) may be given credit for the insight that friendship can be a healing relationship that aids the adolescent in overcoming what has been the source of self-attributions. This view casts friends in the role of therapist and places their communications on the plane of analytic reflection—leaving out, of course, the factor of transference.

A secondary point also follows from Sullivan's writings. He has suggested that friendship may be a vehicle for a kind of self-appraisal that counters the defensiveness engendered by unilateral relations. In the latter, the self is under judgment from someone whose approval is sought and whose standards are predetermined. In such relationships, the self is likely to present only qualities that would be approved, while hiding those aspects that would not be approved. The result could be a distortion of self in which assets were exaggerated and weaknesses were suppressed or denied.

Sullivan argues that having a close friendship during adolescence may be decisive in the individual's autobiography of defensiveness. He claims, for example, that some adult disorders can be traced to the absence of friendship during the important period of adolescence (see also Hartup 1978). Our data bear on his argument as follows. Adolescents do not see friendship as a judgmental relationship, yet they say that the relationship has standards that allow friends to be critics of each other's behavior. The point is brought out in the data on conflict and resolution in which friends demand accounts of untoward actions and typically get them by way of apology, promise, and explanation. While these acts may be defenses, in themselves, they also require admission of the offense and the giving of an account that the other person will accept—if the breach is to be repaired.

This set of results may exemplify the possibilities that lie within friendship for the self's development. Insofar as violations represent failings on the self's part, admission to them, rather than repression of them, may be a step in the self's acceptance of its weaknesses. The important feature is that friends still accept and respect each other, despite their weaknesses. The violator still merits respect if the failing is admitted and if correction is made or compensation is offered. Simultaneously, the strengths of the self are also tempered within friendship. A friend's assets do not stand on their own but may be seen in conjunction with the friend's weaknesses. This would occur through the role alternations of a friend with a problem and a friend who helps the other with a problem (Youniss 1983).

In Sullivan's view, a major defense in a society that prizes intellectual achievement is a sense of uniqueness—an exaggerated feeling regarding the source and content of one's ideas. Friendship is undoubtedly a corrective against this defense. Neither friend alone can claim sole authorship to ideas that have been jointly authored. Moreover, the continuing comparisons that friends make in their private conversations must serve to stem false notions of uniqueness and must promote the belief that much of what one thinks has also been thought by one's friend.

These references to Sullivan would be incomplete without recalling that the points in question were those that differentiated females from males in our results. Importantly, females were, in general, more direct in their handling of resolutions while males were more indirect. For example, females were more likely to confront the violator with the fact that an offense had been committed and had to be undone. Males were more ready to allow the violation to go unmarked and to wait for a spontaneous cessation. These data concur with the general result that females on the average were more openly in continuous communication with their friends than were males on the average. These differences may imply different defensive patterns in the two sexes, a point that surely merits pursuit in subsequent research.

Summary

The two central points in this chapter are (1) that adolescent friendships support the concept of social construction with its meaning for mutual understanding and consensual validation and (2) that friendship is a principled relationship with a prosocial orientation. These results counter the view that adolescents are caught in a struggle that emanates from within and that must be solved wholly through use of their own inner resources. Our results also counter the view that friendship is a relationship of convenience that adolescents exploit to gain personal pleasure and to avoid loneliness. While both of these things are true, neither captures the gist of the relationship insofar as it engenders social responsibility between the self and reciprocating other.

There are serious limits to our analysis that must be admitted here. We have fluctuated between friendship as a dyad and principles that adolescents can state about friendship in general. The data do not deal with adolescents' simultaneous participation in several friendships; with the acquisitions made from experiences in successive relationships; or with the place of friendship within the broader, social ecology of acquaintances, classmates, interest groups, or peer culture (see Krappmann & Oswald 1983). Importantly, the data address only indirectly girl-boy relationships, which undoubtedly play important roles in adolescents' relational and self development (see Miller & Simon 1980). The data should be taken for what they are, an attempt to add to our scant knowledge of this relationship. If adolescents' own descriptions of friendship are taken seriously, then, this relationship serves developmental functions that researchers cannot ignore without missing a core domain of adolescence.

9

Parents and Friends

This chapter presents a comparison of adolescents' relations with their parents and with their friends. Adolescents' perceptions of their relations with parents, initially summarized in chapter 5, will be further discussed. In chapter 5 it was suggested that adolescents perceive their parents as authorities who know more than they do about certain things—in particular, about how adolescents' present behavior bodes for their futures in society. Parental authority is manifest in the way mothers and fathers take unilateral stands, for example, in asserting ideas or by reacting to disagreements. Their orientation toward the future is indicated in parents' discussion of school and future and expectations regarding school performance and conduct that will keep adolescents out of trouble. Adolescents further perceive parental authority as rightful and benevolent. Its legitimacy stems from the parents' greater experience and knowledge of society. Benevolence is based on the belief that parents generally act from a concern that applies to adolescents' immediate happiness and long-term welfare. Adolescents appear not to perceive parental authority as stifling them in finding out about themselves as individuals. They believe that their parents have granted them freedom and that they no longer treat them as children. Although parents assert expectations and enforce rules of behavior, they recognize that adolescents act outside their purview and that they, therefore, cannot monitor all that adolescents do or think.

In the context of greater independence, adolescents begin to perceive their parents' actions in terms of the parental role and to a lesser extent in terms of their parents' individual personalities. The latter is more evident with mothers than with fathers. This may be based on the fact that mothers are engaged in the immediate concerns of their sons' and daughters' personal, emotional, and social lives. Further, mothers share some of their own feelings with adolescents. Fathers, in contrast, are more distant and less open. When mothers and fathers are combined in a single perception, it is possible to see that their respective behaviors are coherent and synchronous. The result is that adolescents sense that they are supported by their families both in day-to-day care, as well as in guidance toward their future adulthood.

All of the foregoing perceptions of the parent-adolescent relationship seem congruent with the general process of individuation. There is enough freedom to permit adolescents to experience themselves as individuals apart from their families. The exploration and testing of individuality, however, occurs in the context of a continuing relation with parents and family. The process seems credible in light of the broader sociological context that includes these elements: adolescents live at home and are dependent on parents; and parents do not see society as benign, but think they have to help their sons and daughters combat society's traps and find a course toward a successful future.

Our findings fail to support the view that modern parents have abdicated their roles as educators and socializers. According to the perceptions of the adolescents in our samples, parents act authoritatively and have not abandoned their sense of responsibility or concern for their offspring's welfare. If these things were not true, parents would not demand and enforce discipline. Much less, would they take unilateral stances in moments of disagreement. The claim that parents have given up their traditional role to become their sons' and daughters' friends, seems highly exaggerated.

The findings also fail to support the image that adolescents' increased cognitive competence allows them to construct identities for adulthood on their own. While increased competence, such as in reasoning, is a fact, adolescents still seek approval and validation from their parents. Adolescents most likely recognize that self-reflection lacks certainty and needs to be checked by other persons. In some areas and to some degree, adolescents call on parents to fulfill this function. And, even when they do not willingly solicit it, parents frequently take the roles of critics by offering counter reasoning to what they think their sons and daughters believe.

These points about parent-adolescent relationships can be elaborated in light of what we have just learned about friendship. Parental authority becomes even more evident as having a unilateral form when it is contrasted with the shared authority that friends manifest. The difference is sharpened by comparing unilateral with mutual procedures of communication. Parental benevolence is not diminished, however, by comparing it with friendship. There is, nevertheless, a distinction between the two: Parental concern is seen to emanate from the parents' role, which is oriented to the future, while the concern that friends have for each other is perceived in terms of a person-to-person agreement.

The advance by adolescents in understanding their parents as persons is clear when compared with children's perceptions of parents as all-knowing figures. However, when this understanding of parents as persons is measured on the same scale as the understanding of friends as persons, it is clear that neither parent has achieved the degree of individuality that friends have. An impediment to mutuality between parents and adolescents is the defensiveness that this relationship engenders. Adolescents seek parental approval, and parents hold standards that serve as criteria for approval. Adolescents have had little hand in making these standards, and they do not always understand either the standards or their supposed implications well. They, therefore, withhold much about themselves from their parents for fear of embarrassment or reproachment. Parents are equally withholding, especially in personal or emotional matters. This part of the parent-adolescent relationship contrasts clearly with friendship in which openness and mutual self-disclosure are regular features.

Friendship is also perceived as a supportive relationship. Friends are helpful, cooperative, and willing to sacrifice self-gain for the other's welfare. This support differs from that given by parents in a key way. Friends share personal knowledge and build a common perspective that allows them to take each other seriously. When one friend has a problem, the other is likely to deal with that problem as it is presented and is unlikely to offer an analysis or solution from an external frame of reference.

The concept of individuation seems to have value also for understanding how friendships contribute to adolescents' psychological development. First, friendship provides a context wherein adolescents can experience themselves as individuals outside the family. Second, within friendship, each person can experience individuality in an accepting atmosphere—friendship does not demand that the friends be alike or similar. Third, friendship is a context in which connectedness is fundamental because the relationship is voluntary and relies on commitment.

The socialization model, which we claim misrepresents parents vis-à-vis our subjects' descriptions, sells friendship short. The model focuses on the relative influence of parents and peers and emphasizes that the present sociological context favors peer influence. Our findings suggest that parental authority has not waned. Our findings further suggest that the influence of friends is clearly prosocial because friends base their relationship on principles. Both parents and friends, then, are influential. The two relationships overlap but are also different in their influence because the two relationships often deal with discrete sectors of the adolescents' lives. In general, but especially for females and their fathers, the parental relationship is more restricted than friendship is—friendship being almost pervasive in scope.

The cognitive model, which stresses adolescent competence, has depicted adolescent reasoning in too narrow a way. The present findings suggest that adolescent friends are conjoined in a continuing process of sharing reflections, exchanging criticism, and seeking consensual validation. The adolescents' descriptions of this process, while incomplete, clearly counter the image of the lone adolescent struggling to comprehend emotions from within and inconsistencies from without. Surely, adolescents do spend time in the privacy of self-reflection. But, from the data we have just seen, adolescents will go to friends to break out of self-reflection. Friends will listen, take them seriously, and work with them toward clarification. The result is that adolescents believe that they learn more about reality and about themselves from their friends than from anyone else. Indeed, it is within friendship that adolescents feel least as if they are living out a role and most like themselves—the personalities they believe themselves to be.

Parental Authority

It was shown in Chapter 5 that parents are perceived as authorities who assert opinions and use standards that they expect their sons and daughters to accept. It was also pointed out that this unilateral stance is diminished to some extent during adolescence. One reason for this change is that parents do not monitor the whole of their sons' and daughters' lives. Consequently, adolescents are given the experience of interpreting their parents' values according to circumstances that come up outside of parental surveillance. Another reason is that parents of adolescents are described as willing to listen and to discuss in a negotiating posture, the views of the sons and daughters. These types of discussions apparently occur more often with mothers than with fathers.

To what degree have parents maintained unilateral procedures, and to what extent have they become more negotiative in their interactions with their sons and daughters? Table 12 presents data for some selected procedures that bear on these questions. The first section of the table presents results from study 7, in which subjects responded in a forced-choice format. That is, a procedure was stated and subjects had to choose the one person—mother, father, same-sex friend, or opposite-sex friend—who was most likely to interact in that manner. All, except the last procedure in each section, began with the phrase, "When we disagree. . . ." Scores for mothers and fathers are combined here in the category of *parents,* and scores for the same-sex and opposite-sex friends are combined in the category of *friends.* The second section of the table presents data from study 6. In this study, mother, father, and friends were judged independently as to the degree each used a procedure. The scores presented here are those indicating usage of the responses "often" or "very often."

The results are self-explanatory. When forced to choose between parents and friends, more than 66% of the subjects, both females and males, designated parents more often than friends as users of unilateral procedures. The results are reversed for the negotiative procedures with one exception being the procedure *talk out differences,* for males.

Table 12. Procedures Used by Parents and Friends in Handling Differences

	Females		Males		Total	
	Parents	Friends	Parents	Friends	Parents	Friends
Forced-choice responses[a]						
Unilateral						
Insists that I change	.72	.17	.57	.35	.65	.26
Says he/she knows more than I	.69	.14	.70	.11	.69	.13
Gets upset if I don't change	.60	.27	.61	.28	.61	.27
Convinces me it is in my best interest to change	.61	.22	.58	.19	.59	.21
Does not consider my advice worth seeking	.67	.21	.44	.28	.55	.26
Negotiative						
Listens to my side	.28	.66	.31	.46	.29	.57
Talk out differences	.21	.65	.50	.36	.35	.51
Accepts my point of view	.17	.73	.31	.59	.24	.66
Depend on each other for advice	.10	.76	.15	.60	.12	.68
Independent responses						
Unilateral						
Expects me to do what he/she says	.53	.01	.66	.03	.59	.02
Simply tells me to do it	.50	.02	.50	.08	.50	.05
Says I'm supposed to do it	.44	.02	.46	0	.45	.01
Keeps telling me to do it	.47	.03	.51	.09	.49	.06
Negotiative						
Asks if I would be willing to	.53	.87	.54	.76	.54	.81

[a]Forced choices do not necessarily sum to 100% because some subjects gave no response or responded to both choices.

The results shown in the "independent responses" are better estimates of usage because adolescents could designate both parents and friends for any procedure. It can be seen that for the 4 unilateral procedures and the 1 negotiative procedure, about 50% of the subjects said that they and their parents interacted in these ways often or very often. It is seen also that less than 10% of the subjects said that they and their friends used unilateral means for settling disagreements. Finally it is clear that negotiative means are used more between friends (81%) than between adolescents and their parents (54%).

The conclusion was drawn in chapter 5 that while adolescents still perceive their parents as unilateral authorities, the relationship has changed relative to what is was during childhood. Specifically, parents negotiate and compromise with their adolescent children. The results in table 12 put this conclusion into perspective. Parents are considerably more unilateral than friends when the two relationships are directly compared. When the two relationships are judged independently, about 50% of the parents were said to interact unilaterally on a frequent basis, while friends were rarely said to. Simultaneously, about 50% of the parents were found to interact negotiatively while 80% of the friends were.

Role versus Person

It was concluded in chapter 5 that adolescents have made a developmental advance over childhood, insofar as they have begun both to appreciate their parents as individual personalities and to be appreciated by their parents as individual personalities. Children seem to accept their relationship with their parents as natural; parents are all-knowing figures and children gain by learning through them. Adolescents at least comprehend that some of what parents do emanates from their role. This understanding, in turn, gives adolescents a sense of obligation to appreciate, and to conform to, parents. Some adolescents go further and view their parents as individuals with needs similar to their own, with articulated personalities that can be enjoyed, and with character flaws that may hurt the relationships. The path from figure-to-role-to-person seems to represent a developmental sequence that is anchored on one end by unilateral authority, with all of its imbalances, and that proceeds on the other end toward greater peer-like mutuality (White, Speisman, and Costos 1983).

When this developmental sequence in the parental relationship is juxtaposed with friendship, it appears to be rather limited. Friends appear to deal with each other at the level of personalities earlier and more regularly than adolescents and their parents do. The reasons for this seem evident. Among other things, friends reciprocally expose their ideas as they seek to clarify personal self-reflections and to exchange views in what adolescents call mutual advising. A primary element in friendship is that friends take each other's views seriously. When one friend expresses an idea or feeling, the other seems to take it as it is. Neither friend is likely to step outside the relationship to review the thought or idea from an external position. That is why friends are seen as not being judgmental. They have no role to flee to, as parents do, for settling differences but must carry on arbitration within the relationship on face-to-face terms.

We suggest that coming to grips with persons is difficult within any authority-based relation, and is especially difficult for parents and adolescents. Contrary to some theorists, however, we do not fault parents but see their actions as following from the structure of the relationship. Our interpretation of our results is that parents look at adolescent behavior on two levels. On one, parents deal in the here-and-now as adolescents come to them. For example, a son has a problem comprehending a feeling, or a daughter has violated some rule of the family's regimen.

On the second level, parents look at behavior as signifying something broader, such as whether or not the adolescent is making adequate progress toward maturity. In this regard, parents have a kind of map with sign posts that are used to gauge progress. Thus, a confused feeling could represent emotional instability or a rule violation could signify lack of discipline. The second level of concern follows from the fact that parents do see themselves as having an obligation to get their sons and daughters through adolescence and on to adulthood. They cannot help but put significance on adolescents' behavior when adolescents themselves may not see their behavior in the same way. An example that was often repeated in the results was the emphasis that parents placed on academic performance and its connection to the adolescents' futures. This was a topic that 80% of the adolescents said that their parents discussed frequently, that over 75% of the parents were said to support with reasoning, that adolescents designated as more likely to be discussed with parents rather than friends (74% versus 26%), and that adolescents said occasioned conflict in the relationship. While school is part of the everyday existence of adolescents, it is not so evident that adolescents put as much weight on its implications for their future as their parents seem to do.

Despite the fact that the school-future nexus was a continuing theme whose rationale was explicated by parents, estimates of mutual understanding by adolescents with their parents on this topic ranged from only 35% to 58% in study 6. The data became clearer when they were placed alongside the results from the studies on friendship where there seemed to be less disparity in personal interests. Again, friends seemed able to accept each other's interests as they are presented and to take them as their own. The intention of the friend who initiates the topic is apparently adopted by the other friend. The two friends then *talk it out* making it their shared concern. As a rule, one friend does not shift the interest to some other topic (the future) but keeps within the perspective of the person who initiated the topic. Should a shift be made, it is probably accomplished with the assent of both friends as is exemplified in the descriptions of routines by which conflicts are sometimes resolved.

Sullivan (1953) provides a theoretical view that helps to clarify this general point. He submits that parents have difficulty perceiving their children as they are because parents' perceptions are encumbered by concerns for long-term implications of here-and-now behavior. Children's perceptions, in turn, are encumbered by attempts to gain parental approval. This insight seems to apply to parent-adolescent relationships as well. Parents seem to look on behavior for what it is and also for what it implies about the adolescents' long-range progress toward adulthood. Adolescents tend to focus on the former more than on the latter and, as we saw, also seek their parents' approval. The result of a mismatch in interests is that neither party can easily deal with the other person, roles being the clouding element. The contrast to friendship, then, is obvious because in this relationship there is no escape to a role.

Lastly on this point, it may be suggested that the role-based character of parent-adolescent interactions may be exacerbated by the stakes. With adulthood being imminent for adolescents, parents might put greater weight on adolescents' than on children's actions. Implications for the future are more obvious. Indeed, several adolescents stressed that in adolescence, as compared to their childhood years, their fathers and mothers treated them as more mature but, as a consequence, have raised their expectations of them and have added responsibilities. The coupling of maturity with higher standards of conduct makes sense in a context where present performance is viewed as predictive of future achievements. In short, the behavior of adolescents counts more because by failing in school and by habitually violating rules, adolescents risk cutting off options that their parents have in mind for their future.

Defensiveness

In their study of 120 adolescents and young adults, White, Speisman, and Costos (1983) noted the slowness with which parent and offspring come to accept each other as individual personalities. The process seems to get an impetus when young adults begin permanent jobs or get married. Until then, most adolescents and their parents still perceive one another through their respective roles. These data are interesting because they imply that theories of adolescence present an accelerated view of the process with their emphases on emancipation and autonomy in early adolescence. Our results concur more with White, Speisman, and Costos's findings than with these other theories.

Our results help to show one of the reasons that the process may be so gradual and slow paced. There is, at least from the adolescents' side, a defensiveness that is inherent to the relationship. Adolescents who are under evaluation and still seek approval from their parents would be expected to be cautious in what they discuss with them, as well as how they discuss their actions, ideas, and feelings. The results of table 13 offer a review of some of the topics that adolescents said they discussed or did not discuss with their parents and friends. These data are offered to demonstrate the cautiousness of adolescents as well as to reiterate the earlier point about the distribution among interests across relationships.

In each group of topics, all but the last item present data from forced-choice situations—the subjects had to select either parents or friends as the more likely discussion partners. Scores for mothers and fathers are combined

Table 13. Comparisons between Parents and Friends across Selected Topics of Discussion

	Females		Males		Total	
Topics[a]	Parents	Friends	Parents	Friends	Parents	Friends
How well I am doing in school	.72	.24	.68	.25	.70	.25
Problems at school	.44	.55	.54	.39	.49	.55
Schoolwork and grades	.86	.83	.89	.80	.88	.82
Career goals	.63	.30	.70	.24	.67	.27
Hopes/plans for the future	.40	.54	.54	.38	.47	.46
Future plans	.87	.81	.88	.76	.88	.78
Feelings about the opposite sex	.07	.92	.14	.78	.11	.85
Problems with the opposite sex	.16	.82	.15	.78	.16	.80
Attitudes toward marriage	.32	.64	.35	.55	.33	.60
Views on sex	.21	.79	.17	.82	.19	.80
Dating behaviors	.45	.73	.43	.73	.44	.73

[a]Forced choices do not necessarily sum to 100% because some subjects gave no response or responded to both choices.

in the category of *parents,* and scores for the same-sex and opposite-sex friends are combined in the category of *friends.* The last item in each group presents data from independent choices (study 6); thus, adolescents could choose either parents or friends, both parents and friends, or neither parents nor friends as discussion partners. On the topic about school, parents were the more likely discussion partners in a forced choice against friends. However, it can be seen from the last item about *schoolwork and grades* that adolescents discuss school equally both with parents and with friends. This was also true of *problems at school* where the split was closer to 50–50. Almost identical results were obtained for *career goals* and for *plans for the future.* Under a forced-choice format, parents were selected over friends. When adolescents were allowed free choice, however, parents and friends were equally likely to be discussion partners. A more even split between parents and friends was shown for *hopes and plans for the future.*

An obvious contrast is shown in the choice of discussion partners for school-future topics and sex-dating topics. Given a forced choice, adolescents consistently selected friends over parents on items regarding feelings for, problems with, attitudes towards, and views on sex and the opposite sex. The last item—dating behaviors—which was answered through independent choice, provides a better estimate of the distribution. About 45% of the adolescents discussed dating behaviors with their parents, while about 75% discussed dating with friends. When the data from all three groups are considered together, they reinforce a general result that has recurred throughout the studies. Parent-adolescent communications are relatively restricted compared with communications within friendship. The data in table 13 show that although parents were highly likely to be included in discussions of school and of the future, they were less likely to be involved in discussions of sexual matters. In contrast, friends were highly likely to be engaged in discussion of all these topics.

These data were selected from our results to illustrate the point made previously that friends more closely share interests than do parents and adolescents. It is obvious that sexual and romantic matters are central to the adolescent period. Most theories of adolescence accept this as fact and consider sexual feelings and attitudes fundamental to the establishment of individuality. It is clear that adolescents prefer their friends as confidants in this area of their lives and that less than half of them claim that they discuss sexual matters with their parents. This is only to confirm the general point that adolescents are wary of what they discuss with their parents. It is plausible that fear of embarrassment or fear of lack of approval lie behind adolescents' withholding of their sexual side from their parents. This finding does not answer why parents are not more often engaged by their adolescent children in discussions of sex.

The results in table 14 provide three additional pieces of evidence which attest to the defensiveness that is built into the parent-adolescent relationship. The first group of results pertains to procedures that seem patently reflective of cautiousness versus openness. They show in brief that adolescents are more careful, hide feelings, and are more hesitant to express self-doubts with their parents than with their friends. They show further that adolescents perceive their parents as less expressive of feelings and, in general, less open than friends. Finally, they show that openness, expression of feelings, and admission of doubts occur more often between friends than between parents and adolescents.

The second section of the table continues the point through a consideration of topics and with whom they are likely to be discussed. The first four items pertain to discussions of feelings about, and problems with, mothers and fathers. It can be seen that females preferred to discuss their mothers more with their friends than with their fathers—males were about equally divided between fathers and friends. On the other hand, both females and males preferred to discuss their fathers more with their mothers than with their friends. This contrast reiterates the point that adolescents may be, in general, more defensive toward their fathers than toward their mothers. These results can be compared with feelings about, and problems with, friends. Adolescents said that they preferred to discuss these topics with friends than with their parents. The last two items in the second section allowed independent choice. With one exception, adolescents said that family and friends are topics they discuss

Table 14. Comparisons between Parents and Friends on Three Measures of Defensiveness

	Females		Males		Total	
	Parents	Friends	Parents	Friends	Parents	Friends
Procedures[a]						
I am careful what I say	.52	.33	.49	.34	.51	.33
I hide true feelings	.57	.21	.47	.36	.47	.28
I would not admit doubts or fears	.58	.18	.43	.31	.51	.24
He does not express true feelings to me	.59	.25	.50	.39	.55	.32
She does not talk openly to me	.67	.18	.41	.39	.54	.29
We talk about doubts and fears	.09	.77	.17	.69	.13	.73
We talk openly	.11	.67	.20	.63	.15	.65
We tell each other true feelings	.12	.86	.23	.52	.17	.69
Topics of Discussion						
Feelings about mother	.20	.77	.46	.47	.33	.62
Problems with mother	.14	.83	.48	.47	.31	.65
Feelings about father	.58	.39	.66	.26	.62	.33
Problems with father	.61	.39	.69	.23	.65	.31
Feelings about friends	.29	.67	.29	.63	.29	.65
Problems with friends	.23	.73	.28	.63	.25	.68
Views on the family	.91	.80	.91	.58	.91	.69
Views on friends	.73	.92	.78	.87	.76	.89
Self Descriptors						
Argumentative	.79	.14	.62	.29	.71	.21
Withdrawn	.80	.17	.64	.31	.72	.24
Uncomfortable	.71	.21	.56	.28	.63	.25
Criticized	.73	.20	.58	.29	.65	.25
Careful	.64	.32	.67	.26	.65	.29
Playful	.02	.89	.09	.82	.05	.85
Relaxed	.19	.75	.14	.81	.17	.78
Outgoing	.08	.91	.14	.83	.11	.87
Open	.15	.81	.21	.71	.18	.76
Myself	.19	.71	.18	.73	.19	.72

[a]Forced choices do not necessarily sum to 100% because some subjects gave no responses or responded to both choices

frequently both with their parents and with their friends. The exception was the topic of *views on the family*—only 58% of the males said they discussed this topic with their friends.

The third group of items presents results from selected descriptors that adolescents applied to themselves in their relationships with parents or friends. The choices seem to represent the difference in defensiveness across the two kinds of relationships in an obvious way. Adolescents described themselves as more *argumentative, withdrawn, uncomfortable, criticized,* and *careful* with their parents than with their friends. In contrast, the same subjects described themselves as more *playful, relaxed, outgoing, open,* and *myself* with friends than with parents. These data confirm the overall pattern of the two kinds of relationships from a new angle. They suggest that one product of the parent-adolescent relationship is a sharpened perception of the two sides of self—one that is open and accepted in friendship, the other that is cautious and under judgment with parents.

Our interpretation of the results is that the relative defensiveness of adolescents toward parents stems from the structure of the relationship and is neither an aberrance nor a sign of disturbance. This defensiveness follows from the enactment of responsibility by parents as authoritative adults seeking to guide their sons and daughters along a course to successful adulthood. It follows equally from adolescents who while seeking guidance and approval from their parents, also fear being called immature by, looking childish in front of, or feeling inferior with their parents. In any case, adolescents withhold their ideas and feelings from parental judgment.

It should be pointed out that from the adolescents' perspectives, parents equally withhold their feelings. While parents articulate reasons behind their views and standards—for example, stating why rules of discipline are important—they are perceived in general, as less than open—particularly in expressing their feelings. An obvious example concerns sexual matters. While we are not privileged to the actual conversations that parents and adolescents have regarding sexual matters, it is possible that these conversations are carried on at abstract levels that stress standards and consequences. While adolescents said that they do not express feelings or discuss details with their parents regarding sex, it is reasonable to infer that parents also do not express feelings regarding sexual matters in their own lives. It can be seen, then, that cautiousness applies to both sides in a relationship built upon unilateral authority.

The last result, which fits into this sequence, came from the adolescents in study 3 who were presented the following item: *I usually feel comfortable telling my mother (father; best friend) just about everything about myself.* Thirty-one percent of the adolescents said *true* when the other person was their mother or father. There was no difference between females (33%) and males (28%). The same question was asked of adolescents from this sample regarding disclosures to friends. In this case, 73% of them said *true*—80% of the females and 63% of the males.

Harmony

Much has been made of the question whether or not adolescents' relations with their parents are contentious or harmonious. The question is part of the general belief that adolescents need to be emancipated from their parents and, in service of this goal, take positions that demonstrate independence. While we do not consider this to be a critical issue, the present findings have some bearing on it and merit a brief discussion. One of the values of the concept of individuation, as we see it, is that it allows emancipation to be considered in context rather than letting it connote something absolute.

As will be shown shortly, the typical adolescent is not in a battle to assert independence against parents who thwart it. There is plenty of allowance for self-assertion within the parental relationship. Parents take unilateral stands as a rule, but they do not appear to be rigid or authoritarian. Not only do parents partake of more mutual procedures, at least some of the time, but, further, they cannot monitor all that adolescents do. Moreover, parents allow adolescents the freedom to have private lives with friends and with other peers. As was seen, at least for friendship, this social sphere is hardly conducive to conspiracy against parental values. The principles of friendship are utterly conservative and are congruent with those that parents teach as being socially correct.

This does not mean that adolescents agree with everything their parents teach, or expect of, them. The fact is that the parental relationship is rife with moments of disagreement and conflict. Adolescents do violate most rules that parents construct for them and do not always perform up to their parents' expectations. If these data reflect lack of harmony, they must be compared with friendship that was marked by an equal amount of disagreement, rule violation, and expectation failure. We suggest that these data are not surprising given that adolescence is a period of self-exploration. It should not be uncommon that part of this exploration requires self-assertion and that the self at some time must go against the other person's interest in a relationship.

Two further points seem to put conflict in perspective. The first is that in both relations with parents and with friends the persons care enough about their relationships to admit to acts that provoke conflict and to deal with them so that the breach is repaired rather than left to widen. And second, adolescents tend to view both relationships as being respectful of, and fair to, the persons within them. Respect was indicated by this statement: *My mother (father, best friend) acts as if I am as important as she(he) is in our relation.* When parents were the persons in the statement, 66% of the adolescents said *true.* For friends, 80% of the subjects answered *true.* Fairness was assessed as follows: *My mother (father, best friend) expects more of me than she(he) is willing to give back.* Of subjects answering for parents, 72% said *false.* Of subjects answering for friends, 71% said *false.*

Parent-Peer Influence

As is well known, several psychologists and sociologists have made parent-peer influence the primary issue in the study of adolescence and considered the counterinfluence of parents and peers to be of a pressing nature. Their reasoning is, in brief, that as family structure weakens (e.g., divorce), adolescents come more under the sway of peers who have little investment in upholding the standards that are necessary for cohesiveness in adult society. Our studies were not specifically addressed to this theory. We did not directly compare these two kinds of influences, and we focused on friends rather than peers. Moreover, our samples included adolescents only from families with two parents. Further, the adolescents were all currently enrolled in high school and were probably not regular truants. Still, the data may be used to appraise aspects of this theory that remain of interest both within and outside the social sciences. Four points merit emphasis:

First, according to adolescents' descriptions, friendship is no less principled or less demanding of adherence to principle than are relations with parents. The point is made several ways a primary example being the issues articulated in cases of conflict. These issues include keeping promises, not disclosing privileged information, being attentive, being sensitive to a friend's needs, not becoming insulting, not lying, not intruding on other relations that a friend has, respecting the friend's property, acting in a self-respecting way, not acting selfishly, and not becoming overdemanding.

We submit that these rules overlap with the supposed standards that socilization theorists attribute to parents. The results demonstrate further that these rules are enforced in friendship. Friends confront one another when the rules are broken, and remedial action must be taken—or else there is a risk of losing the relationship. Thus not only are the rules of friendship similar to the standards that adults promote, but their enforcement is equally evident. The picture that results clashes with the image that has been sketched for the "peer culture"—that is, everyone seeks immediate gratification; no one checks anyone else; cooperation is merely collusion; and self-gain reigns over the common good. These rules may apply somewhere, but they do not apply to the friendships described by the adolescents whom we interviewed.

Second, influence depends on the content of parental teaching. According to adolescents' descriptions, their parents do teach standards that are both general, as well as directed to specific instances. However, the data show that parental instruction does not cover all of the areas that constitute adolescents' lives. Dating and sexual matters are glaring exclusions given their importance to adolescence. Further, it is evident that many specific instances of adolescents' experiences are left outside the parents' purview. These events may be touched on by parents' general dictums, but their specific applicability is determined by adolescents themselves. The gap is especially notable between fathers' focuses and adolescents' opinions and feelings about noninstrumental matters.

Third, while adolescents acknowledge their parents' authority, they recognize another kind of authority with friends. The distinction hinges on the how, or the form, of instruction. As was seen, parents tend to give advice by stating reasons behind the dos and don'ts. In this, they try to transmit their experience to their sons and daughters in a reasoned manner. This unilateral form can go only so far; once a reason is stated, the initiative passes to the adolescent who can adapt to, or reconstruct, it for the self. In contrast, friends do not stop with the assertion of reasons. Rather, the two friends exchange ideas critically but in a context controlled by the aim of reaching consensus and mutual understanding. We infer that the general terms *talking out* and *sharing advice* denote particular interactions in which the weight of authority comes from reciprocal critiques that sharpen ideas as truth for us is negotiated.

Fourth, the theory of parent-peer influence does not address the issues of belief or understanding. Both parents and adolescents acknowledge their disparity in experience. Socialization theorists presume that the greater experience of parents resolves into better or wiser perspectives. It is not necessarily the case, however, that adolescents concur. Were this true, adolescents would regularly bring their confusions and problems to their parents for clarification and resolution. It is obvious that they do not. One reason has already been cited in our discussion of adolescent defensiveness. Another may be that adolescents feel that their parents do not always have the best solutions for their problems. They may think also that their parents' solutions do not quite fit their needs.

Table 15 reviews data that bear on the issue of belief and understanding. The results shown from study 7 indicate that adolescents feel they (1) learn more from their friends than from their parents, (2) go to friends more than to parents with personal problems, (3) are understood better by friends than by parents, and (4) feel more fully themselves with friends than with parents. The results shown from study 3 sharpen the differences between self-disclosure to friends and to parents.

Table 15. From Whom Do Adolescents Learn and by Whom Are They Understood: Parents or Friends?

	True	False
Study 7		
I feel I learn more from my close friends than from my parents	.70	.30
I am as likely to go to my parents with personal problems as to my close friends	.41	.59
I feel that my close friends understand me better than my parents.	.70	.30
I feel that parents understand me as well as my close friends do.	.34	.66
I feel I am more myself with close friends than with my parents.	.69	.31
Study 3		
I usually feel comfortable telling my parents just about everything about myself.	.31	.69
I usually feel comfortable telling my best friend just about everything about myself.	.73	.27

It follows from this set of findings that a key element is missing from the socialization model. Parent-adolescent influence does not proceed as an electrical signal across a neutral conduit. Communication depends on the relation between the persons—what their interests are, and whether or not they are working toward mutual understanding. This applies to parental, as well as to close-friend relations. We cannot say from the finding which element is more important or how the elements are connected. It seems plausible, however, that several things interfere with parent or peer influence; among them are defensiveness, engagement in the discussion, and involvement to the extent that one's views are heard and understood. In this more complex context, the question of who is more influential—parents or peers—skirts the reality of communication as dependent on the relationship in which it occurs (cf., Urwin 1984).

Individuation

In chapter 5, it was suggested that the concept of individuation could be usefully applied to our results in either of two ways. In one, individuation was used to differentiate maternal from paternal relations, with the former being more advanced developmentally than the latter. Mothers and adolescents were more likely to interact as individuals, expressing themselves through their feelings and ideas than in roles with mothers acting as authority figures and adolescents seeking their approval. Additionally, the bond of support between mothers and adolescents was strong and direct because mothers tried to take adolescents' concerns seriously and, in turn, adolescents were open to using their mothers to care for their needs. This was accompanied by the belief that adolescents could be helpful in meeting their mothers' needs with reciprocity. Adolescents' relations with their fathers seem to differ on each point. Fathers were shown to meet disagreements with unilateral instruction and were less ready to take on the adolescents' interests as their own. Further, the adolescents were not open in their communication with their fathers; few said that their fathers met their emotional needs, and the adolescents reported that they did not respond reciprocally to their fathers' intiatives.

A second way of looking at these data is through the combined effects of both parents in which case individuation is made a property of the adolescents' relations to their families. From this perspective, mothers' and fathers' actions are seen as working in consort. For example, mothers' direct actions that encourage adolescents to assert themselves are supplemented by fathers' indirect actions of not monitoring their sons and daughters; thus, room is left for self-exploration outside the fathers' purview. In addition, mothers' direct actions of listening to and supporting adolescents were accompanied by fathers' readiness to step in and help when their sons or daughters had a serious difficulty.

Grotevant and Cooper (in press) have provided a historical analysis of the concept of individuation. They track its formulation in Mahler's writings on childhood and the extension of Mahler's ideas by Blos (1967) to adolescence, which he sees as a second period of individuation. They show further its incorporation into family-systems theory that gives emphasis to clinical implications. Lastly, they show the concept's more recent introduction into the experimental literature where terms are defined more rigorously in reference to specific behavioral events. For example, in another of their works (e.g., Cooper, Grotevant, & Condon 1983), they show that expressions of self can be denoted through adolescents' willingness to state their views when they are communicating with their parents. For another example, taking responsibility for one's views can be referred to adolescents' holding to views when, in fact, parents have contrary views.

It is clear that the historical applicability of the concept of individuation has been to the parental relationship where the central issue is how the child or adolescent can define self after having been dependent on parents, especially the mother, in an enveloping, pervasive relationship. If the concept is looked at in terms of process, as we have in this book, then friendship may be brought in, and brought to bear on, parental relationships. Technically, friendship may be inapplicable to individuation since its problems are somewhat the reverse of those of parental relations. The question for friendship is how two individuals form a bond, while the historical issue of individuation has been how can a person establish individuality after having defined self through years of definition through the parental bond.

Throughout this book, the individuation concept has been used heuristically because it provides such an obvious match to the findings. The concept recognizes two sides of relationships: the fact that the members are individuals, and the fact that the members support each other. Most other theories emphasize one or the other aspect. The data do not fit a one-sided model—for example, adolescents are obviously distant from their fathers, yet they respect them and believe that their fathers will support them in times of trouble. Similarly, friends accept the fact that they are each an individual, yet they demand each other's attention and get upset when one forms new bonds with persons outside the friendship. Clearly, something like individuation is needed to incorporate such findings that show dual tendencies within any relationship.

The general presumption is, as White, Speisman, and Costos (1983) have stated, that under present sociological conditions, the tendency for parent-child relations is more in the direction of greater peer-like mutuality—that is, from unilateral dependence to mutuality, or interdependence, between two individuals. We agree also with White and her colleagues that the process is gradual and typically proceeds into adulthood. In the usual case, achievement of peer-like mutuality between parents and children only moves ahead but is not accomplished during adolescence.

In keeping with the heuristic tone adopted so far, we suggest two possible extensions that allow friendship to be seen as part of the individuation process. The first suggestion is that friendship provides a contrasting experience that may help adolescents evaluate their position in their parental relationships. The effect of friendship on parental relations works by way of contrast. The clearest example is found with females' relations to friends and to their fathers. With friends, females gain a clear sense of agency for themselves. They can generate ideas, articulate views, confront feelings, and think of themselves as individuals. Simultaneously, the self's agency is put to use in helping one's friends—for instance in giving advice or clarifying confusing feelings. The connection between female friends testifies to the advantages of interdependence; the relationship is available when validation is needed, yet it is not so intrusive as to obliterate independent action on either friend's part.

When the same females interact with their fathers, their experience with their fathers seem to contrast on almost every point to those with their friends. Fathers are seen as likely to emit unilateral instructions when they see differences between their views and those of their daughters. Fathers are seen to show little interest in their daughters' daily emotional concerns; in turn, daughters are not open to disclosing their feelings to their fathers. Daughters believe that because of these stilted communications, in which they hide their feelings as much as their fathers do, their fathers do not understand them well. While they think that fathers are fair and respect them, daughters believe that they cannot directly reciprocate to their fathers for what their fathers have done for them. The daughters wish they were closer to, communicated more with, and were appreciated by their fathers as individuals with ideas worth being taken seriously.

We cannot point to specific evidence that would show how experiences within friendship entered into the daughters' relations with their fathers. The suggestion is only that the contrast is obvious enough to make it possible for the disparity to provoke the adolescents' reflection. One way this might work is through the mediation of mothers with whom duaghters said they discussed feelings toward, and problems with, fathers. The possibility here is that when daughters come to the realization that their fathers do not adequately appreciate them as individuals, they consequently back-off to a position of distant respect and invest their energy in other relationships, where their individuality is accepted and is fostered.

The second suggested interplay of friendship with parental relations is that friendship allows adolescents to test the limits of both their individuality and connectedness. For example, self-assertion occurs to some degree in relations with parents. It appears to occur with greater frequency within friendship.

Similarly, mutual understanding is found in parental relations at least some of the time on some topics. In friendship it seems to be more pervasive and more regular.

From this perspective, friendship may contribute to the adolescent's exploration of individuality by providing a testing ground for how far he or she may go in expressing a separate self while still being accepted within a relationship. This is plausible because the risks involved seem less weighty than if all of the testing had to be done with parents. While adolescents prize friendship, the sociological fact is that loss of one friendship does not preempt forming other friendships. The same is not true about parental relationship where the risks are higher and the consequences more severe. Adolescents are still materially dependent on their parents and must live with them. A step too far toward asserting individuality might result in tension and conflict.

It follows that individuality, which is probably a primary issue between parents and adolescents, develops gradually through a series of accommodations. A likely prospect is that it begins first in friendship, then proceeds in the realtionship with mothers, and lastly with fathers. In all of these relationships, the issue is: How far can I go in being an individual while remaining responsive to the relationship? Individuality is, therefore, not absolute since it can proceed to higher levels in one relationship than in another at any given time. Thus, at any one time, the availability of all three relationships—mother, father, friend—gives adolescents opportunities to experience individuality in differing degrees (cf., Grotevant & Cooper, in press).

Conclusion

The tendency in the literature has been to compare parents with peers as to their respective influences and, further, to stress the differences between parents and peers. This view does not take adequate account of the structure of the parental relationships or of the relationships between friends. When structure is taken seriously, then one begins to see that each relationship has a distinctive dynamic, generates its own issues, and contributes to the development of adolescents in separate ways. Little is gained by ignoring relational structure and by positing that influence occurs through a neutral transmission process. These relationships differ in the contents that they deal with, in the forms of communication that they allow, and in the results of communication.

Contemporary adolescence has also been viewed in a context of weakened family ties and of more powerful peer persuasion. Again, this view has not adequately looked at the structure of the parental relationships or of relationships between friends. Contrary to the popular image, the descriptions from the adolescents in our samples showed that contemporary parents have not abandoned their authoritative stances or responsibilities for their sons' and daughters' socialization. Also, in contrast to another image, our studies showed that friendship appears to be a relationship that functions according to traditional prosocial principles and is not a laissez-faire association that encourages egoism.

In summary, parents are not friends, and friends are not parents. Both relationships require submission, by adolescents, of self to the common good. The respective structures of the two relationships require distinctive accommodations to make this general principle real. Hence, these two relationships contribute different, but equally valuable, experiences for the task of adolescent development.

10

The Individual and Relations

Our studies were undertaken to gain insight into the manner in which adolescents' relations with their parents and friends are means for adolescent development. In conventional approaches to adolescence, relationships are one of many elements that help adolescents gain information about themselves as they strive for self-growth and identity. From our studies we have found that relationships in adolescence are fundamental to self-definition, and their development is synonymous with the individual's development. This position was based on our previous work with children (Youniss 1980) and appears to be part of an emerging view about adolescence (e.g., Cooper, Grotevant, & Condon 1983; White, Speisman, & Costos 1983). The goal of the present chapter is to review how the relational perspective has enriched our understanding of adolescence and to demonstrate why this approach has significance for placing adolescence within a broader life-cycle context.

Two concepts in particular seem to gain clarity from a relational analysis. The first is emancipation, which refers to adolescents' insights into their past dependence on the parental bond. Children do not apparently know the degree to which their definition of self is formed in response to this bond. Adolescents, however, penetrate this mysterious hold by becoming conscious of it in what theorists consider to be a first step toward self-conscious exploration. By implication, the insight supposedly leads to weakened dependence on, and emancipation from, parents. Thus, adolescents gain the room they need to test out their new found individuality. The results of our studies, however, suggest that emancipation may not be the consequence of these insights. Rather, emancipation is a limited term because the parental relationship still retains its force. A more appropriate description seems to be that the relationship is transformed, not severed, so that adolescents still remain responsive to parental authority while they experience greater freedom from it.

The second concept that seems to require revision is that of autonomy. It ordinarily refers to the capacity of adolescents to rely on self-reasoning in place of parental approval. Autonomy cannot develop prior to emancipation but ought to follow it once adolescents experience a sense of their own agency. The results of our studies bear on this concept in several ways. First of all, even after emancipation has begun, adolescents still appear to seek parental endorsement for their ideas. Secondly, when adolescents shift their focus from parents to friends, cooperative co-construction rather than autonomous reasoning seems to be typical. These findings suggest that previous theories about autonomy may have exaggerated self-reliance at the expense of recognizing the importance of social construction and its relational basis.

Emancipation and autonomy are terms found in psychological theories. They are also, however, concepts that fit a particular sociological orientation called functionalism. According to this view, adolescence is a time to begin adapting to the society that adolescents eventually will face in adulthood. This functional society, among other things, does not respect family background, has little room for sentiment, and requires individual action that can be supported through rational justification. It is not difficult to see that this functionalist version of society meshes with and supports the traditional views about emancipation and autonomy. In this regard, psychological and sociological theory are closely intertwined.

In recent years, the functionalist position has been criticized for its depiction of society and about the model of the individual that supports that society. Among other things, the critics have pointed out that contemporary persons actually engage in more cooperative social action than the functionalists' model of individuality would predict. Further, the formal institutions that constitute society seem to operate less rationally, in a neutral sense, and more sentimentally, in the sense of regard for persons, than functionalism grants. These facts have led theorists to investigate the ties that persons maintain and the reasons why persons act for the good of their relationships rather than for individual gain. This outlook has placed adolescent relationships and adult relationships with family and friends in a new light.

Our findings are in keeping with the emerging perspective on several important points. Following emancipation, both parents and adolescents appear to participate in the transformation of their relationship—thus, making it possible for the relationship to continue in subsequent years. Simultaneously, adolescent friendships seem to be much more than relationships of convenience or for entertainment. These friendships seem to teach adolescents the advantages of cooperation—even bringing it to the point of becoming a need. In particular, adolescents recognize that self-understanding needs a reference outside of the individual. In friendship, adolescents discover that their self-reflection gains clarity when they are understood by another person and, when they reciprocally understand another person. It is plausible that this insight is carried beyond adolescence into adulthood because its importance bears so fundamentally on self-definition.

Emancipation

The evidence in our results is that adolescents do experience a kind of emancipation in which they perceive differences between their present and past relations with their parents. Our results support this point clearly when they are compared with findings about children (Damon 1977; Huard 1980; Youniss 1980). Adolescents were able to articulate the contrast crisply: "I used to listen to everything [my father said] and thought he was always right. Now I have my own opinions." Some adolescents stated this insight further in that they were conscious of the complementary nature of the way in which their dependence was conjoined to parental protectiveness: "She looked out for me." "He was concerned for my safety." "I know he's there to help." "I used to be daddy's little girl." "I was mommy's nice boy."

Insights about emancipation were expressed a second way. Adolescents perceived that their parents do not know everything and that they are persons rather than inpenetrable figures in the following statements: "I realize he's not perfect, but still he's a good man." "I'm a little bit more understanding of what it's like to be an adult." And, "I'm aware of my father as a person rather than a role; I know his faults and strengths as a person." The piercing of this mystique about parents is accompanied by adolescents seeing their parents treating them more as persons than just as sons and daughters: "He deals with me as a person, not as a child." "Now I'm really not a little girl he's beginning to realize it." "He treats me more as an equal." "He sees me as someone he can talk to—not an equal." And, "He still has the upper hand, but treats me more seriously."

The question then turns to what occurs after these insights have been made and adolescents have some understanding of how much of who and what they are is owed to the parental relationships. Here, the results are equally clear. Adolescents do not necessarily turn away from the relationship or reject it as no longer important. Instead, parental authority retains its hold as the relationship is transformed into a balance of dependence and freedom. For example, "We can talk a little now. I am not afraid to do something against his will. . . . I talk to him more." "Ask him more advice but not on personal matters. I still want to be nurtured and protected. I want his approval." And, "We're closer. I can be more open now. I'm still reserved but will air opinions. I'm still careful what I say. He feels closer to me. He will be more open and say what he's feeling if I initiate it. He may be a little afraid because I'm growing up and he can't be [the] full authority."

In excerpts such as these, the transformation seems to have begun from both the parents' and the adolescents' sides. The parents retain authority by giving more freedom to adolescents by recognizing their personal needs and capabilities. In turn, adolescents act more individualistically while still relying on their parents for advice and guidance. It is clear that parental relationships have not been discarded nor have they lost their binding power. In fact, the adolescents said that the transformation helped to bring them and their parents closer.

But even in the cases where the transformation seems to be one-sided—the adolescents view parents as persons—these adolescents still desired to retain their relationships. For instance, these adolescents said: "It was better 5 years ago. I get more defensive and fresh. He's being more pushy." "I'm not afraid to say things now. I still feel respect and look up to him." Or, "Now I'm angry. I still see him as my father. He give me more freedom, but still demands a certain amount of respect from me." And, "We did not get along at all when I was 14. Now we get along better. I don't show when I'm mad; I try to understand him." "I know he won't change. He still treats me like I'm 13 and expects me to listen to him."

A further clarification may be seen in the sort of escalation of authority that parents use as their sons and daughters proceed closer to adulthood. Although parents grant adolescents more freedom, the adolescents said their parents worry more about such things as their school performance and keeping out of trouble: "He's being more pushy . . . about school. He does more prying into my business. Still I respect him." "I know he's there to help. Sees me as his little girl. He respects me more; knows I'm older. . . But he's more demanding [and] expects more of me." Or, "He lets me do more things and he expects more of me." And, "He respects me more, knows I'm older and want to be on my own more. He's more demanding; expects more of me."

We suggest that our findings as a whole, which are resketched through the foregoing excerpts, help to clarify the concept of emancipation in several ways. The awareness by adolescents of their childhood dependence on the parental relationship leads not to detachment but to a transformation that allows the relationship to be retained. Adolescents are given, or take, greater responsibility for themselves but still seek the endorsement of their parents. One reason parents retain, and are granted, authority is that the stakes for adolescents are higher as adolescents move closer to adulthood. Parents raise their expectations, and adolescents seem to sense that they need their parents' guidance even more as they come closer to adulthood. While the alternative of detachment may occur in some instances, it is hardly the rule for the adolescents in our samples. The typical case seems to be that of a persisting relationship in which the old complementary nature of the roles is modified, but in which parental authority coexists alongside greater agency for the self.

Autonomy

The concept of autonomy has both general and specific meanings in psychological theories. In general, it refers to greater self-determination in adolescence than was possible in childhood—since children unknowingly form views to gain their parents' approval. More specifically, with the advent of cognitive theories, autonomy has come to refer to adolescents' use of self-reflective reason for coneptualizing reality and the self within it. The cognitive addition leads to two issues that may be clarified from our results. One is the degree to which adolescents rely on their self-reflection to reason out how reality is and how it ought to be ordered. And the other is the extent to which the order that is sought is directed to self-understanding.

Self-reliant Reasoning

It has already been argued that emancipation does not result in a loss of power for parental authority. Adolescents still call on their parents for advice rather than take full responsibility for their own views: "I look at him as a kind of leader . . . value his opinions. I go to him for major things." We suggest that our results, on the whole, indicate that adolescents show only a moderate kind of autonomy, one in which they still rely on their parents for verification of their own constructions. That is to say, self-reflection does not stand on its own but is coupled with social construction in which reflection is mutual rather than individual.

It seems to be the case that the concept of autonomy is most often used with reference to parental relations. In this regard, it gains obvious explanatory power through a contrast between the assertion of personal agency and the constraint of agency by parental domination. This contrast implies a shift from an earlier social construction that is paced by unilateral parental authority to a subsequent kind of construction that is more under the individual's own control. We suggest that this developmental scheme becomes substantially tempered when adolecents begin to focus on friendship, rather than on their parental relationships. To wit, within friendship, construction seems to be as much social and cooperative as it is individual.

First of all, adolescents seem to be nearly unanimous in describing friendship as a relationship in which private reflections are shared for the purposes of personal clarification and mutual understanding. Let us look now at the former element to illustrate an important point. The following excerpts are taken from the data in which adolescents described their obligations within friendship: "You have to give a friend advice when he has a problem because a lot of times when a person is involved in a problem he can't see it too well. He needs advice from the outside." Or, "If you didn't listen to your friend's problems, she wouldn't have anyone to talk to and everything would build up. You're her only hope." And, "That's what a friend is for. He takes the place of a psychologist."

These excerpts seem to represent awareness that self-reflection can be unreliable and that individuals need an external voice even for self-understanding. As one subject said: "You can't always decide what you want to do yourself. You need a second opinion." Or, as another said: "It's important to have a friend to talk to. It's rotten to have problems inside and not know what to do." It seems clear, then, that adolescents are wary of their own self-reflection and are conscious that by staying locked into their own privacy they risk getting caught in uncertainty. This reinforces the persistent result that friendship is a relationship in which adolescents open their private self-reflections with the hope of getting advice from friends—friends who will seriously take their interests as their own. This is why adolescents said: "A friend is an advisor." And, "It's really important that [adolescents] have someone who will listen to them."

We will not repeat the argument here that friendship is far more than play and that the very terms of the relationship make it possible for cooperative co-construction to occur on a regular basis. The point here is that the conventional meaning of autonomy excessively stresses what adolescents achieve through their own reasoning when the data illustrate adolescents' own emphasis on joint reasoning. The foregoing excerpts indicate that self-reflection does not begin and end within the boundaries of the individual. Adolescents take their self-reflections to friends in a process that is obviously social. Opinions are exchanged, emotions are shared, and choices are talked out. In the process, each friend's reflection is affected by the other's in a form of turn taking that is cooperative in spirit and neither competitive nor directed to conformity.

We suggest that autonomous thinking and co-construction are not incompatible theoretically because they are not incompatible in the lives of adolescents. It is recalled that friendship is the relationship in which adolescents showed the least defensiveness and felt the most like *myself*. Perhaps here, a point made earlier bears repeating. Cooperation in construction does not require conformity in the sense of giving up one's view by adopting another's view. Friendship does not obliterate the self but provides external reference which self-understanding needs. Adolescents stated: "Friends have different interests." "I look for people who think like me but if they don't agree, they keep an open mind." "Now [friends] don't have to be the same as me anymore." "I look for a person who accepts, not judges—we accept each other's bad points now." "Friends can be different now—don't have to think the same." And, "I always express myself freely now. . . I can be friends with anyone now just as long as they understand the way I am."

Mutual Understanding

One of the themes that accompanies the cognitive theorists' emphasis on autonomy is that reasoning is employed for self-understanding. Not only do individuals think on their own, they apply their thinking to themselves. Again, the reference is to parental relations and the child's unwitting effort to think in ways that will merit parents' approval. Once adolescents abandon the parental refuge, however, they face another problem of deciding how reality should be ordered so that it makes sense to them. This notion dovetails nicely with the notion that adolescents are searching for order in their new found selves. With the old prop of parents knocked out from under them, the search for order is serious since adolescents have nothing to fall back on.

This aspect of autonomy seems equally an exaggeration of the adolescent's individuality. As our results have shown, the search for order is not a lonely struggle. Adolescents join with their parents and friends who share their concerns about finding order and avoiding personal confusion. An additional question, however, is: what constitutes order? Here the stress on individuality can be misleading. Emphasis on the individual's needs clouds the possibility that social understanding is synonymous with self-understanding. As was already demonstrated, adolescents are already conscious that self-contained reflection is faulty. An accompanying awareness may be that order, itself, must be found through consensual validation and not simply in oneself.

The issue may be stated another way: What is the basis of self-understanding? To what degree are individuals self-reliant in this regard? And, how much do they rely on others for verification? We have already seen parts of the answers to these questions in adolescents' remarkable openness with their friends. During adolescence, friends appear to confide in each other with trust and honesty. One reason why adolescents do this is clearly that they believe they can learn from friends in a context which is nonthreatening: "He won't be shocked." And, "You won't be embarrassed."

We suggest that the missing element from the conventional view of self-understanding is the lack of explicit reference to the other person's part in the process of social construction. For the adolescents we interviewed, self-understanding includes two components: wanting to be understood by the other and understanding the other. Some of the adolescents said: "Now I look for a person who is interested in me." "Now I'm concerned more about them." "When I was 13, I tried to be accepted by the popular group. Now I don't care [about popularity]. I value the person." "I am more caring and understanding. I can be friends with anyone now just as long as they understand the way I am." "Before friendships were activity centered . . . Now I try to really know someone." And, "Now you have to be able to talk and be open—so someone can really relate to what you're saying."

While friendship provides an obvious case for the point at issue, the parental relationship shows equally that adolescents want to be understood by, and to understand, their parents. In citing obligations to parents, adolescents said: "You should tell him things. Talk to him. Tell him what you're doing." "Keep him posted; fill him in on your life." Or, "Talk to him . . . take your problems to him." And, "Talk to him. Try to get to know him." As we saw, most adolescents believe that their parents do not understand them well. Most also believe that they do not understand their parents, especially fathers who hide behind their work and withhold their feelings. However, adolescents' descriptions show that they desire mutual understanding and that, in some instances, they and their parents are making gains toward it. For example, one said, "We can talk now and express our feelings. . . He realized there was a communication gap and tried to overcome it. That made us closer." And even when the process has not begun, adolescents wish it had: "I've become more hostile. He doesn't understand me—doesn't know what I'm thinking."

Piaget's Perspective

It may be helpful to conclude this discussion on autonomy with a brief analysis of Piaget's writings. They have played a checkered role in generating the conventional emphasis on self-guided reasoning used for self-understanding. The cognitive theorists have used Piaget's theories to couple autonomy with formal operations, the latter being the supposed underpinning for the former (e.g., Inhelder & Piaget, 1958). However, Piaget ([1932] 1965) addressed autonomy in a relational context, in a manner much more in keeping with present findings.

Piaget argued that psychological theorists endowed autonomy with too much individualism. In that way, individualism came to signify persons standing on their own, trusting their reason, and resisting conformity. For Piaget, these meaning represent *egoism* and not autonomy because they leave out the possibility that mature autonomy comes when the individual can submit to ideas that have been validated through rules of fair and open discussion. That is, the autonomous person "takes up its stand on norms of reciprocity and objective discussion" ([1932] 1965, 95) and "knows how to submit to [norms] in order to make itself understood" ([1932] 1965, 96). Autonomy ensues from cooperation rather than through egoism, since it is in cooperative construction that the individual will "not only discover the boundaries that separate . . . self from other persons but will learn to understand the other person and be understood by him" ([1932] 1965, 95).

The importance of the relational position to the concept of autonomy has been elaborated on previously (Youniss 1980; 1981). What our present data add is a demonstration that during adolescence when autonomy begins to be developed, adolescents very much sense a responsibility to other persons, namely, their friends and their parents. It seems impausible to argue that adolescents suddenly find no need to make themselves understandable to those persons upon whom they previously most relied for self-understanding. That they might suddenly step back into the privacy of self-reflections, after that procedure has proved unreliable, seems implausible. That is why we suggest that a relational analysis adds a critical element to the concept of autonomy. Adolescents not only cooperate with others in constructing reality, but they do so with an awareness they they need to explain themselves to others or risk self-delusion or egoism.

Social Development

The results of our present studies on adolescents appear continuous with our previous findings about children. From roughly middle-childhood onward, there is a gradual but definite movement toward greater individuality. Its main elements are experiencing the self's agency and coming to know the self more clearly and fully. In this respect, our findings are congruent with most theories that stress self-awareness and increasing independence. What our findings add, however, is the simultaneous development of a social sense of self—the realization that the self does not stand alone but is responsible to other persons. This recognition develops as clearly as self-awareness does, and the two are intimately connected. Responsibility refers to realizing what is owed to others for the self's development and to recognizing that others are needed for the self's current functioning.

This formulation has ontological and sociological implications that merit further consideration. The former bears on the question raised earlier: How does a self develop out of relationships? It has been argued previously (Youniss 1980), that Piaget ([1932] 1965) and Sullivan (1953) offer a perspective that has not been pursued seriously enough by psychological theorists. The core of the perspective is that the self develops *through* relationships as they develop. This contrasts with the more conventional view that at some moment, the self steps outside relationships to assert its own independence. In such a view, relationships are an impediment to the self's growth because they constrain what the self could be were it on its own. The implicit assumption seems to be that relationships make the self dependent while the mature self is independent.

A key to seeing the perspective we propose in lieu of the conventional position is that relationships and the self develop together. There is a self, for example, in the parental relationship of childhood. That self is constrained by the need for parental approval and the awestriking power of parental authority. There is also a self in the parental relationship of later adolescence, but it is not the same self, nor is it the same relationship as was found in childhood. The relationship has been transformed so that parents' authority emanates not from uncontestable authority but from authority that needs to be justified. Adolescents can then ask for reasons behind their parents' expectations. In turn, adolescents can be called on by their parents to justify their own beliefs.

The point is made just as clearly in friendship. Adolescents say that friends can have different views and do not have to think alike. However, when differences come to the fore, either in discussion or in conflict, the friends incur the responsibility to explain themselves to one another. In neither relationship—between adolescents and parents nor between friends—is development toward the point when an individual asserts self by turning inward with recourse to self-reflective reasoning alone seen. Self-reflection is only part of a larger process, which ultimately requires that reasoning done on one's own must stand the test of social criticism and verification.

This perspective is missing from psychological theories of adolescence that make self-development contingent upon emancipation from relationships and that picture autonomy in terms of self-reliance. In the view we are proposing, the self relies on relationships and needs them to escape egoism. Self-understanding does not proceed solely through private discourse wherein the self reflects on its own reasoning. That leads to an internal spiral of infinite regression in which a self could become embedded in its own subjectivity. The way out of this inward tunnel is to take one's reflections to others for their review. It is through the movement outward that the self can learn whether others understand it and find out how others have reasoned about similar topics.

We propose a further point: Relations are more than mirrors to be used to see the self reflected in another person. The question then is how much adolescents need relationships and how committed they are to relationships for maintaining their own autonomy. Our argument is that as adolescents become aware of their interdependence with others, other persons become that much more critical to their autonomy. Not just any other persons will do, but the persons who are equally cognizant of interdependence and willing to accept the work that is required to make it real are needed. All of this hinges on the thesis that self-understanding entails reciprocity—being understood by others and understanding them. This is the gist of Piaget's definition of autonomy: "Now apart from our relations to other person, there can be no moral necessity. The individual as such knows only anomie. Autonomy therefore appears only with reciprocity, when mutual respect is strong enough to make the individual feel from within the desire to treat others as he himself would wish to be treated" (Piaget [1932] 1965, 196).

Theories of adolescence have recently begun to stress the importance of cognitive development and to use it to explain adolescent social development. The rationale is that adolescent reasoning is logical and, therefore, reliable enough to render understanding of social reality and of the self's place within it. Adolescent reasoning is also seen to be sturdy enough to yield a moral vision of what social reality ought to be. This orientation is clearly focused on the individual as an independent thinker. It fails to take adequate account of the social nature of reasoning or the relational existence of the individual. The only thing social about this cognitive position is the objects to which thinking is applied—for example, other persons as they are or should be. These theories fail to recognize that reasoning is social in "the doing," that social construction is every bit as basic as construction by the individual is. A second omission concerns relationship both in the process of construction and in the outcome.

As to the latter, an interesting dynamic seems to be at work. Cooperation in social construction depends on a reserve of shared understanding and trust between the two persons. The more that two persons participate in such social construction, the more they may come to respect each other for their participation. Implied also is a commitment to maintain relations with such persons with whom interdependence has been established. This may be why adolescents try so hard to transform their relations with their parents rather than to detach themselves from their parents. This may also be why adults, when asked who their intimate friends are, name persons with whom they were friends during their youth (Fischer 1977, chapter 5).

In summary, growth of the self need not be incompatible with the development of relations. The two can be conceived as simultaneous and interconnected. The problem occurs when relations are viewed as an impediment to self-growth. But relationships are not static, as is evident in the apparent transformation of parental relations from childhood to adolescence. The warp found in conceptions of autonomy seems to be due to an exaggerated emphasis on individual self-reliance, abetted by the orientation of cognitive theorists. While it seems correct that adolescent reasoning is developed well beyond that of children, it does not follow that adolescent reasoning is any more individualistic. Indeed, the opposite may be the case. Adolescents seem aware of how much of themselves they owe—in what they think and who they are—to others. Their consciousness of these obligations need not lead to stepping out of relations. On the contrary, what seems to follow is a serious pursuit of relationships that cultivate interdependence so that self-understanding can be enhanced through mutual understanding.

The Sociological Context

There is a debate among sociologists today as to how individualistic and how rational contemporary persons are, or must be, as they adapt to modern society. The focal point is the Parsonian functionalism of the 1950s and 1960s, which is now seen more and more as a paean to individualism and rationality. It will be recalled that Parsons attempted to correct the abstract character of the person found in behavioristic theories. He was committed to analyzing action but not action devoid of meaning. His remedy was to assess action with society as a context so that action could be seen as a useful adaptation to society's systems and structures. It followed from this position that the personality and the person's value orientation were socially conditioned (e.g., Parsons & Bales 1955).

In Parsons's view, and for functionalism in general, the psychological makeup of individuals is not independent of the societal structure in which individuals live. How one views society, then, very much determines what one emphasizes psychologically. It is recalled here that for functionalists, modern society was seen as something new and distinctive from societies in the past. Among other things, its structure was such as to favor achievement over ascription, specificity over diffuseness, and generalism over particularism (Johnson 1975). These well-known pattern variables were means of saying that modern society rewarded persons who defined themselves through personal achievements and pursued their aims through rational calculation.

The implications for psychology are clear. One example is seen in Parsons's analysis of socialization in the family (Parsons & Bales 1955). Adaptive socialization is that which orients offspring toward their individuality by promoting achievement through objective standards. In a society that rewards individuals for what they have accomplished rather than because of their family background (e.g., who their parents were), demanding too strong a tie to family would be maladaptive. An additional instance can be seen for the diffuseness-specificity variable. Socialization that is adaptive would orient offspring toward segregating transactions according to topical domains, each domain requiring its own rational analysis. For example, an economic transaction would be appraised with a kind of cost-benefit analysis that discounts the particular individuals who are involved, feelings toward them, or effects that might follow for secondary parties.

It is not difficult to see that the functionalist depiction of society provides a ready context for the psychological concepts of emancipation and autonomy. The two reinforce each other, however implicit their connection may be. They become even more entwined when other assumption are added. For example, those who recognize that society is continually changing note that parents can contribute less and less to their children's socialization. For instance, in the late nineteenth century, fathers could not apply their own work experiences to prepare their sons for work. Fathers could not even envision the kinds of work their sons would be doing in white-collar, corporate positions—dealing with the management of personnel, distribution, procurement, or marketing (e.g., Sennett 1974). This generation gap in the intergenerational transmission of experience has continued through the present century and is still evident today. How many parents born in the 1940s are, today, able to prepare their adolescent sons or daughters for employment in modern technological positions? Or, how do these parents prepare adolescents for marriage given the rich mixture of trends involving reduced and delayed fertility, greater prospects of divorce, changed values toward female employment, and debate about the division of labor within the family?

Perhaps a more compelling example of the tie between sociological perspectives and psychological concepts is seen in the popular notion of identity search. Surely, in the recapturable history of adolescence in western society, identity searching was not an obvious problem for adolescents (see Gillis 1981; Kett 1977). It is, however, recognized as a problem for contemporary adolescents whose choices for future work, place of residence, and sex role seem open, and not fixed. Although theorists, who focus on the identity-search issue, do not refer to the social context explicitly, it may serve as the presumptive wellspring for their psychological characterization of the adolescent.

Relationships Still Count

In the sociological reaction to functionalism, two clear themes have begun to emerge. The first is that society may not have changed so much as the functionalists suggest. Specifically, individualism has not replaced the need for relationships or the commitment to the responsibilities of relationships. This seems to be the gist of sociological studies that demonstrate the importance of membership in networks in which persons exchange ideas, provide reciprocal support, and keep track of one another (e.g., Bott 1971; see Smith 1980, for the relevance of such studies to the debate on functionalism).

As Fischer (1977) states the findings, who you know has not been eclipsed by what you know. Particularism and diffuseness have not been replaced by universalism or specificity. Persons are still evaluated as wholes—not just for what they do—and the evaluation includes affect and sentiment; it is not solely rational. Rather than defining themselves as free-standing individuals, contemporary adults see themselves as intimates with their parents, siblings, and friends for all of whom they feel responsible and to whom they feel closely tied (e.g., Wellman 1979). The importance of these findings is that the relations that adults maintain cannot be assessed solely in instrumental terms that allow one to identify what the self's gain or advantage is. The relations seem to be maintained out of respect for the past, for the psychological pleasure they provide, or for the comfort that is derived from them.

Important evidence on this point has come from those investigators who have looked closely at the presumed historical shift that differentiates traditional from modern society. An interesting example is found in the work of Hareven (1982), who studied family life in the textile-manufacturing setting of Manchester, New Hampshire, from the early 1800s to the early 1900s. Among other things, she noted that immigrants who came to the mills and found work could be called individualistically modern in the sense that they had left their families and communities for employment opportunities (self-gain) elsewhere. She observed, however, that these same immigrants invited their relatives to join them, helped them find jobs, and set up communal, mutual-aid subsocieties within the new industrial setting. Industrialization did not create individualism nor destroy family ties. Rather, persons took advantage of industrialization to better, not only their own conditions, but the conditions of those to whom they felt relationally committed.

Historians also have been able to address more closely the bearing of industrialization on the parent-adolescent bond. Tilly, Scott, and Cohen (1979) reported that in western Europe, female youths who moved away from their families for employment in cities did not sever their ties with their families or construct values, such as sexual exploration, that would give them more individual freedom (cf., Shorter 1975). Rather, these daughters sent part of their wages back home to help their parents and seem to have retained conservative attitudes toward sexual practices and marriage, as if their parents had been present, monitoring them.

Katz (1981) has looked more closely at the intergenerational issue during industrialization in Hamilton, Ontario. The problem that parents began to face was whether to have their sons work so that their wages could be added to the family's income or to take their sons out of the labor market in order to enhance their education. The latter choice was obviously less instrumentally beneficial than the former. The latter had prospects of bettering the sons' futures at the cost of immediate family income. The latter, however, was the choice most parents made (see also Gillis 1981; Kett 1977).

These historical data hardly seem inconsistent with our results. For one thing, contemporary parents sacrifice their own savings for their sons' and daughters' educations under the apparent belief that benefit will accrue to them through the betterment of their sons' and daughters' futures. It is not surprising to find, then, that offspring, after they have become successful, feel committed to their parents, even to values their parents hold that seem outdated for contemporary society.

Gillis has provided a sane voice which brings the historical data sharply to bear on the exaggerated claims regarding the maladaptiveness of family ties and the adolescent's individualism:

> Young members of a particular class experience the world differently from the way their elders experience it, but both share a common heritage. The popular notion of "generation gap" ignores this totality and should be used only with great caution. There are, of course, different generations, whose placement in the overall historical process causes them to view the world in contrasting, sometimes conflicting ways; but there is also enormous continuity within a particular class, gender, or ethnic group that binds together the generations in common outlook and behavior. . . The essential continuity of generations within class, sex, and ethnic groups is borne out by recent American studies that have underlined the solidarity within these groups (1981, 219).

Gillis is equally clear in noting the positive value of social solidarity among youth:

> Historical experience provides the tools with which each generation hammers out its orientation to the world. . . Layer upon layer of youth cultures have been laid down over the centuries. . . Categorizing them into normal and deviant subcultures does violence to both the present and the past by obscuring the way in which the present variety of youth cultures has developed historically and how each serves to express authentic, though conflicting, interests and values. . . Young people are

makers as well as receivers of tradition. Each generation redefines its traditions to meet its particular needs (1981, 218–19).

The Place of Relations

The second point in the sociological reaction to functionalism is that relations, which have persisted, serve a special role in existence. They are essential to individual functioning—without them the individual runs the risks of alienation and uncertainty. Individuals need to know that others understand them and think as they do. The individual needs to feel transcendent beyond self, as belonging to something with others. This sense of cohesion is every bit as fundamental to the person as is individual identity (Furth 1983; Macmurray 1961). Theorists, such as Habermas (1979), who recognize the shift from traditional to modern society also see a *split* in modernity. On the one hand, objective social systems require individualistic adaptations. On the other hand, and at the same time, individuals seek, and live in, relations with others. The aim of individualistic adaptations is to gain self-advantage, as the individual is pitted against the rules of systems and other individuals. In contrast, the goal of individuals seeking relations with others is intersubjective understanding, which is oriented toward consensus (see also Held 1980, 332).

Intersubjective, or mutual, understanding is not a frivolity but a fundamental. It is as necessary to existence as is self-understanding. The two are intertwined. An analogy is seen in a proposal offered by Kropotkin (1902): In evolution there are two laws, not just one. The law that most recognize is one of competition. A law of equal strength, that fewer recognize, is the law of mutual aid. Evolution would be different if only one of these laws were in effect. The two laws, which are simultaneous, give humans their peculiar character. They can compete in the economic sphere one moment and tend to family traditions or pursue religious interests the next.

One gets a clearer sense of why relations are fundamental and not derivative, or secondary, elements from reading more closely the story of western society's history. Braudel (1979) provides a set of interesting examples as he tries to trace the growth of capitalism in Europe. After describing elements such as fairs, markets, shops, exchanges, and banks, he takes on individual cases of trade that required a minimum of four transactions before a profit could be made on a commodity. Several persons were involved in these transactions. Braudel's question was: How did the process become reliable? How did the initiator of the transactions avoid risk when there were so many intermediaries involved in these transactions that covered several continents and long time spans?

In the cases he cites, the reliability of the process was insured by the explicit use of interpersonal relations. One device was to spread family members around the globe so that each was located at a strategic point. Another was to use marriage so that different banking houses became interlocked through kinship. Another was to stay within ethnic confines that were established through well-placed networks, for example, of Armenians or Jews. And a fourth device was to use religious bonds, such as Hugenots forming solidarity unions within Europe's large trading centers. These examples are similar to Hareven's in that relations are used to exploit the modern system. These instances are critical because one sees directly that the objective social system did not disassemble the traditional patterns of relationships. Rather, the traditional patterns were turned on the system for the group's advantage.

The theme of a split in modernity has been carried beyond the economic sector to government—another obvious example of where individualism seems called for. From Gouldner (1960), to Lowi (1969), to Bell (1973), one sees the coexistence of two modes of functioning. In one, the system is specific, universal, and individualistic and operates impersonally for strategic efficiency. In the other, the rules are diffuse, particular, and collective. The distinction is between the formal decision-making process, when for example technical information is gathered and submitted to cost-benefit analysis, and politics. The former is clearly a rational enterprise. The latter is run by the meeting of interest groups who must bargain and negotiate to reach a decision that is a political compromise among the interested parties.

These examples taken from the view of objective social systems are designed to show that relations still have binding power and have not dissipated in force with the rise of the individual in modern society. They may at first seem far removed from psychology and the problems of adolescence. We suggest that they are relevant because they illustrate the place of relations in the sociological context. If adolescence is a time for replacing childish adaptations by preparing for adulthood, then, the kind of society into which the adolescent is moving must be made clear. There is a sort of maladaptation for relation in the society the functionalists have sketched. Their view of society supports individuals who are detached from their relationships and who have faith in their own reasoning. There is, however, a central place for relations in the two-layered society depicted in the above examples. In the latter, bonds among persons serve adaptation in a society whose apparent structure is objective but whose infrastructure is intersubjective.

Lastly, we would add that when relations are viewed in this light, relations with parents and with friends become more similar than different. Both, but each in its own way, teach the adolescent how to deal with the tasks of intersubjectivity. In both relationships, the aim is to understand and be understood. And, in both, the process is more that of cooperation than competition. The aim and process differ, of course, when the focus turns to the individual and to social systems. The importance of this point can be seen further by recognizing that family relationships do not near an end during adolescence, today, as they once historically did (cf., Degler 1980; Kett 1977). In contemporary life, the prospect for a long and continuing bond between adolescents, their parents, and siblings is real. The kind of mutual aid the family provides vis-à-vis society, for the adolescent may continue through adulthood—even to the point when the relationship is reversed between the adult offspring and their elderly parents. Needless to say, the sort of mutual aid and consensus understanding that is available in the friendships of adolescents remain available through the same as well as in new friendships that are established in their adult years.

Appendix A

Appendix B

Study 4

Below are a list of statements given to us by other teenagers describing the kind of things that cause conflict between them and their mothers.

For each statement, we would like to know how often this happens in your relationship with your mother and how serious a conflict it causes when it does happen. After each item, put an X in the column that best fits what happens in your relationship with your mother.

	Happens often	Happens Sometimes	Never Happens	Caused a Conflict	Did not cause Conflict
1. I don't do what my mother tells me to do.					
2. I came in two hours later than my mother told me to.					
3. I went someplace where my mother told me not to go.					
4. I didn't clean my room like my mother asked me.					
5. I got lower grades in school than my mother expected of me.					
6. I drank too much and my mother caught me.					
7. When my mother scolds me for doing something wrong, I talk back to her.					
8. I yell at my mother when I'm in a bad mood.					
9. I stopped talking to my mother for a week when she made me mad.					
10. I lied to my mother about something important.					
11. I didn't tell my mother about my feelings when I was depressed.					
12. My mother is unfair.					

	Happens often	Happens Sometimes	Never Happens	Caused a Conflict	Did not cause Conflict
13. My mother grounded me for a week when I did a little thing wrong.					
14. My mother expects me to do too much work around the house.					
15. My mother tries to tell me which friends I can and cannot see					
16. My mother searches my room to check on things.					
17. My mother criticizes me a lot.					
18. My mother won't listen when I have a problem.					
19. My mother lied to me about something important.					
20. There are some things about my mother's personality that I don't like.					
21. My mother won't let me go to some place I want to.					

For each statement we would like to know how often this happens in your relationship with your close friend (whether or not you or your friend caused the problem) and how serious a conflict it causes when it does happen. After each item, put an X in the column that best fits what happens in your relationship with your close friend of the same sex.

	Happened More than once	Happened Once	Never Happened	Caused a Conflict	Did not cause a Conflict
1. My close friend spends more time with another girl(boy) than with me.					
2. I made some new friends that my close friend doesn't like very much.					
3. My close friend will just ignore me for a week.					
4. I have a boyfriend(girlfriend) and don't have much time for my close friend anymore.					
5. My close friend made plans to go to a party with me but didn't show up.					
6. I had a party but didn't invite my close friend.					
7. I went to a picnic with a close friend but he(she) spent all his time with other people.					
8. My close friend told me a secret and I told someone else.					
9. I knew my close friend had a personal problem but he(she) wouldn't talk to me about it.					
10. I lied to my close friend about something important.					
11. My close friend talked about me behind my back.					
12. I believed a rumor about my close friend before finding out if it was true or not.					
13. My close friend criticizes me.					
14. I got in trouble once and blamed my close friend and got him(her) in trouble.					
15. I asked my close friend for help with schoolwork but he(she) said he didn't have time.					
16. I argued with my close friend over a difference of opinion instead of just accepting it.					
17. My close friend and I had a fight over a disagreement instead of trying to compromise.					
18. I wasn't very careful with my close friend's things and broke something.					
19. When I asked my close friend for a loan, he(she) said no.					
20. My close friend helped me when I needed it, but I didn't help her(him) when he(she) needed it.					
21. My close friend accidentally damaged something valuable belonging to me.					
22. I used something my close friend owned without asking for permission first.					
23. My close friend has a problem with drinking too much.					
24. My close friend had a personal problem and I gave him(her) a lecture about it.					
25. My close friend criticized someone who is a friend of mine.					
26. I started fooling around with my close friend's boyfriend (girlfriend).					

Appendix C

The following statements are about you and your MOTHER.

Think of the times when your MOTHER wants you to do something when you want to do something else. How often does your MOTHER do the following things when she wants you to do something?

	Hardly Ever	Not Often	Often	Very Often
1. My MOTHER keeps talking to me about what she wants me to do hoping I would start wanting to do it.	1	2	3	4
2. My MOTHER says I'm supposed to do what she tells me to do.	1	2	3	4
3. My MOTHER says I would enjoy doing what she wants me to do.	1	2	3	4
4. My MOTHER simply tells me to do it.	1	2	3	4
5. My MOTHER says she expects me to do what she tells me.	1	2	3	4
6. My MOTHER tells me that she would do favors for me at other times if I would go along with her now.	1	2	3	4
7. My MOTHER keeps telling me to do it until I do it.	1	2	3	4
8. My MOTHER asks me if I would be willing to do it.	1	2	3	4

The following questions are about you and your FRIEND who is of the same sex as you. Answer the following questions with that FRIEND in mind.

Seven topics of conversation are listed and underlined below. What happens when you and your FRIEND talk about these topics?

	Not Often	Some-times	Often	We don't discuss this
About the way you handle your school work or what you should do to make better grades.				
a) My FRIEND explains the reasons for his(her) ideas.	1	2	3	0
b) My FRIEND really tries to understand my ideas.	1	2	3	0
About the way you behave toward your friends or problems you may have with your friends.				
a) My FRIEND explains the reasons for his(her) ideas.	1	2	3	0
b) My FRIEND really tries to understand my ideas.	1	2	3	0
About your future school and job plans.				
a) My FRIEND explains the reasons for his(her) ideas.	1	2	3	0
b) My FRIEND really tries to understand my ideas.	1	2	3	0
About what you should, or should not, do on dates.				
a) My FRIEND explains the reasons for his(her) ideas.	1	2	3	0
b) My FRIEND really tries to understand my ideas.	1	2	3	0
About the way you behave toward your family or problems you may have with your family.				
a) My FRIEND explains the reasons for his(her) ideas.	1	2	3	0
b) My FRIEND really tries to understand my ideas.	1	2	3	0
About religious beliefs such as what you think about God and other religious teachings.				
a) My FRIEND explains the reasons for his(her) ideas.	1	2	3	0
b) My FRIEND really tries to understand my ideas.	1	2	3	0
About social issues such as racial and sexual discrimination, draft for military service, and welfare programs.				
a) My FRIEND explains the reasons for his(her) ideas.	1	2	3	0
b) My FRIEND really tries to understand my ideas.	1	2	3	0

Appendix D

Age _____

Sex _____

Grade _____

Dear Student:

This questionnaire is part of a large study we have been conducting over the past 5 years. We are interested in finding out what teenagers think about their relationships with their friends and parents and what goes on in these relationships. We believe that this information will lead to a better understanding of teenagers in America and will help social scientists, teachers and parents understand the kinds of issues and problems that teenagers deal with in their day-to-day lives.

We really appreciate your help in this work. We understand that some of these questions may seem personal to you, but sometimes it is necessary for us to ask "personal" questions in order to find out the things we want to know. Remember, do not put your name on this questionnaire. In this way we can assure you complete confidentiality with regard to your answers.

Again, thank you very much for your help.

Sincerely,

Jim Youniss

Jackie Smollar

Part I: Section A

In this section, we would like you to tell us what kinds of interactions are most likely to take place in your relationships with your close friend of the same sex as you, your close friend of the opposite sex, your mother, and your father. For example, does the statement: "This person and I talk openly to each other." best describe what goes on in your relationship with your same-sex friend? your mother? or, your father? If your answer is "same-sex friend," please put a check mark (✓) in the column with the heading "Same-Sex Friend." Remember, you are to check only the person with whom this behavior is MOST LIKELY to take place. IMPORTANT: Please check only one person for each statement unless you feel that the behavior is equally likely to take place with two people. Then you may check two people. Also remember that the same-sex friend and opposite-sex friend are not to be brothers or sisters.

Interactions	Mother	Father	Same-Sex Close-Friend	Opp-Sex Close-Friend
1. This person and I always talk openly to each other.				
2. I am not interested in any advice this person has to offer.				
3. When we disagree, this person usually insists that I change my point of view.				
4. This person and I are not embarrassed to talk about our doubts and fears to each other.				
5. When we don't agree, this person usually listens carefully to my side of the issue.				
6. This person does not consider my advice worth seeking.				
7. I am usually very careful what I say to this person.				
8. When we disagree, this person usually says I should change my opinion because he/she knows more than me.				

Part I: Section B

In this section we would like you to tell us how you feel in each of these four relationships. For example, if the description "Helpful" describes the way you act or how you feel in each of these four relationships. For example, if the MOTHER, put a check mark (✓) in the column with the heading MOTHER next to the description. "Helpful." Check only ONE PERSON for each self description. Again, remember that same-sex and opposite-sex friends are not to be brothers or sisters.

I AM MOST LIKELY TO BE:

| | | | WHEN I AM WITH MY: | |
| | | | Same-Sex | Opp.-Sex |
	Mother	Father	Close-Friend	Close-Friend
Outgoing				
Judgmental				
Helpful				
Honest				
Agrumentative				
Open				
Withdrawn				
Sensitive				
Myself				
Selfish				
Dishonest				
Insensitive				
Careful what I say				
Cooperative				

Interactions	Mother	Father	Same-Sex Close-Friend	Opp-Sex Close-Friend
9. When there is a disagreement between us, this person usually talks out the differences with me.				
10. I usually hide my true feelings from this person.				
11. When we disagree, this person usually gives me good reasons why I should change my point of view.				
12. This person has never admitted any fears or doubts to me.				
13. This person always accepts my point of view even if it is different from his/hers.				
14. This person and I usually depend on each other for advice.				
15. This person does not express his/ her true feelings to me.				
16. When we disagree, this person usually gets upset if I don't change my point of view.				
17. I would never admit my doubts or fears to this person.				
18. This person and I always tell each other our true feelings.				
19. This person does not talk openly to me.				
20. When we disagree, this person usually tries to convince me that it is in my best interest to adopt his/her point of view.				

Part I: Section C

In this section, we would like to know what you talk about in each of these same four relationships. For example, if you have a problem in school, who are you MOST likely to talk to about it? This time we also want you to tell us who you are LEAST likely to talk to about this topic. In this section, we would like you to go through the list of topics once, indicating with an "M" in the correct column the person you are MOST likely to talk to about a particular topic. Then, please go through the list again and put al "L" for the person who you would be LEAST likely to talk to about each topic. Again, remember that same-sex and opposite-sex close friends are not to be brothers or sisters.

TOPICS OF CONVERSATION	Mother	Father	Same-Sex Close-Friend	Opp.-Sex Close-Friend
1. How well I am doing in school.				
2. My views on religion.				
3. My career goals.				
4. Problems I may have with my mother.				
5. My feelings about a close friend. (of the same sex)				
6. My views about sex.				
7. Doubts I may have about my own abilities.				
8. Problems I may have at school.				
9. My feelings about my brother or sister.				
10. My hopes and plans for the future.				
11. Problems I may have with a close friend (opposite-sex).				
12. My political beliefs.				
13. My attitude toward marriage.				
14. My feelings about my mother.				

I AM MOST LIKELY TO BE:	WHEN I AM WITH MY:			
	Mother	Father	Same-Sex Close-Friend	Opp.-Sex Close-Friend
Serious				
Playful				
Phony				
Accepting				
Relaxed				
Trusting				
Uncomfortable				
Secure				
Accepted				
Loved				
Distrustful				
Criticized				
Unwanted				
Distant				
Close				
Insecure				

Part I: Section D

In this section, we would like to know what kinds of things happen in your relationship with your parents which either upset you or upset your parents. In an earlier study, students your age wrote down a list of things that tended to make their parents or themselves upset. We have chosen a few of those and we would like to know if they happen in your family, and, if so, do they happen more often with your mother or with your father. We would like you to put a check mark (✓) in the column that best fits each statement. For example if the statement: "My parents gets upset when I don't do my chores after I've been told to." describes something that NEVER HAPPENS in your home, put a check mark (✓) in the column with that heading. If it does describe something that happens in your home, indicate with your checkmark whether it happens more often with your mother or more often with your father.

	Never Happens	Happens with mother more often than with father	Happens with father more often than with mother
1. My parent gets upset when I don't do my chores after I've been told to.			
2. My parent gets upset when I stay out later than I'm supposed to.			
3. My parent gets upset when I don't tell him/her my problems.			
4. My parent get upset when I don't tell him/her what's going on in my life outside the home.			
5. My parent gets upset when I con't do well in school.			
6. My parent gets upset when I get into trouble at school.			
7. My parent gets upset when I purposely ignore him/her.			
8. My parent gets upset when I yell at him/her.			
9. My parent gets upset when I don't help out when I'm asked.			
10. My parent gets upset when I don't let him/her know when I'm going to be late coming home.			

TOPICS OF CONVERSATION	Mother	Father	Same-Sex Close-Friend	Opp.-Sex Close-Friend
15. The fears I may have about life.				
16. Problems I may have with my father.				
17. My moral standards, what I think is right and wrong.				
18. My feelings about a close friend. (opposite sex)				
19. Problems I may have with my brother or sister.				
20. My views on society.				
21. My feelings about my father.				
22. Problems I may have with a close friend. (same-sex friend)				

IMPORTANT: Please REMEMBER to go through the list again and put an "L" in the column of the person who you are LEAST likely to talk to about each topic.

Part II: Section A

In this section we are interested in your friendships. Below is a list of statements to be answered either TRUE or FALSE about your friendships or your views about friendship. If the statement is TRUE or MOSTLY TRUE about your friendship, please put a T in the blank in front of the statement. If it is FALSE or MOSTLY FALSE, please put an F in front of the statement.

IMPORTANT: Please answer each statement with either a T or an F. DO NOT use both T and F for one statement.

___ 1. I have always had some difficulty making friends.

___ 2. I have at least one very close friend who means a lot to me.

___ 3. Most of the time, I would rather be by myself than with other people.

___ 4. Right now in my life, I feel my close friends understand me better than my parents do.

___ 5. I believe that my friends value my friendship.

___ 6. I usually spend more of my "free time" with my parents than with my friends.

___ 7. I have always had a lot of problems in my friendships.

___ 8. Friends are nice to have but they are not really important to me.

___ 9. If I have a personal problem, I am as likely to go to my parents for help as to my close friend.

___ 10. Once I become friends with someone, we usually stay friends a long time.

___ 11. I think it's nice to have people to do things with, but I don't like to get too close to my friends.

___ 12. I feel I am more my real "self," more myself, when I'm with my close friend than when I am with my parents.

___ 13. Even when I was younger, my friendships never seemed to last very long.

___ 14. I usually spend about the same amount of "out-of-school" time with my friends as with my parents.

___ 15. I don't really care whether other people want to be friends with me or not.

___ 16. At my age now, I feel I learn more important things from my relationship with close friends than I do from my relationships with my parents.

___ 17. I usually make friends easily.

___ 18. I have never had a relationship I would describe as a really close friendship, even when I was younger.

___ 19. I feel that at this stage in my life, my parents understand me as well as my close friends do.

	Never Happens	Happens with mother more often than with father	Happens with father more often than with mother
11. I get upset when my parent won't let me go out somewhere when I want to.			
12. I get upset when my parent makes me do something I don't want to do.			
13. I get upset when my parent criticizes me.			
14. I get upset when my parent yells at me.			
15. I get upset when my parent doesn't listen to me when I have a problem.			
16. I get upset when my parent doesn't try to understand my point of view.			
17. I get upset when my parent says one thing but does another.			
18. I get upset when my parent doesn't tell me the truth.			

Part II: Section B

In this section we are also presenting statements to be answered either with a T if the statement is more true for you or with an F if the statement is mostly false for you. These statements deal with things you feel your parents or your friends do for you. In addition, we would like you to tell us what you do, in return, for your parents and your friends. Please give us as specific information as possible. This information will help us to understand the kinds of give-and-take that go on in different types of relationships.

_____ 1. My mother usually makes sure that I get the things I need. For example she gives me money to by things, good food, and clothes.

Since my mother does this for me, I usually _____ for her.

Since my mother does not do this for me, I usually _____ for her.

_____ 2. My mother is usually sensitive to my feelings. For example, she listens when I have a problem.

Since my mother does this for me, I usually _____ for her.

Since my mother does not do this for me, I usually _____ for her.

_____ 3. My mother usually helps me get along with people. For example, she gave me advice on how to get along with family members and friends.

Since my mother does this for me, I usually _____ for her.

Since my mother does not do this for me, I usually _____ for her.

_____ 4. My close friend usually sees to it that I have something if I need it. For example, if I need to borrow money or a book for school, my friend will give it to me.

Since my close friend does this for me, I usually _____ for her/him.

Since my close friend does not do this for me, I usually _____ for her/him.

_____ 20. For as long as I can remember, friendships have never really been that important to me.

_____ 21. I don't have a lot of problems in my friendships, they usually run pretty smooth.

_____ 22. I feel that I am my real "self" when I'm with both my parents and my close friend.

_____ 23. I don't like to have really close friendships because when they break up, it hurts too much.

Part II: Section C

In this section we would just like you to answer some questions. Please be specific in your answers.

1. Name one thing you most like doing with your mother

2. Name one thing you most like doing with your father

3. Name one thing you most like doing with your best friend of the same sex.

4. Name one thing you most like doing with your best friend of the opposite sex.

5. Name one thing that your mother does that hurts your relationship with her.

6. Name one thing that you do that hurts your relationship with your mother.

7. Name one thing that your father does that hurts your relationship with him.

8. Name one thing that you do that hurts your relationship with your father.

9. Name one thing that your best friend does that hurts your friendship.

10. Name one thing that you do to your best friend that hurts your friendship.

11. Name one thing that could be done to improve the relation between you and your mother.

12. Name one thing that could be done to improve the relation between you and your father.

13. Name one thing that could be done to improve the relation between you and your best friend.

14. Name one thing that could be done to improve the relation between you and your boyfriend/girlfriend.

---

5. My close friend is usually sensitive to my feelings. For example, when I have a problem, she listens to me.

Since my close friend does this for me, I usually _____ for her/him.

Since my close friend does not do this for me, I usually _____ for her/him.

6. My close friend usually helps me get along better with people. For example she/he will give me advice on how to get along with family members and friends.

Since my close friend does this for me, I usually _____ for her/him.

Since my close friend does not do tfis for me, I usually _____ for her/him.

7. My father usually makes sure that I have the things I need. For example, he gives me money when I need it or buys me things I need for school.

Since my father does this for me, I usually _____ for him.

Since my father does not do this for me, I usually _____ for him.

8. My father is usually sensitive to my feelings. For example, he listens when I have a problem.

Since my father does this for me, I usually _____ for him.

Since my father does not do this for me, I usually _____ for him.

9. My father usually helps me get along better with other people. For example, he gives me advice on how to get along better with family members and friends.

Since my father does this for me, I usually _____ for him.

Since my father does not do this for me, I usually _____ for him.

References

Adelson, J., and M. J. Doehrman. 1980. The psychodynamic approach to adolescence. In J. Adelson, ed., *Handbook of adolescent psychology*, 99–116. New York: Wiley.

Advisory Committee on Child Development. 1976. *Toward a national policy for children and families*. Washington, D.C.: National Academy of Sciences.

Ainsworth, M. D. S. 1969. Object relations, dependency, and attachment: A theoretical review of the infant-mother relationship. *Child Development* 40:969–1025.

Arend, R., F. L. Gove, and A. L. Sroufe. 1979. Continuity of individual adaptation from infancy to kindergarten. *Child Development* 50:950–59.

Aries, P. 1962. *Centuries of childhood: A social history of family life*. New York: Knopf.

Barker, R. G., and H. F. Wright. 1955. *Midwest and its children*. New York: Harper and Row.

Baumrind, D. 1975. Early socialization and adolescent competence. In S. E. Dragastin and G. H. Elder, Jr., eds., *Adolescence in the life cycle*, 117–43. New York: Halstedt.

Bell, D. 1973. *The coming of post-industrial society*. New York: Basic Books.

Bell D. C., and L. G. Bell. 1983. Parental validation and support in the development of adolescent daughters. In H. D. Grotevant and C. R. Cooper, eds., *Adolescent development in the family*, 27–42. San Francisco: Jossey-Bass.

Bengtson, V. L., and L. Troll. 1978. Youth and their parents: Feedback and intergenerational influence on socialization. In R. M. Lerner and G. B. Spanier, eds., *Child influences on marital and family interaction: A life-span perspective*, 215–40. New York: Academic Press.

Bernard, J. 1981. *The female world*. New York: Free Press.

Berndt, T. J. 1979. Developmental changes in conformity to peers and parents. *Developmental Psychology* 15:608–16.

———. 1982. The features and effects of friendship in early adolescence. *Child Development* 53:1447–60.

191

Bigelow, B. J. 1977. Children's friendship expectations: A cognitive developmental study. *Child Development* 48:246–53.

Bigelow, B. J., and J. J. LaGaipa. 1975. Children's written descriptions of friendship: A multidimensional analysis. *Developmental Psychology* 11:857–58.

Blasi, A. 1980. Bridging moral cognition and moral action: A critical review of the literature. *Psychological Bulletin* 88:1–45.

Blos, P. 1962. *On adolescence: A psychoanalytic interpretation*. New York: Free Press.

————. 1967. The second individuation process of adolescence. *The Psychoanalytic Study of the Child* 22:162–86.

Bott, E. 1971. *Family and social network*. 2d ed. London: Tavistock.

Braudel, F. 1979. *The wheels of commerce: Civilization and capitalism 15th to 18th century*. Vol. 2. New York: Harper and Row.

Braungart, R. G. 1980. Youth movements. In J. Adelson ed., *Handbook of Adolescent Psychology*, 560–97. New York: Wiley.

Brittain, C. V. 1963. Adolescent choices and parent-peer cross-pressures. *American Sociological Review* 28:385–91.

Bronfenbrenner, U. 1970. *Two worlds of childhood: U.S. and U.S.S.R.* New York: Basic Books.

Burke, R. J., and T. Weir. 1979. Helping responses of parents and peers and adolescent well-being. *Journal of Psychology* 102:49–62.

Burlin, F. 1976. The relationship of parental education and maternal work and occupational status to occupational aspiration in adolescent females. *Journal of Vocational Behavior* 9:99–104.

Campbell, M. M., and K. Cooper. 1975. Parents' perceptions of adolescent behavior problems. *Journal of Youth and Adolescence* 4:309–20.

Chaffee, S. H., J. M. McLeod, and B. D. Wackman. 1973. Family communication patterns and adolescent political participation. In J. Denis, ed., *Socialization to politics*, 349–64. New York: Wiley.

Cline, F. 1980. Adolescent-parent conflict. *Nurse Practioner* 5:55–56.

Coleman, J. 1961. *The adolescent society*. New York: Free Press.

Cooper, C. R., H. D. Grotevant, and S. M. Condon. 1983. Individuality and connectedness in the family as a context for adolescent identity formation and role-taking skill. In H. D. Grotevant and C. R. Cooper, eds., *Adolescent development in the family: New directions for child development*. 43–60. San Francisco: Jossey-Bass.

Cott, N. F. 1977. *The bonds of womanhood: Woman's sphere in New England, 1780–1835*. New Haven: Yale University Press.

Csikzentmihalyi, M., and R. Larson. 1984. *Being adolescent: Conflict and growth in the teenage years*. New York: Basic Books.

Damon, W. 1977. *The social world of the child*. San Francisco: Jossey-Bass.

Davis, K. 1940. Sociology of parent-youth conflict. *American Sociological Review* 1:523–35.

Degler, C. 1980. *At odds: Women and the family in America from the revolution to the present*. New York: Oxford University Press.

Douvan, E., and J. Adelson. 1966. *The adolescent experience*. New York: Wiley.

Eder, D. and M. T. Hallinan. 1978. Sex differences in children's friendships. *American Sociological Review* 43:237–50.

Elder, G. H., Jr. 1980. Adolescence in historical perspective. In J. Adelson, ed., *Handbook of Adolescent Psychology,* 3–46. New York: Wiley.

Emmerich, H. J. 1978. The influence of parents and peers on choices made by adolescents. *Journal of Youth and Adolescence* 7:175–80.

Erikson, E. H. 1968. *Identity: Youth and crisis.* New York: Norton.

Fischer, C. S. 1977. *Networks and places: Relations in the urban setting.* New York: Free Press.

Fischer, J. L. 1981. Transitions in relationship style from adolescence to young adulthood. *Journal of Youth and Adolescence* 10:11–23.

Fox, G. L. 1981. The family's role in adolescent sexual behavior. In T. Ooms, ed., *Teenage pregnancy in a family context,* 73–130. Philadelphia: Temple University Press.

Freud, A. 1968. Adolescence. In A. E. Winder and D. L. Angus, eds., *Adolescence: Contemporary studies,* 13–24. New York: American Book Co.

Furth, H. G. 1980. *The world of grown-ups* New York: Elsevier.

———. 1983. Freud, Piaget, and Macmurray: A theory of knowledge from the standpoint of personal relations. *New Ideas in Psychology* 1:51–65.

Gecas, V. 1972. Parental behavior and contextual variations in adolescents' self-esteem. *Sociometry* 35:332–45.

Gillis, J. R. 1981. *Youth and history: Tradition and change in European age relations.* New York: Academic Press.

Gottman, J. M. 1983. How children become friends. *Monographs of the Society for Research in Child Development* 48:Serial No. 201.

Gouldner, A. W. 1960. The norm of reciprocity: A preliminary statement. *American Sociological Review* 25:161–78.

Greenberg, M. T., J. M. Siegel, and C. J. Leitch. 1983. The nature and importance of attachment relationships to parents and peers during adolescence. *Journal of Youth and Adolescence* 12:373–86.

Grotevant, H. D., and C. R. Cooper. in press. Individuation in family relationships: A perspective on individual differences in the development of identity and role taking skills in adolescence. *Human Development.*

Habermas, J. 1979. *Communication and the evolution of society.* Boston: Beacon.

Hareven, T. K. 1982. *Family time and industrial time.* New York: Cambridge University Press.

Hartup, W. W. 1970. Peer interaction and social organization. In P. H. Mussen, ed., *Carmichael's manual of child psychology,* 3d ed. Vol. 2, 361–456. New York: Wiley.

———. 1978. Children and their friends. In H. McGurk, ed., *Issues in childhood social development,* 130–70. London: Methuen.

Held, D. 1980. *Introduction to critical theory: Horkheimer to Habermas.* Berkeley: University of California Press.

Hinde, R. A. 1978. Interpersonal relations: In quest of a science. *Psychological Medicine* 8:373–86.

———. 1979. *Towards understanding relationships.* London: Academic Press.

Hirschi, T. 1969. *Causes of delinquency.* Los Angeles: University of California Press.

Hollingshead, A. B. 1949. *Elmtown's youth: The impact of social classes on adolescents.* New York: Wiley.

Huard, C. A. 1980. A cognitive-developmental analysis of children's conceptions of interpersonal authority. Ph. D. diss., the Catholic University of America, Washington, D.C.

Hunter, F. 1983. Procedures of socializing influence in adolescents' relationships with mothers, fathers, and friends. Ph.D. diss., the Catholic University of America, Washington, D.C.

Hunter, F., and J. Youniss. 1982. Changes in functions of three relations during adolescence. *Developmental Psychology* 18:806–11.

Inhelder, B., and J. Piaget. 1958. *The growth of logical thinking from childhood to adolescence*. New York: Basic Books.

Jacob, T. 1974. Patterns of family conflict and dominance as a function of child age and social class. *Developmental Psychology* 10:1–12.

———. 1975. Family interaction in disturbed and normal families: A methodological and substantive review. *Psychological Bulletin* 82:33–65.

Johnson, B. 1975. *Functionalism in modern sociology: Understanding Talcott Parsons*. Morristown, N.J.: General Learning Press.

Jourard, S. M. 1971. *Self-disclosure: An experimental analysis of the transparent self*. New York: Wiley.

Jourard, S. M., and P. Richman. 1963. Factors in the self-disclosure inputs of college students. *Merrill-Palmer Quarterly* 9:141–48.

Kandel, D. B., and G. S. Lesser. 1972. *Youth in two worlds: U.S. and Denmark*. San Francisco: Jossey-Bass.

Kanter, R. M. 1977. *Men and women of the corporation*. New York: Basic Books.

Katz, M. B. 1981. Social class in North American urban history. *Journal of Interdisciplinary History* 11:579–605.

Kett, J. F. 1977. *Rites of passage*. New York: Basic Books.

Kohlberg, L. 1969. Stage and sequence: The cognitive-developmental approach to socialization. In D. A. Goslin, ed., *Handbook of Socialization Theory and Research*, 347–480. Chicago: Rand McNally.

———. 1971. From is to ought. In T. Mischel, ed., *Cognitive development and epistemology*, 151–235. New York: Academic Press.

Kon, I. S., and V. A. Losenkov. 1978. Friendship in adolescence: Values and behavior. *Journal of Marriage and the Family* 40:143–55.

Krappmann, L., and H. Oswald. 1983. *Types of children's integration into peer society*. Paper presented at the Society for Research in Child Development, Detroit.

Kropotkin, P. 1902. *Mutual aid*. London: Sargent.

Krosnik, J. A., and M. Judd. 1982. Transitions in social influence at adolescence. *Developmental Psychology* 18:359–68.

LaGaipa, J. J. 1979. A developmental study of the meaning of friendship in adolescence. *Journal of Adolescence* 2:201–13.

Larsen, L. E. 1972. The influence of parents and peers during adolescence: The situation hypothesis revisited. *Journal of Marriage and the Family* 34:67–74.

Lasch, C. 1979. *Haven in a heartless world*. New York: Basic Books.

Laumann, E. O. 1973. *Bonds of pluralism*. New York: Wiley.

Leahy, R. L. 1981. Parental practices and the development of moral judgment and self-image disparity during adolescence. *Developmental Psychology* 17:580–94.

Lever, J. 1978. Sex differences in the complexity of children's play and games. *American Sociological Review* 43:471–83.

Lewis, M., and L. Rosenblum, eds. 1975. *Friendship and Peer Relations.* New York: Wiley.

Lin, N., W. M. Ensel, and J. C. Vaughn. 1981. Social resources and strength of ties. *American Sociological Review* 46:393–405.

Loevinger, J. A. 1966. The meaning and measurement of ego development. *American Psychologist* 21:195–217.

Loew, L. 1982. Changes in structure in the father-adolescent son relation. Ph.D. diss., the Catholic University of America, Washington, D.C.

Lowenthal, M. F., and C. Haven. 1968. Interaction and adaptation: Intimacy as a critical variable. *American Sociological Review* 33:20–30.

Lowi, T. J. 1969. *The end of liberalism.* New York: Norton.

Macmurray, J. 1961. *Persons in relations.* London: Faber and Faber.

Marks, P. A., and D. L. Haller. 1977. Now I lay me down for keeps: A study of adolescent suicide attempts. *Journal of Clinical Psychology* 33:390–99.

McGuire, K. D., and J. R. Weisz. 1982. Social cognition and behavior correlates of preadolescent chumship. *Child Development* 53:1478–84.

Miller, P. Y., and W. Simon. 1980. The development of sexuality in adolescence. In J. Adelson, ed., *Handbook of adolescent psychology,* 383–407. New York: Wiley.

Minuchin, S. 1974. *Families and family therapy.* Cambridge: Harvard University Press.

Montemayor, R. 1982. The relationship between parent-adolescent conflict and the amount of time adolescents spend alone and with parents and peers. *Child Development* 53:1512–19.

Nie, N. H., C. H. Hull, J. G. Jenkins, K. Steinbrenner, and D. H. Bent. 1975. *Statistical Package for the Social Sciences.* New York: McGraw-Hill.

Offer, D., and J. B. Offer. 1975. *From teenage to young manhood.* New York: Basic Books.

Offer, D., E. Ostrov, and K. I. Howard. 1981. *The adolescent: A psychological self-portrait.* New York: Basic Books.

Parsons, T., and R. F. Bales. 1955. *Family socialization and interaction process.* Glencoe, Ill.: Free Press.

Patterson, G. R., and J. B. Reid. 1970. Reciprocity and coercion: Two facets of social systems. In C. Nearinger and J. L. Michael, eds., *Behavior modification in clinical psychology,* 133–77. New York: Appleton Century Crofts.

Piaget, J. [1932] 1965. *The moral judgment of the child.* New York: Free Press.

Platt, A. 1969. *The child savers.* Chicago: University of Chicago Press.

Potvin, R. H., and C. F. Lee. 1980. Multistage path models of adolescent alcohol and drug use. *Journal of Studies on Alcohol* 41:531–42.

———. 1981. Religious development among adolescents. *Social Thought* 7:47–61.

Reiss, D., M. E. Oliveri, and K. Curd. 1983. Family paradigm and adolescent social behavior. In H. D. Grotevant and C. R. Cooper, eds., *Adolescent development in the family,* 77–92. San Francisco: Jossey-Bass.

Riesman, D. 1953. *The lonely crowd.* Garden City, NY: Doubleday.

Rivenbark, W. H., III. 1971. Self-disclosure patterns among adolescents. *Psychological Reports* 28:35–42.

Ryan, S., and J. Smollar. 1980. Children's conceptions of obligations to parents and friends. Manuscript.

Sahlins, M. D. 1965. On the sociology of primitive exchange. In M. Banton, ed., *Relevance of models of social anthropology,* 139–238. New York: Praeger Press.

Sampson, E. E. 1977. Psychology and the American ideal. *Journal of Personality and Social Psychology* 35:767–82.

———. 1981. Cognitive psychology as ideology. *American Psychologist* 36:730–43.

Selman, R. L. 1980. *The growth of interpersonal understanding.* New York: Academic Press.

Selman, R. L., and D. Jaquette. 1977. Stability and oscillation in interpersonal awareness: A clinical-developmental analysis. In C. B. Keasey, ed., *Nebraska Symposium on Motivation* 25:261–304. Lincoln: University of Nebraska Press.

Sennett, R. 1974. *Families against the city.* New York: Vintage Books.

Sharabany, R., R. Gershoni, and J. E. Hofman. 1981. Girlfriend, boyfriend: Age and sex differences in intimate friendship. *Developmental Psychology* 17:800–808.

Shorter, E. 1975. *The making of the modern family.* New York: Basic Books.

Siegelman, E., J. Block, J. Block, and A. Von der Lippe. 1970. Antecedents of optimal psychological adjustment. *Journal of Consulting and Clinical Psychology* 35:283–89.

Smith, C. J. 1980. Social networks as metaphors, models, and methods. *Human Geography* 4:500–524.

Smollar-Volpe, J. 1980. The development of concepts of parent-child and friend relations and of self within these relations. Ph.D. diss., the Catholic University of America, Washington, D.C.

———. 1981. The development of concepts of self: An interpersonal perspective. In J. A. Meacham and N. Santilli, eds., *Social development and youth,* 131–44. Basel: S. Karger.

Smollar-Volpe, J., and J. Youniss. 1982. Social development through friendship. In K. H. Rubin and H. S. Ross, eds., *Peer relations and social skills in childhood,* 279–98. New York: Springer-Verlag.

Sroufe, A. L., and E. Waters. 1977. Attachment as an organizational construct. *Child Development* 48:1184–99.

Stone, L. 1981. Family history in the 1980s. *Journal of Interdisciplinary History* 12:51–87.

Sullivan, E. V. 1977. A study of Kohlberg's structural theory of moral development: A critique of liberal social science ideology. *Human Development* 20:352–76.

Sullivan, H. S. 1953. *The interpersonal theory of psychiatry.* New York: Norton.

Sullivan, K., and A. Sullivan. 1980. Adolescent-parent separation. *Developmental Psychology* 16:93–99.

Tilly, C. 1981. *As sociology meets history.* New York: Academic Press.

Tilly, L. A., J. W. Scott, and M. Cohen. 1976. Women's work and European fertility patterns. *Journal of Interdisciplinary History* 6:447–76.

Urwin, C. 1984. Power relations and the emergence of language. In J. Henriques, W. Hollway, C. Urwin, C. Venn, and V. Walkerdine, eds., *Changing the Subject: Psychology, social regulation, and subjectivity,* 264–322. London: Methuen.

Verbrugge, L. M. 1979. Multiplexity in adult friendships. *Social Forces* 57:1286–1309.

Waterman, A. S. 1981. Individualism and interdependence. *American Psychologist* 36:762–73.

————. 1982. Identity development from adolescence to adulthood: An extension of theory and a review of research. *Developmental Psychology* 18:341–58.

Watzlawick, P., J. H. Beavin, and D. D. Jackson. 1967. *Pragmatics of Human Communication*. New York: Norton.

Wellman, B. 1979. The community question: The intimate networks of East Yorkers. *American Journal of Sociology* 184:1201–31.

White, K. M., J. C. Speisman, and D. Costos. 1983. Young adults and their parents: Individuation to mutuality. In H. D. Grotevant and C. R. Cooper, eds., *Adolescent development in the family*, 61–76. San Francisco: Jossey-Bass.

Wolf, E., J. Gedo and D. Terman. 1972. On the adolescent process as a transformation of the self. *Journal of Youth and Adolescence* 1:257–72.

Wright, P. H., and T. W. Keple. 1981. Friends and parents of a sample of high school juniors: An exploratory study of relationship intensity and interpersonal rewards. *Journal of Marriage and the Family* 43:559–70.

Youniss, J. 1980. *Parents and peers in social development: A Sullivan-Piaget perspective*. Chicago: University of Chicago Press.

————. 1981. Moral development through a theory of social construction. *Merrill-Palmer Quarterly* 27:385–403.

————. 1983. Piaget and the self constituted through relations. In W. F. Overton, ed., *The relationship between social and cognitive development*, 201–27. Hillsdale, N.J.: Erlbaum.

Youniss, J., and J. Volpe. 1978. A relational analysis of children's friendship. In W. Damon, ed., *Social cognition*, 1–22. San Francisco: Jossey-Bass.

Index